S. ALEXEYEV

RUSSIAN HISTORY
IN TALES

PROGRESS PUBLISHE

MOSCOW

S. Alexeyev

RUSSIAN HISTORY IN TALES

Translated from the Russian
Designed by V. CHISTYAKOV
Illustrated by L. GOLDBERG

С. АЛЕКСЕЕВ.
Рассказы из русской истории

На английском языке

First printing 1975

Second printing 1981

Third printing 1982

А $\frac{70803\text{-}001}{014(01)\text{-}82}$ без объявл.

4803010102

FROM THE AUTHOR

Dear Reader:

Before you is a book concerned with the past of Russia, the country in which I was born and which I deeply love, just as each of you love your own native land.

The history of Russia is rich in turbulent events. More than once it suffered the invasions of enemies who encroached upon this rich land and the independence of its state. The people of Russia have accomplished many heroic exploits in the defence of their homeland.

For ages the country was ruled by tsars and landlords.

More than once the working people of Russia rose up in struggle against their oppressors. In this struggle they performed great feats to achieve their dream, to achieve a better life, social justice and a radiant future.

Russian History in Tales is a book about the glorious, intrepid and revolutionary past of the peoples of Russia.

The introductory stories take us back to the XVII century.

1670. The Russian state was in turmoil.

"Razin, Razin is coming!"

"Stepan Timofeyevich Razin!"

This cry resounded in many cities and villages in the confines of the Russian state during the summer of 1670. The humiliated and deprived people of Russia rose up in armed struggle against their enslavers. A full-fledged war was launched by the working people against the power of the tsar, feudal barbarity and the horrors of serfdom in Russia. The leader of this revolt was the wise and decisive folk hero Stepan Timofeyevich Razin.

"Razin is coming! Razin!"

The peasant troops moved in the direction of the state capital, Moscow.

The old boyar Rus trembled and quaked.

Thus the first section of the book acquaints the reader with episodes from the peasant war led by Stepan Razin.

The second section is concerned with the epoch of the reign of Tsar Peter the First, who went down in history as Peter the Great.

Peter the First was an outstanding Russian tsar, a tsar-reformer. Though he remained, of course, the tsar of the boyars and nobility he nevertheless did much to develop and transform the Russian state.

The name of Peter the Great is also linked with Russia's struggle to gain an outlet on the Baltic Sea. Russians had long been considered good seafarers. They set out on long journeys and traded with distant peoples. But enemies tried to take away from Russia all access to the sea. An especially bitter struggle developed in the eastern reaches of the Baltic Sea where the Russians were hard-pressed by the Swedes.

At that time Sweden was a very powerful state. Her army was considered one of the best in the world and she boasted of a large and heavily armed navy.

In 1700 war broke out with the Swedes. This conflict, called the Northern

War, lasted for 21 years and ended with total victory for Russia.

The second section of this book is composed of stories offering episodes from the Northern War and vignettes from the life of Russia during the time of Peter the First.

The third section of the book is devoted to Suvorov and his soldiers.

The Russian soldier is known as one of the best in the world. Stubborn in battle, possessing great stamina to endure the difficulties of life on the march, humanitarian to the losers—these are but a few of his traits. The great Russian general, Alexander Vassilyevich Suvorov, and the soldiers who fought under him serve as the standard of Russian military valour.

Suvorov lived during the XVIII century.

"When striking, use brains not brawn", "Help a friend, even if it means your own end", "The brave are always in the front, the cowards are always killed in the rear", "If the training's hard, the fighting's easy"—all these sayings belong to Suvorov.

Suvorov lived for more than seventy years, and fifty of them were spent in the army. He began his career as a simple soldier and ended it as a Field Marshal and Commander-in-Chief.

1812. A threatening cloud hung over Russia. The troops of Napoleon, the French Emperor, swarmed over its borders. The Russian army fell back. As circumstances would have it, even Moscow was abandoned to the enemy.

But faith in final victory was never lost, Napoleon's troops were in fact smashed and the remnants of his army left the territory of Russia without having won any laurels.

The peoples of Russia supported the army in its struggle against Napoleon's assault. Partisan warfare emerged on a large scale. It was a people's Patriotic War for independence.

You may read about the Patriotic War of 1812 in the section entitled "Martial Glory".

In the two following sections of the book, "The Red Banner of Labour" and "The Tsar is Overthrown", the reader may witness the life and struggles of the workers in tsarist Russia, the Great October Revolution of 1917 and the benefits which the revolution brought to the working masses of the country.

The Revolution of 1917! A total reconstruction of the entire social and spiritual life of Russia was begun. It was an epoch when everything was in change: the social system and old conceptions about life, relationships to property, to work, and between humans. A new phenomenon emerged on the stage of history—socialist society, and a new community of people soon appeared bearing the title of Soviet people. The former tsarist Russia became the Union of Soviet Socialist Republics.

The leader of the Russian Revolution and the working masses was Vladimir Ilyich Lenin. With his teachings he showed the path to victory. Under his leadership the revolution was implemented. With him the new Soviet state found its first leader.

Tales about Vladimir Ilyich Lenin form the next section of the book. The book draws to a close with stories about the Great Patriotic War, 1941-1945.

1941. The 22nd of June. The day of the summer equinox. Morning. Daybreak. At this very time Hitler's Germany perfidiously, without a declaration of war and in violation of a pact of non-aggression which had been signed between the USSR and Germany, threw its mechanised hordes against the lands of the Soviet Union.

The aggressors brought pain and suffering, death and enslavement to our land. Soviet people rose up to liberate the country in the Great Patriotic War.

The cruel and deadly struggle against the nazis lasted almost four years. The Soviet Union, jointly with other countries allied in a coalition against Hitler, emerged victorious in this war. Nazism was crushed, and Hitlerite Germany surrendered unconditionally.

The concluding section of this book will acquaint the reader with episodes from World War II.

I must confess that I worked with great trepidation on this book. It is with no less a feeling of anxiety that I now await this encounter with you, the reader from a foreign land.

It will give me pleasure if this modest introduction to the history of my Russia is even a small step in bringing our cultures together and in contributing to mutual understanding.

My warmest regard to you, the reader of this book.

Sergei Alexeyev

STEPAN RAZIN, THE COSSACKS AND PEASANTS IN REBELLION

THE HORSEMAN

The mounted horsemen passed through the peasant fields and climbed a small hill. Their eyes fell upon a strange sight. The peasant was ploughing the land. Harnessed to the plough, however, were instead of a horse three human beings: the wife and mother of the peasant and his young son.

They strained against the plough, pulled, stopped and once again set to work.

The horsemen approached the ploughman. The leader cast a stern glance at him:

"What in the world are you doing, hitching up people instead of cattle!"

The peasant looked about—before him stood a gigantic person, wearing a cap tipped with red and green Morocco-leather boots. His **caftan** was elegant and under it a bright shirt was visible. He held a braided whip in his hands.

"It must be a **boyar**, or maybe the governor himself," thought the peasant.

He fell to his knees before the lord, his body resting upon the furrows in the soil.

"We are orphans, orphans we are. We have no horse, they took our provider away to cover our debts."

The horseman's face clouded over. He dismounted and turned to the peasant.

The peasant edged backwards, stumbling and slipping in fear, then turned on his heels and ran.

"Hold on there! Stand still! Where are you off to?" boomed out a mocking voice.

The peasant meekly retraced his steps.

"Here, take this horse," the horseman held out the reins.

CAFTAN — a cotton or silk ankle-length garment with very long sleeves and a sash fastening

BOYAR — the highest rank of the service aristocracy in XIV—XVII centuries in Russia

The peasant was dumbfounded. His wife and mother froze in their tracks. The young son's mouth gaped wide as they all stared in disbelief.

The horse is stately, dappled, fit for a prince.

"Sire is joking," the peasant decided. He held still, motionless.

"Take it or I may just reconsider," threatened the other. And walked away on foot across the field.

The horsemen raced after him. Only one youthful rider lingered for a moment, he had accidentally dropped his tobacco pouch.

"The Lord, it must have been the Lord who sent this," the thunderstruck peasant muttered. He turned to the steed and was struck by fear. Could this be sorcery? He reached out to the horse and received a swift kick in reply. The peasant clutched at the bruised spot.

"He's real alright!" he cried out in joy. "Who are you all, where are you from?"—the peasant threw himself at the youth.

"We are wanderers. Free hawks. The spring winds," mysteriously winked the youth.

"Well, who can I pray for? Who was the one in the cap?"

"Razin, Stepan Timofeyevich Razin"—the words floated back as the horseman disappeared.

BOATS
OF THE STRELTSY

"Razin, Razin is coming!"

"Stepan Timofeyevich!"

The year was 1670. Russia was in chaos. The **boyars** and tsarist servitors were in a state of panic. An oppressed, dependant people stirred and rose in revolt. Peasants, Cossacks, Bashkirs, Tatars and Mordvinians. Hundreds of them, and then many thousands.

The peasant legions were led by the dashing **ataman** of the Don Cossacks, Stepan Timofeyevich Razin.

"Long live Stepan Razin!"

The insurgents moved in the direction of Tsaritsyn. They stopped just above the town on the steep shore of the Volga. Camp was set up.

"Why wait, let's take Tsaritsyn now," the Cossacks could be heard saying.

In the darkness of night residents of the city approached Razin:

"It's time to move, Father, and take power. The townspeople await you in Tsaritsyn. There are only a few **streltsy**, and they'll be no problem. We'll open the gates for you."

"Take the town, take Tsaritsyn, Ataman," his advisors urged.

Razin was in no rush however. He knew that upon the Volga a large force of **streltsy** was moving by boats upon Tsaritsyn. The **streltsy** had more than enough cannons, muskets, arquebuses and gunpowder. They were well-trained and led by Lopatin, an able commander. "How can we take on such a superior force," thought Razin. "We can't hide ourselves in the town. We might be able to hold out longer there, but we want to attack in Cossack fashion and knock them out."

Lopatin's boats approached nearer and nearer to Tsaritsyn.

"Take the stronghold, **Ataman**!" shouted the Cossacks.

The **ataman** was in no hurry.

Lopatin sent out scouts every day. They brought back information on the behaviour of the Cossacks.

"They're staying on the heights. They haven't touched the town."

"What a fool," Lopatin laughed. "They don't have much of a commander."

"Father, Sire, take Tsaritsyn," begged the insurgents of the **ataman**.

Razin remained silent, as if he had heard nothing.

At that time Lopatin's caravan came to a point even with the heights on which the Cossacks stood. They opened fire.

"Fire away, fire away," mocked Lopatin. "That's what's important, who can shoot his way to victory!"

STRELTSY — musketeers, the permanent regular regiments of the armed forces

ATAMAN — a title held by elected Cossack military commanders

They edged further away from the dangerous shore. Tsaritsyn came into view. Now it was close by. A cannon fired in salute from the fortress.

Lopatin was content. He rubbed his hands.

And suddenly... What's going on?! Cannon fire spewed forth from the walls of Tsaritsyn. One, a second, a tenth. They fell upon the **streltsy** boats which bowed and went under like paper ships.

Somebody noticed a broad-shouldered Cossack dressed in the ataman's **caftan** on the high city wall.

"Razin, Razin's in Tsaritsyn!"

"The bandits are in the city!"

"Hold it! Turn around!"

But at this time, as if by command, from the left and right banks of the Volga dug-outs filled with Cossacks descended upon the caravan. Like bees upon honey Razin's legions swarmed over the **streltsy** boats.

"Beat them! Destroy them!"

The **streltsy** boats surrendered.

"Cunning, cunning that **ataman**," said Razin's men after the victory. "Look how he fooled the head of the **streltsy**. He waited until the last moment to take Tsaritsyn."

"At the head of them stands only one head, but Razin has two," joked the men of Razin for a long time after.

SHE WON'T CONDEMN

The **boyar** Truba-Nashchekin was torturing his serf. They bound the arms and legs of the unfortunate and tied him to a bench with reins. The **boyar** stood next to him with whip in hand and lashed away at his bare back.

"Take that, and that, dirty peasant. Receive that from me, slave. I'll teach you to remove your cap in front of a **boyar**."

Truba-Nashchekin struck him with the whip, so ferociously that his skin turned to pulp. Resting for a bit, he sprinkled salt water on the wounds, then took to the whip again.

"Sire, Livonty Minaich," begged the peasant, "I beg you, don't murder me. I didn't do it on purpose. I didn't see you coming."

The **boyar** paid no attention to the pleas and moans and continued his murderous business.

The last strength was ebbing out of the peasant. He pulled himself together and said:

"You wait, Sire. Razin soon will come."

And suddenly...

"Razin, Razin is coming," the sound carried across the **boyar's** home. Truba-Nashchekin's face contorted in fear. He cast aside the whip and left the peasant. He lifted the folds of his **caftan**, rushed to the door and fled.

Razin's Cossacks tore into the **boyar's** estate and killed his servitors. The head himself, however, had disappeared.

Razin summoned the peasants together in an open area. He announced them free and then suggested that they choose an elder from amongst themselves.

"Cross-eyed Guryan! Him, him!" shouted the assembled peasants. "He's the wisest and the justest."

"Let it be him," pronounced Razin. "Where is he? Have him come here."

"He's home. He's been badly beaten by the **boyar**."

Razin left the group and went to the home of Cross-eyed Guryan. He entered the home. The tortured man lay on a bench. He lay without movement. His back was partially revealed—not a back but rather a bloody mess.

"Guryan," the **ataman** said.

The peasant turned slightly, opening his eyes a slit.

"No longer to wait. You've come," whispered the peasant. A smile appeared on his face. Appeared and just as quickly disappeared. Guryan died.

Razin returned to the assembled peasants and Cossacks.

"Where is the **boyar**?" he roared.

"We couldn't find him, **Ataman**."

"Where is the **boyar**?" repeated Razin, as if he hadn't heard the first answer.

The Cossacks once again threw themselves into the search. Soon the **boyar** was found. He had hidden in a stove in the bath-house, and there he sat. Truba-Nashchekin was dragged to Razin.

"Hang him, string him up," shouted the crowd.

"Drag him to a birch!" ordered Razin.

"I beg you. Don't murder me," Truba-Nashchekin pleaded. "Please," he whimpered in a high, penetrating, feminine voice.

Razin chortled in disdain.

"Finish him off, **Ataman**, finish him off. Don't drag it out," the peasants urged him.

Suddenly a little girl approached Razin. A tiny thing. She looked up at Razin.

"Have mercy on him, uncle."

The peasants grew silent. They looked at the little girl. Where in the world did she come from?

"Maybe we are committing an ungodly act," somebody suddenly uttered. "Can it be to the good if a little child condemns it?"

Everybody stared at Razin expectantly.

Razin glanced at the little girl, upon the peasants, then in the distance, upon the sky.

"She will grow up and understand, then she won't condemn. Hang him," he uttered sharply to the Cossacks.

HE-E-ELP!!!!

Razin sat on the bank of the Volga. It was late evening. He leaned against his sabre, lost in thought.

"Where should we turn next? To the south, along the Volga, to Astrakhan and the Caspian Sea? Or perhaps to the north, to Saratov, Samara, Kazan and then—to Moscow?

"Moscow, Moscow. The city of cities. Now there's the place to go! We would arrive and drive out the **boyars**. It would be heaven. Our strength isn't up to it yet. We're short of cannons, powder and muskets. The peasants aren't used to fighting. Their clothes are in tatters. We've got to head to the

south," Stepan Timofeyevich reasoned, "stock up with food and clothing and bring the troops to a fighting trim. And then..." here Razin caught his breath, "we'll have all of the **boyars** by the throat."

Razin was sitting on the bank of the Volga lost in these thoughts. Suddenly a shout came over the river. At first it was so quiet that Razin thought he had imagined, but the shouts grew louder and louder:

"Help!"

Darkness enveloped all. Blackness. Nothing was visible. But it was clear that someone was drowning, struggling against the current.

Razin raced to the river. He dove into the water without pausing to undress.

He swam in the direction of the voice, one stroke upon the next.

"Whoever's there—hang on!"

There was no answer.

"Too late, too late," grieved Razin. "Some poor fellow died for nothing." He swam another ten yards or so and decided to turn back. At that very moment, however, he caught a glimpse of a shaggy beard and a hand sticking out of the water.

"Help!" wheezed the bearded one, and again he went under.

"Eh, this time you won't get away!" exclaimed Razin. He dove and dragged the man up. He carried him to the shore and stretched him out on the sand. Placing his knee on the man's chest he pressed and forced the water up and out his mouth.

"You drank your fill!" laughed Stepan Timofeyevich.

The rescued man soon opened his eyes and looked up at the **ataman**:

"Thanks, Cossack."

Razin surveyed the unfamiliar face. A sickly, pasty--faced peasant, he was dressed in torn trousers and a tattered canvas shirt.

"Who are you?" Razin addressed him.

"A fugitive. I'm heading to Razin. Have you heard of him?"

The peasant groaned and fainted.

At this time voices could be heard from the shore:

"Razin! **Ataman!** Stepan Timofeyevich!"

Evidently those approaching had gone out to look for Razin. Razin stepped into the darkness.

The Cossacks came upon the peasant. They bent over and listened for a heartbeat.

"He's breathing!"

Two of them dragged the rescued man to the camp while others continued along the shore of the Volga:

"Razin! **Ataman!**"

In the morning his captains informed Razin that in the previous evening one of the Cossacks had saved a fugitive peasant. Only no one knew which Cossack. No one in the ranks admitted of the deed.

"Clearly, you haven't asked everyone?" grinned Stepan Timofeyevich.

YAIK—CITY OF STONE

The River Yaik. The Caspian Sea. Yaik—a small city built with stone.

The city's towers were high, the width of its walls could be measured in metres, its gates were of oak. A stronghold rather than a city.

"Here my Cossacks can get some rest," thought Razin.

"But it'll be no picnic taking this town. Half of our men will fall in the attempt."

At this time Razin was informed that his men had captured some thirty men in the steppes, monks and pilgrims heading in the direction of Yaik.

Razin was about to say: "These are holy men, they're peaceful. Let them go, let 'em on their way." But suddenly he caught himself short:

"Hold it. Bring them here."

The monks appeared.

"Undress!"

He called his Cossacks.

"Put on their clothes!"

The two groups exchanged clothes.

The mood was unsettled in Yaik Fortress. The **streltsy** knew and the local commander knew that

Razin was somewhere nearby in the steppes. He could show up at any moment.

The commander doubled the guard at the fortress. He gave strict order not to let anyone in or out without the proper papers. By night-time all gates were to be bolted shut.

The sun was setting in the west. The sentries stood at watch. They peered attentively into the steppe.

Suddenly they saw a group of people moving toward the city. They looked again—monks.

The pilgrims approached the gates:

"Open up."

The guards were confused:

"Where are you going?"

"To the Yaik church. We want to pay our respects to the holy icons."

"Spend the evening in the steppes. Outsiders are not allowed in."

"You have no God, eh?" grumbled the monks. "The Lord will remember this."

The guards went inside to inform the commander.

"How many are there?"

"Thirty."

"Let them in. Just make sure that no others slip in." By this time it was completely dark. The guards returned and unbolted the gates. A bearded guard, letting them in one by one, began to count the pilgrims.

"One, two ... twenty ... thirty. Hold it!"

"You with the beard, you can't even count," a voice was heard, "twenty still haven't come in."

"What the devil," the guard exclaimed, puzzled.

Forty, and then fifty had passed through. Now some peasants burst in. The muzzle of a horse poked its way in. One horseman, behind him a second, and then a third.

"Stop, hold it!" shouted the guard.

What next? A brawny fellow ran up to him and bound his mouth with a ready gag.

By this time the fortress was awakened to what was happening. By the time the alarm was sounded, it was already late.

Thus Razin won over Yaik Fortress without a battle. To be sure, on the streets there were some shots. But that doesn't really count. It was a **boyar** town, but it came into the hands of Razin.

HANDS

A group of fugitive peasants were making their way along the Volga to find Razin.

They travelled by night. During the daytime they made up for lost sleep in the forests and thickets. They kept off well-travelled roads and bypassed settlements. They travelled in this fashion for a whole month.

The eldest of the peasants, the pockmarked Mityai, drilled the others:

"He, **ataman** Stepan Timofeyevich, is frightening. He doesn't like men who can't fight. If he asks: can you hold a sabre—answer him, you can. If he asks: can you handle a lance—you can."

The peasants appeared before Razin:

"Take us on, **Ataman**, into the ranks of the Cossacks."

"Can you hold a sabre?"

"We can."

"Can you use a lance?"

"We can."

"You don't say," exclaimed Razin. He ordered a horse brought up. "Mount up, greybeard," he said to Mityai. "Hold the sabre."

Mityai hadn't expected to be checked. "It looks pretty bad. They'll execute me for lying to the **ataman**." He began to prevaricate:

"Uh, we do better on foot."

"A Cossack on foot?! Come on, climb up!"

"You see, we're exhausted from our trip."

"A military man doesn't know the word fatigue."

Mityai resigned himself. Cossacks seized him by the arms and tossed him on the horse. The peasant seized the sabre.

The Cossacks whooped. The horse galloped across the field. Mityai was not used to being in the saddle

and it was the first time that he'd held a sabre. He waved the sabre and precisely at that point it fell out of his hands.

"The sabre is obstinate, capricious. It sure is stubborn," guffawed the Cossacks.

"Why does he need a sabre, he'll beat the enemy with his **lapti**," loudest of all guffawed Stepan Timofeyevich.

The peasant was touched to the quick. He gathered up his courage, approached Razin and said:

"You laugh in vain, **Ataman**. Get behind the plough and we'll have a laugh or two."

Razin, his laughter bettering his good judgement, said:

"Sure enough, I'll hold a plough."

A plough was brought to him, a mare harnessed up. But Razin, like all Cossacks, had never ploughed in his entire life. He thought it was a simple business. But when he began he found out otherwise.

"Come, come, your furrow is crooked," shouted Mityai.

"You're cutting up such a thin chunk of soil. Deeper, deeper into the ground," urged peasants.

The **ataman** threw his weight into the plough and in so doing, broke the share.

"The plough is obstinate, capricious. It sure is stubborn," laughed the peasants.

"Why does a Cossack need a plough, he can plough the land with his sabre," snickered Mityai.

Razin looked at the peasants. He broke into laughter.

"You're alright, greybeard," he slapped Mityai on the shoulder. "Thanks for the lesson. Hey," he shouted to the Cossacks, "don't offend the ploughmen: give them horses and all the essentials. They're a match for a Cossack."

Then he thought and added: "The ploughman and the soldier are like the two hands belonging to the same man."

LAPTI — peasant footwear, made of bast

ONE THIRD OF AN ARSHIN

When towns were taken Razin strictly forbade giving insult or injury to the merchants. Razin understood: without merchants there would be no salt and no nails.

"We won't touch them, **Ataman**," answered his men, "if only they don't offend us."

"Who would dare!" grinned Stepan Timofeyevich. "But if they do cheat you in weights or measures, we'll take care of them. I give you my word, the word of Stepan Razin."

Razin's men moved into Astrakhan. Merchants opened their stores and spread out their goods. Razin himself walked the rows and even bought a pair of boots. Tiny red boots, a gift for his daughter Parasha.

Stepan Timofeyevich returned to his **ataman**'s tent. He was pleased. Trade had been lively and peaceful.

A crowd was gathering at the booth of the merchant Okayemov. The merchant dealt in satin and silk. The Cossacks were buying red, green and yellow pieces for their holiday dress. The merchant, measuring out the material, thought to himself: "Either I'm not a merchant, or I have no horse sense, why shouldn't I cheat just a bit?" The merchant gave the sign of the cross and began to short each customer by a third of an **arshin**.

Half a day passed when suddenly one of the Cossacks caught the merchant red-handed. The Cossacks began to check their own silk purchases. First one, then a second, then a fifth, then a tenth realised that he was one third of an **arshin** short.

"Hold him, the scoundrel!"

"You'll answer for this, swindler!"

The customers seized the merchant. Dragging him from his booth they set up court there and then. In an hour the captain on duty reported to Razin:

"The people are furious. They've cut short a merchant."

"How's that—cut short?" frowned Razin.

"By a third of an **arshin**."

"Come again! By a third of an **arshin**?"

"The head from the shoulders."

ARSHIN — a measure of length, equal to 28 inches

"Rats!" cursed Razin. "I want to see the offenders."

The Cossacks appeared before Razin.

Razin shouted at them in a fierce rage: "For a third of an **arshin** you deprived a merchant of his life. You spilled blood over rags!"

"Don't lose your temper, **Ataman**, think it over," answered his Cossacks. "Do you really think we're concerned over a matter of **arshin**. To chop off the head of a thief—it can only bring good. If only this can serve as an example for us all, for our grandchildren and our great-grandchildren. Don't be angry, **Ataman**."

Razin calmed down.

"Alright, be on your way." He thought to himself: "Merchants are necessary. We can't get along without trade. But with those of Okayemov's ilk, they can only bring harm. Maybe my men are right after all."

THE WORD
OF A COSSACK

Two young Cossacks, Gus and Prisevka, argued over the question of who was more dedicated to the cause of the people.

"I am," shouted Gus.

"No, I," Prisevka assured him.

"I wouldn't hesitate to give up my life," Gus said, pounding his chest.

"I wouldn't utter a sound under the worst of tortures," swore Prisevka.

"If you like, I'll cut off a finger as proof."

"So what's a finger? I'll tear off my whole hand."

The Cossacks caused quite a commotion, neither willing to yield ground to the other.

At this time Razin was wandering about the camp and heard the ongoing argument. He paused to listen, grinning.

The antagonists caught sight of the **ataman** and fell silent.

Stepan Timofeyevich looked at the young bucks:
"My, such loudmouths: life, torture, fingers and hands. Would you like to test yourselves?"

"Just give the order, **Ataman**! We give you our word as Cossacks."

"Do you know how to read and write?"

"No, Stepan Timofeyevich."

"Well, here's what I propose. Whoever masters this knowledge first, that one is the most dedicated to the people."

The Cossacks were disconcerted. They had expected nothing of the sort. But, after all, it was the **ataman** who had spoken. What else could they do? They couldn't take it all back, for the word of a Cossack had been given.

The question of literacy was no joke to Razin. He needed men who could read and write, and there were few indeed, for the skill didn't come easily to the peasant soldier.

The Cossacks raced to the church in search of the deacon.

"Teach us, long-hair!"

They started with the letters of the alphabet. What a chore! How they exerted themselves!

The trouble was—science is grudging in its rewards. The first week passed, then a second.

"I'm running out of strength," Gus cried like a baby.

"A quick death from a **streltsy** bullet would have been far better," moaned Prisevka.

Yet another week passed.

"My head's going to explode. This business is killing me," agonised Gus.

"Why torment us with such a hellish thing," complained Prisevka.

They moaned and cursed their fate, our Cossacks did. They moaned, and yet they kept at it. The word of a Cossack had been given.

Two whole months inched by.

"Well, be on your way," the deacon finally said.

As if spirited by the winds the Cossacks rushed to Razin.

"We mastered, **Ataman**, the wisdom you wanted."

"You don't say!" said Razin sceptically.

"Check us if you doubt."

Razin handed them a piece of paper with writing on it.

"Go ahead, read."

Gus read. To be sure, not very smoothly, but all was correct, he hit no snags and figured everything out.

"Well done, Cossack!" praised Razin.

He got another piece of paper, this time clean, and handed it to Prisevka.

"Go ahead, write!"

Prisevka wrote. To be sure, not very swiftly. But everything was correct, he confused no letters.

"Well done, Cossack," exclaimed Razin in surprise.

Stepan Timofeyevich drew these Cossacks into his circle of affairs. He assigned them to handle important papers and communications. They turned out to be very efficient assistants.

Razin often praised the two Cossacks, for he was impressed that they hadn't disgraced the name of a Cossack.

Gus and Prisevka were embarrassed by this praise.

"After all, we did it for the people!"

RAZINKA

In a battle near Simbirsk Razin received a serious wound in the head.

The faithful Cossacks carried him home to his native Don. Between the Volga and the Don they spent one evening at a small farmstead. The wounded man was carefully carried into the peasant hut.

After a short interval a little boy approached Razin and offered him an apple:

"Have a bite, Stepan Timofeyevich . . . Razinka."

"What's that?"

"They're called Razinka," the boy explained.

Razin's eyebrows lifted somewhat in surprise. The **ataman** fell to thinking.

It was in 1667 that Razin and his Cossacks had first ventured forth on the Volga. At that time he had passed the night on this very same farmstead.

The head of the household, an old man, had been planting apple trees the next morning. Stepan Timofeyevich had been intrigued by the process:

"Let me help you."

"That's nice of you," answered the old man.

Razin had dug a hole and planted an apple seedling; a frail tiny seedling, so small it had no leaves.

"Come back, Stepan, after three years and try a Razinka," the old man invited the **ataman**.

Not three but four years had passed. "Fate does have some good things in store after all," thought Razin.

"Where's the old man?" he asked the little boy.

"He died, in the spring, when all was in bloom. He called out for you as he was dying, Stepan Timofeyevich. He went on and on about the apple tree. He asked us and everyone born after us to look after this tree."

In the morning Razin took a look at the tree. It stood young, strong and laden with fruit. Powerful branches reached out from its trunk. From them hung bright, large—the size of two Cossack's fists—fragrant apples.

"Razinka," Stepan Timofeyevich said to himself. He asked to be carried to the grave site of the old man, paid his respects and then ordered that they take to the road again.

During the whole journey Razin talked about apple orchards.

"What amazing beauty. We will plant them along the whole Don, along the Volga, all over the world, these marvels. We will drive out the **boyars** and plant orchards. The earth will blaze with a white fire in the springtime. The branches will be so laden they will droop to the ground in the autumn. In the same fashion we will begin life anew. We will replough, turn over the soil again with ploughshares. The weeds will be eliminated, ears of rye and wheat will be visible everywhere. We will bring happiness and joy to the common people."

Razin didn't live to see his dream fulfilled, the insurgents didn't succeed in overthrowing the tsar and the **boyars**. After he reached the Don Razin was seized by wealthy Cossacks. He was thrown in irons, led to Moscow and executed on Red Square.

The executioner's axe was raised over his head. It was raised and descended.…

Stepan Timofeyevich Razin perished. He perished but the memory of him remains. Eternal praise, eternal glory to him.

1

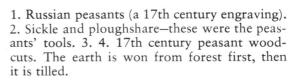

2

1. Russian peasants (a 17th century engraving).
2. Sickle and ploughshare—these were the peasants' tools. 3. 4. 17th century peasant woodcuts. The earth is won from forest first, then it is tilled.

3

4

5. The "Quiet", the name given by court historians to Tsar Alexey Mikhailovich Romanov. During his reign the oppression of the people resulted in the uprising led by Stepan Razin. 6. 7. Wooden block with chain and shackles for the feet and an iron collar for the neck—for rebels.

6

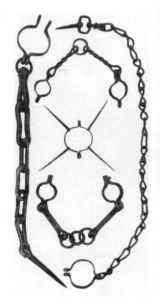

ОБРАЗ ВЕЛИКАГО ГДРА ЦРА И ВЕЛИКАГО КНЗА · АЛЕ&SА МІХАІЛОВІЧА ВSЕА ВЕЛІКІА ІМАЛА ІБѢЛЫА РОSІІ САМОДЕРЖЦА.

5

7

8

8. Who to petition? Thus the serf Ivan Ivanov wrote a complaint against his owner to the governor: "He beats and tortures me without end and for no good reason; he wears me out and keeps me in irons, and I am guiltless..." (a 17th century petition). 9. A map of the Russian state. Insert, upper-left corner: a map of Moscow, 1614. 10. 11. This is what they looked like, the servitors of the tsar, the rulers of the state and the Russian people—*boyars* and merchants.

9

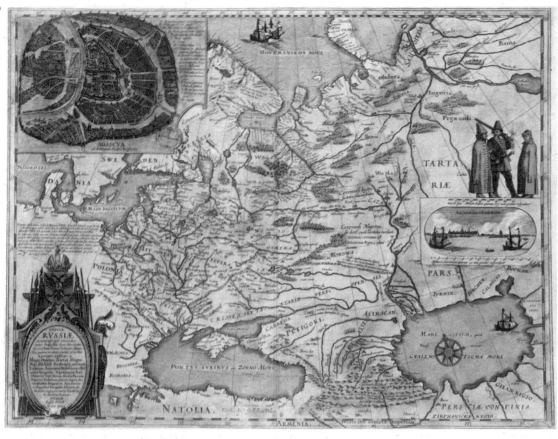

10

11

12

13

14

12. A portrait of Stepan Razin. 13. A primer in penmanship—literacy was the privilege of the "haves". 14. "The Manifesto of Enticement"—Razin's appeal to the people to join the uprising (September 1670).

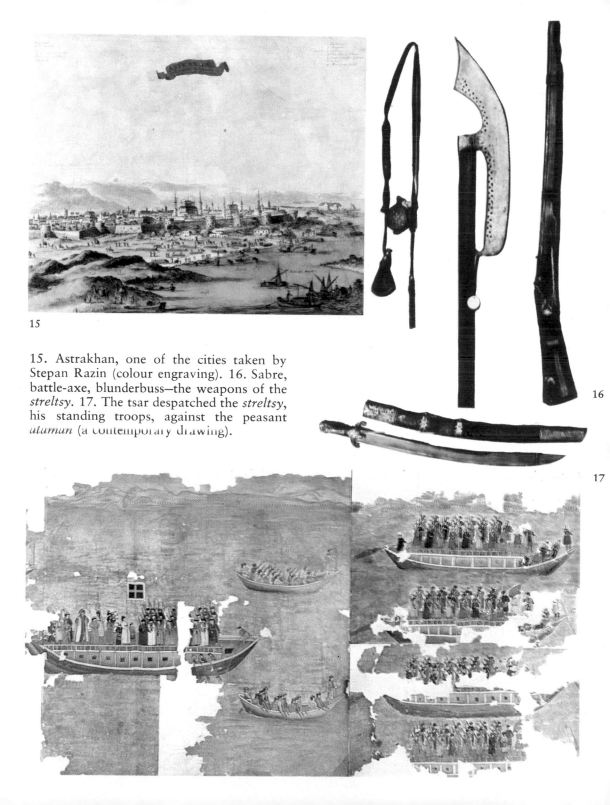

15

15. Astrakhan, one of the cities taken by
Stepan Razin (colour engraving). 16. Sabre,
battle-axe, blunderbuss—the weapons of the
streltsy. 17. The tsar despatched the *streltsy*,
his standing troops, against the peasant
ataman (a contemporary drawing).

16

17

18

20

21

19

22

18. Painting by Vassili Surikov entitled "Stepan Razin". 19. Weapons of Razin's peasant army: axe, bludgeon, *gorbusha*. 20. The dug-outs employed by Stepan Razin (contemporary engraving). 21. The ethnic groups of the Volga region were active participants in the revolt led by Razin. A Bashkir (colour engraving). 22. Battle between Razin's supporters and the tsar's troops in Astrakhan, 1670 (engraving).

 his Brother

RAZIN the Rebell

23

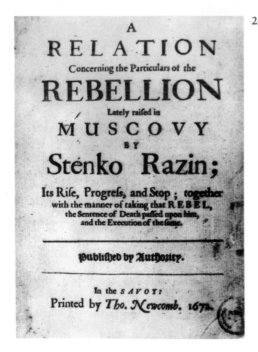

A
RELATION
Concerning the Particulars of the
REBELLION
Lately raised in
MUSCOVY
BY
Stenko Razin;

Its Rife, Progrefs, and Stop; together
with the manner of taking that REBEL,
the Sentence of Death paffed upon him,
and the Execution of the fame.

Publifhed by Authority.

In the SAVOY:
Printed by Tho. Newcomb. 1672.

24

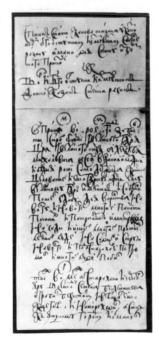

25

23. Stepan Razin and his brother Frol being led to their execution (contemporary sketch). 24. A Relation Concerning the Rebellion in Muscovy by Stenko Razin (English publication of 1672. Title page). 25. The tsar's verdict against Stepan Razin.

PETER THE GREAT AND HIS TIMES

CAPTAIN
OF THE ARTILLERY COMPANY

The Russian army moved towards the Narva.

"Tra-ta-ta, tra-ta-ta!" the regimental drum beat out the march.

The troops marched past the ancient Russian towns of Novgorod and Pskov. They marched to the beat of the drums, to the sound of songs.

The autumn had been dry, but suddenly rain swept down. The leaves were washed from the trees, the roads churned into mud. The air turned cold. The soldiers continued their march upon the rain-soaked roads, sinking up to their knees in mud.

The going was difficult. At the crossing of a small stream a cannon got stuck on the bridge. One of its wheels hit a rotting plank and sunk all the way to the axle.

The soldiers shouted at the horses and beat them with whips. The horses were worn out from the long journey—literally skin and bones. They strained with all their might, but to no use. The cannon wouldn't budge.

The soldiers crowded around at the bridge, threw their shoulders to the cannon and tried to push it out.

"Forward!" cried one.

"Backwards!" commanded another.

The soldiers bustled and argued but the cannon stayed in place. The sergeant circled about the cannon, not knowing what to do next.

Suddenly the soldiers looked about—an elaborately carved enclosed coach was rushing along the road.

The sleek horses galloped up to the bridge and came to a halt. An officer climbed out of the coach. The soldiers saw that he was a captain of an artillery company. His height was enormous—a full seven feet—

his face round, with large eyes. Over his lip, as if glued, was a tar-black moustache.

The awed soldiers drew to attention and froze in position.

"The situation looks bad, brothers," uttered the captain.

"It sure does, Artillery Captain!" the soldiers shouted in reply. "Now we're going to catch it," they all thought.

So it was. The captain approached the cannon, looked over the bridge.

"Who has seniority here?" he asked.

"I do, sir," the sergeant said haltingly.

"So that's how you take care of our military equipment!" the captain turned on the sergeant.

"Well, uh ... we, you see..." sputtered the sergeant.

But the captain didn't bother to listen, he turned and clubbed the sergeant in the neck! Then he approached the cannon once again, took off his **caftan** adorned with red lapels and crawled under the wheels. He applied his huge shoulder to the wheel of the cannon and lifted it up. The soldiers were so astonished that they whistled out loud. They ran up to the cannon and swarmed over it. It budged, the wheel emerged from the hole and came to a halt on solid timber.

The captain straightened his shoulders, smiled and shouted to the soldiers "Thanks, friends!", smacked the sergeant on the shoulders, sat in the coach and galloped away.

The soldiers stood agape, watching the captain disappear in the distance.

"How's that for you!" said the sergeant.

Soon after a general and a group of officers overtook the soldiers.

"Hey, you," cried out the general, "did the tsar's coach pass by?"

"No, Your Honour," answered the soldiers, "we've only seen a captain of the artillery."

"Captain of the artillery?" repeated the general.

"Precisely," answered the soldiers.

"Fools! Captain indeed! That was the tsar himself. Peter Alekseyevich!"

WITHOUT NARVA
WE'LL NEVER SAIL THE SEAS

The well-fed steeds raced along merrily. The tsar's coach overtook troops stretched out over many versts, passed by carts stuck in the mud.

Next to the tsar sat another man. The same height as Peter, he was somewhat broader of shoulder. This was Alexander Menshikov.

Peter had known Menshikov since childhood. At that time Menshikov had worked for a pastry shop. He had walked the streets and frequented the markets in the city selling **pirozhki.**

"Hot cakes, hot **pirozhki!**" he had shouted at the top of his lungs.

Once Alexashka Menshikov was fishing on the river Yauza, across from the village of Preobrazhenskoye. He looked up and saw another boy walking along. From his clothes he guessed—it was the young tsar.

"Do you want me to show you a trick?" Alexashka turned to Peter.

"Sure."

Menshikov grabbed a needle with thread and pierced his own cheek, but so skilfully that he managed to pull the thread through without drawing blood.

Peter cried out in surprise.

More than ten years had passed since that time. You wouldn't recognise Menshikov, the changes that had taken place in the interval. He was the best friend and confidante of the tsar. "Alexander Danilovich", the former Alexashka was now respectfully called.

"On, you team!" cried the soldier sitting on the coachbox.

The steeds rushed forward at breakneck speed. Sticky mud flew off in all directions. The coach hurtled down the uneven road.

Peter sat silently, gazing at the broad back of the soldier, recollecting his own childhood games and **Poteshnye voiska.**

At that time Peter had lived on the outskirts of Moscow, in Preobrazhenskoye. Most of all he had loved war games. A group of boys had been gathered

PIROZHKI — pies

POTESHNYE VOISKA — play troops; group of boy-soldiers gathered under the young Peter I

together for him and given arms and cannons. The only thing lacking had been real powder. They had fired away with stewed turnip. Peter would gather his troops together, divide them into two groups, and the battle began! Then the losses were counted. One had broken an arm, a second took it in the side, and a third in the head...

From time to time **boyars** would arrive from Moscow and begin to scold Peter for his war games, but he would aim the cannon at them and—bam!—stewed turnip would fly into their fat stomachs and bearded faces. The **boyars** grabbed the folds of their embroidered clothes and scattered in all directions. Peter would seize his sword and shout:

"Victory! Victory! The enemy have shown us their backs!"

Now the **Poteshnye voiska** had grown up. They had become two full regiments—the Preobrazhensky and Semenovsky. The tsar called them guards. These regiments marched with the rest to Narva, together they had endured sticky impassable mud. "How will these old friends and acquaintances perform?" wondered Peter. "We're not dealing with the **boyars** now."

"Sire," Menshikov brought Peter out of his meditations. "Sire, Narva is in sight."

Peter looked. On the left, on the steep bank of the Narova stood a fortress surrounded by a stone wall. At the very edge of the river the Narva castle came into view—a fortress within a fortress. The main tower of the castle—"Long German" it was called—soared high into the sky.

Opposite Narva, on the right bank of the Narova was yet another fortress: Ivan-Gorod. And Ivan-Gorod was enclosed by insurmountable walls.

"It won't be easy, Sire, to take a fortress like that," said Menshikov.

"No, not easy," answered Peter. "But necessary. Without Narva we can't get along. Without Narva we won't have access to the sea."

"YOUR HIGHNESS, ALLOW ME TO SAY"

The Russians were beaten at Narva. It turned out that the country was poorly prepared for war. There were shortages of weapons; outfits were lacking; the troops were poorly trained.

Winter, frost, wind. An elaborately carved sleigh rushed over the snow. The horseman raced over the pits and bumps. Flakes of snow flew up from the horses' hooves. Peter raced towards Tula; he was heading towards the arms factory of Nikita Demidov.

Peter had known Demidov for a long time, ever since Demidov had been simple blacksmith. Any time Peter had business in Tula, he would stop by at Demidov's and say: "Teach me, Demidov, the blacksmith trade."

Demidov would put on his apron and pull a piece of searing hot iron from the furnace with his pincers. He pounded at the metal with a small hammer and showed Peter how to shape metal. Peter held the hammer in his hands. He turned to the points Demidov had shown him—Wham! Sparks flew off to the side.

"Here, this way," suggested Demidov.

Hardly had the tsar made a mistake when Nikita would shout:

"Clumsy oaf!"

Then added:

"Please, Your Highness, don't get angry. Any craft takes a lot of shouting. Shouting is part of the apprenticeship!"

"Alright," answered Peter.

So here was the tsar, once again in Tula. "There's more in it than meets the eye," thought Demidov. "The tsar does not pay calls just for pleasure!"

He was so right.

"Nikita Demidovich," said Peter, "have you heard about Narva?"

Demidov didn't know what to say. Idle words would only infuriate the tsar. How could one not have heard of Narva when it was being gossiped about everywhere. After all, hadn't the Swedes done us in? Demidov remained silent, trying to conjure up an answer.

"Alright now, don't try to be clever," said Peter.

"I heard about it," Demidov got out.

"Now here's the story," Peter added. "We need cannons, Nikita Demidovich. Do you understand, cannons."

"How couldn't I understand, Sire."

"In fact we need many cannons," Peter finished.

"I understand, Peter Alekseyevich. The only thing is, our Tula factories are poor. We have no iron, no fuel at hand. Misery, not factories, that's the word."

Peter and Demidov were silent. Peter sat on a carved bench and looked out at the factory courtyard through the window. Peasants in tattered clothes and worn out **lapti** were dragging along an aspen log.

"There you have it, the free and easy life in Tula. We beg for firewood like paupers." And then he leaned towards Peter and began to talk quietly, stealthily: "Your Highness, allow me to say..."

Peter, silent for a second, glanced at Demidov and said:

"Go ahead, say it."

"My men," said Demidov, "went looking around the Urals... And I went with them. That's where the iron is! And the forests, a regular ocean, there don't seem to be any end to them. That's where to set up your factories. They'll start giving you cannons, shells, weapons... anything else you might need, right away."

"The Urals you say?" Peter repeated.

"That's what we're talking about," reiterated Demidov.

"I've heard about the Urals. But they're so far away, Demidov, the very edge of the earth. Just think how much time it would take just to build the factories!"

"Don't worry about that," said Demidov with conviction. "We'll lay out the roads, there are some rivers as well. Distance? It's just a matter of how you look at it. As to the time, well, we'll be around tomorrow. You wait and in two years Ural cast iron and Ural cannons—everything will be in order."

Peter stared at Demidov and understood that Nikita had been thinking for a long time about the Urals. The latter kept his eyes pinned on Peter, waiting for a response from him.

"Alright, Nikita Demidovich," Peter finally said, "we'll have it your way. I'll write out an order and you'll head for the Urals. You'll receive money from the treasury and men as well... and God be with you. But take heed! You know, there isn't a more important business at hand for us. Remember this. If you let me down you'll suffer for it."

In a month's time, having gathered together the best miners and gunsmiths, Demidov set off for the Urals.

During the same time Peter had succeeded in sending men to Bryansk, Lipetsk and other cities. In locations all over Russia Peter ordered that iron be extracted and factories built.

BELLS

"Danilych," Peter once said to Menshikov, "we're going to take the bells off the churches."

Menshikov was stunned.

"Why are you staring at me?" Peter shouted at him. "We need copper, we need cast iron, we will melt the bells into cannons. Into cannons. Into cannons, do you understand?"

"That's right, Your Highness, that's right," Menshikov affirmed. In truth he didn't know whether the tsar was pulling his leg or talking seriously.

Peter wasn't joking. Soldiers were soon dispersed to fulfill the tsar's orders.

Some of these soldiers arrived in the large village of Lopasnya, where Uspensky church was located. The soldiers arrived at dark and entered the village as the evening bells were ringing. The bells sang out in the evening air, many tones flowing into one. The sergeant counted out on his fingers—eight bells.

While the soldiers unharnessed the frozen horses, the sergeant went to the home of the priest. Having learned what was going on the priest frowned, his forehead forming lines of wrinkles. However he met the sergeant graciously, saying:

"Come in, come in, soldier, and call your men. Surely you are exhausted from your travels and cold."

The soldiers entered the home cautiously, very carefully cleaning the snow from their felt boots and making the sign of the cross.

The priest fed the soldiers and brought out the wine.

"Drink up, soldiers, and eat your fill," he said warmly.

The soldiers drank more than their fill and soon dozed off. In the morning when the sergeant stepped into the street and looked up at the belfry only one bell was swinging there.

The sergeant rushed to the priest.

"Where are the bells?" he shouted. "What did you do with them?"

The priest spread his hands and said:

"Our parish is poor, there's only one bell in the entire area."

"How can that be, only one?" the sergeant said angrily. "I saw eight of them yesterday, I even heard them all."

"What are you talking about, soldier!" the priest waved his arms. "What kind of fantasies are you having? You were drunk and you dreamt it all up."

It occurred to the sergeant that not for nothing had they been wined and dined. He gathered his soldiers, searched the whole church, scurried into every cellar. In vain. It was as if the bells had disappeared under water.

The sergeant threatened to report the incident to Moscow.

"Go ahead and report it," the priest replied.

The sergeant, however, decided not to write. He knew that he would be held responsible as well. He decided to remain in Lopasnya and conduct an investigation.

The soldiers remained there a week, and then a second one. They wandered the streets and visited homes. Unfortunately nobody seemed to know anything about the bells. "There were some, but where they are now we just don't know," was the common response.

During their stay a little boy attached himself to the sergeant. He was called Fedka. He looked over the soldiers, weapons and asked questions about war. He was a clever little one and constantly at work trying to steal a bullet from the sergeant.

"Don't be a pest!" said the sergeant. "Find out where the priest hid the bells and the bullet is yours."

"You mean you'll give it to me?"

"That's right."

For two days Fedka was nowhere to be seen. On the third day he came racing to the sergeant and whispered in his ear:

"I found them."

"No, really?" said the sergeant dubiously.

"Honest to God, I did. Give me the bullet."

"Nothing doing. We'll see about that later."

Fedka led the sergeant out of the village and raced on homemade skis along the shore of the river, the sergeant barely keeping time with him. Fedka was at home on skis but the sergeant stumbled and fell in the snow up to his waist.

"Let's go, come on!" Fedka prodded him. "It's not far now."

They reached a spot some three versts from the village and descended a steep bank down to the ice.

"Here we are," said Fedka.

The sergeant looked about and saw a hole in the ice. And nearby another and further yet another. From each hole could be seen a cable frozen to the ice. Now the sergeant understood where the priest had hidden the bells: under the ice in the water. Gladdened by the news the sergeant gave Fedka the bullet and raced back to the village. The sergeant ordered the soldiers to harness up the horses: he himself paid a visit on the priest. He told him:

"Forgive me, Father, apparently I really did imagine those bells in a state of drunkenness. We're leaving Lopasnya today. Please, don't hold a grudge against me, pray to God for us."

"Have a nice trip!" smiled the priest. "I wish you well, soldier. Of course I'll say a prayer."

The very next day the priest summoned together his parishioners.

"Well, it's all over with. Calamity has passed us by."

The parishioners went to the river to drag out the bells, reached down through the holes, but nothing was there.

"Blasphemers! Tyrants!" shouted out the priest. "They left and took the bells with them. Our bells are gone!"

The wind swept over the river, sweeping under the priest's cassock, tearing at the peasants' beards, and kicking up clouds of fine snow along the steep banks.

HAY, STRAW

The Russians learned from Narva that it didn't pay to throw untrained troops against the Swedes. Peter decided to create a standing army. When there was no war the soldiers could learn how handle weapons properly and accustom themselves to discipline and order.

Once Peter was passing by the soldiers' barracks. He noticed that they had formed ranks and were marching in formation. Next to them marched a young officer issuing commands. Peter began to listen: the commands were somewhat out of the ordinary!

"Hay, straw!" cried out the officer. "Hay, straw!"

"What's going on?" thought Peter. He stopped his horse to get a better look: something was tied to the feet of the soldiers. He could see hay on the left feet and straw on the right.

The officer caught sight of Peter and commanded: "Attention!"

The soldiers came to a halt: the lieutenant ran up to Peter:

"Captain, sir, officer Vyazemsky's company is being taught drill patterns!"

"At ease!" Peter commanded the company.

Vyazemsky's attitude pleased Peter. He had been ready to become enraged over the "hay, straw" business, but now his approach changed. He asked Vyazemsky:

"Why in the world did you make your soldiers attach this stuff to their feet?"

"It's not just stuff, Captain," answered the officer.

"What do you mean, not just stuff!" objected Peter. "You're disgracing the soldiers. Don't you know the regulations?"

Vyazemsky stood his ground.

"That's not the case," he said. "The whole idea is to make matters simple. Ignorance, Captain, is the problem. They can't tell which is the left and which is the right foot. But hay and straw, that makes sense to them. They can tell the two apart because they're from the villages."

The tsar was surprised at this device, but grinned.

Soon Peter was surveying a parade. The smartest marchers were in the last company.

"Who's the commander?" Peter asked a general.

"His name's officer Vyazemsky," answered the general.

THE BOYARS' BEARDS

The boyars Buinosov and Kurnosov lived in Moscow. They could trace their ancestors far back, their homes in the city fairly burst with treasures and each owned the lives of thousands of serfs.

The boyars, however, were most vain of their beards. Their beards were in fact full, luxurious. Buinosov had a wide square one. Kurnosov's, on the other hand, was long and formed like a horse's tail.

Suddenly the tsar's rescript appeared: all beards were to be shaven off. Peter was changing the way of life of old Russia: he ordered that people cut off their beards, begin to wear foreign fashions, drink coffee, smoke tobacco, to name but a few.

When they learned about the new regulation Buinosov and Kurnosov moaned and sighed. They decided not to cut their beards, but in order to avoid the eyes of the tsar decided also to feign illness.

But soon the tsar remembered these boyars and summoned them to call on him.

The two began to argue, who would go first. "You go," said Buinosov.

"No, you," replied Kurnosov.

Finally they cast dice and Buinosov lost out. He went to see the tsar, and threw himself at his feet.

"Don't ruin me, Your Highness, don't disgrace me in my old age!" He crawled his way along the floor, grabbed the tsar's hand and tried to kiss it.

"Get up!" commanded Peter. "Your brain isn't located in your beard, it's in your head."

But Buinosov got up on all fours and continued insisting:

"Don't disgrace me, Your Highness."

Peter lost his temper, called for his servants and ordered them to cut off his beard without delay.

Buinosov returned in tears to Kurnosov, holding his hand up to his newly-shaved chin and chattered to him incoherently.

Kurnosov was afraid of confronting the tsar. He decided to pay a call on Menshikov to ask for help and advice.

"Help me, Alexander Danilych, have a word with the tsar for me," he asked.

Menshikov thought and thought, how could he broach this topic with Peter. Finally he went to him and said:

"Your Highness, what if the boyars payed a tax for their beards? It certainly wouldn't hurt the treasury!"

Peter knew that the coffers were indeed low at the time. He thought for a bit, then agreed.

Kurnosov was overjoyed, hastened to pay the money and received a copper medal with the inscription: "Money paid in full." Kurnosov wore the medal around his neck as if it were a cross. Whoever stopped and bothered him about his beard, he would raise up his beard and reveal the medal.

Now Kurnosov was even more proud and arrogant, but in vain. After a year had passed the tax collector arrived at his door and demanded a new payment.

"What are you talking about?" Kurnosov said angrily. "I've paid my money," and showed his medal.

"Oh yes, that medal," said the tax collector. "Well, it's expired. You've got to pay for a new one."

What could he do? He bought another medal. And after another year had passed the process repeated itself. Kurnosov then began to think, to estimate and project the costs. It turned out that at the rate of expenditure he was forced to make for his beard his whole fortune would soon be exhausted. He would be left with a beard and not much else.

When the tax collector came for the third time, he looked up and saw a beardless Kurnosov staring at him with indignant eyes.

On the next day Menshikov related the situation to the tsar. Peter broke into laughter.

"So much for them the fools, let them get used to the new way of things. As far as the money is concerned, you were pretty clever, Danilych. Kurnosov's beard must have covered the expense of outfitting a whole division!"

WHAT DID THE YOUNG BOYARS LEARN WHILE ABROAD

These insults were still fresh in the minds of Buinosov and Kurnosov when new ones were suddenly heaped on. Peter ordered that fifty of the brightest sons of the boyars be rounded up and sent abroad to study. Buinosov and Kurnosov were forced to part with their sons.

Weeping and wailing prevailed in the homes of the boyars. The nurses raced about, the homes were in turmoil, the farewells were not joyous but bitter; to them the parting was funeral.

The wife of Buinosov completely lost control of herself.

"Our only son, off to a strange land, into the clutches of the Germans. I won't have it!" she cried. "I won't give him up!"

"Shut up!" Buinosov cursed his wife. "The tsar has so ordered. What would you have? Siberia? The gallows?"

The Kurnosov home was just as agitated. Kurnosov was also forced to shout at his wife:

"You can't chop wood with a pen knife. You can't buck the tsar. You'll just have to be patient, woman."

A year later the young boyars returned home. They were summoned to the tsar's chambers to receive their assignments in the bureaucracy.

"Tell me, Buinosov," demanded Peter, "what was it like living in a different country?"

"It was fine, Your Highness," young Buinosov answered. "The people were friendly, hospitable, not like our peasants, ready to tear at each other's throats."

"Yes, but what did you learn?"

"A lot, Your Highness, we learned to say 'Vater' instead of 'father' and 'Mutter' in place of 'mother'."

"But what else?"

"We learned how to bow properly, two and three times, how to dance, and how to play the fashionable games."

"My, you sure did pick up a lot," Peter said.

"What do you have to say?" Peter turned to the young Kurnosov.

"How can I begin, Sire. Ask me questions."

"Alright. Tell me, Kurnosov, what is fortification?"

"Fortification, Sire, is a military science, having as its goal the defence of one's troops from the enemy."

"You're talking sense," said Peter. "Now tell me, what is navigation map?"

"Navigation map, Sire," replied Kurnosov, "is the description of the sea or a river, including information on spits and shallows, depth readings and currents, anything which might present an obstacle to a ship's journey."

"Well put," said Peter. "And what else did you learn?"

"I looked into all kinds of matter, Sire," answered Kurnosov. "For example, how to build ships, how to extract ore, how medicine is practised there. Those German and Dutch, they know what they're doing. They have skills and knowledge. Only I don't think we should look down our noses at our own people. Our country is no worse, and our people are just as good. And we're no poorer!"

"You're a fine fellow!" exclaimed Peter. "You justified my hopes, it warms my heart." And Peter kissed the young Kurnosov. "But you," Peter turned to Buinosov, "evidentially, were a fool when you left, and haven't changed much. Get out of my sight!"

Thus Buinosov remained in obscurity. But Kurnosov soon became an important figure in government circles.

THE ABC'S

Literacy was uncommon in Peter's Russia. Parish churches taught the rudiments of knowledge to children and once in a while a wealthy home would hire a tutor. That was about the extent of it.

During Peter's time an effort was made to develop a school system. These primary schools taught grammar, arithmetic and geography.

One such school was opened in the town of Serpukhov, situated half way between Moscow and Tula. A teacher arrived in the town.

The teacher showed up at the school and awaited the arrival of his pupils. He waited one day, a second and then a third. No sign of pupils. At this point the teacher began to visit homes to find out what was the matter. He entered one home, asked for the head of the household, a local merchant.

"Why," he asked, "doesn't your son come to school?"

"He has no need for it!" answered the merchant. "We've got along without education, and so can he. Knowledge only brings on trouble."

The teacher went to a second home, that of a shoemaker.

"You really mean to say that we have the wits for such things!" said the shoemaker. "Our business is to make shoes. Why waste your time listening to lies?"

At this point the teacher payed a call on the local mayor to tell him what was going on. The mayor, however, just shook his head in helplessness.

"What can I do about it?" he asked. "It depends on the parents. For some education is necessary. For others, it's a luxury."

The teacher stared at the mayor and understood that help was not going to come from these quarters. Angered, he said:

"If that's how it is, I'll write directly to the tsar."

The mayor looked at the teacher. He did in fact have a determined air. He could tell that the teacher meant what he said.

"Alright, alright," he said, "don't be in a rush. Go back to the school."

The teacher returned to the school and began to wait. Soon he heard footsteps outside. He looked out of the window: soldiers with weapons were escorting the children.

This process went on for a whole week. Then things took a turn for the better, the parents apparently made their peace and accepted the situation. The children began to come to the school of their own will.

The teacher began to teach his children the alphabet.

"A," said the teacher.

"A," replied the class in unison.

"B," said the teacher.

"B," repeated the children.

"C . . ."

Next they turned to arithmetic.

"One and one," said the teacher, "make two."

"One and one are two," echoed the pupils.

Soon he was teaching the children to write the alphabet as well, and to add. They learned where the Caspian, Black and Baltic seas are located. They picked up a lot of new information.

Peter happened to be passing through Serpukhov on his way to Tula. He spent the night in the town and in the morning decided to pay a visit to the school. He had overheard that the parents had been reluctant to send their children to school. He decided to confirm this. Peter entered the class and saw that it was packed with children. Amazed, he asked the teacher how he had managed to gather together so many pupils.

The teacher related the whole story.

"That's really something," Peter laughed. "That mayor did well. That's right in our style. I think I'll order that they do the same in other regions. Our people are somewhat feeble-minded, don't even understand what's good for them. They don't give a darn about the business of state. And how we are crying for educated help. The lack of knowledgeable people could be fatal for Russia."

BE SATISFIED WITH A LITTLE
AT FIRST: MORE WILL COME

"It's high time we had our own newspaper," Peter told his friends on more than one occasion. "It would be of use to all: merchant, boyar and city dweller."

Once Peter disappeared from the court. He didn't appear as evening approached and many began to wonder apprehensively if some harm had come to him. In reality Peter was at this time selecting material for the first number of Russian newspaper with the help of the printer Fedor Polikarpov.

Polikarpov, a tall thin man with glasses resting on the tip of his nose, stood at attention before the tsar. Like a soldier he stood and read.

"Sire, there's something here from Verkhotursk in the Urals. It says that they're turning out a lot of cannon there."

"Let's use it," said Peter. "Everyone should know that it's not such a disaster to have lost a battle at Narva. If we really want to, we can do an awful lot."

"Here's something else, Sire," continued Polikarpov. "It says that in Moscow four hundred cannons were made from the cast iron collected from bells."

"Write that one in too," said Peter. "Let people know that we're not taking away their bells for nothing."

"From Nevyansky factory—Demidov's—they write that the factory peasants rioted and now the boyars and merchants can find no peace."

"Leave out that one," said Peter. "It's better to send out troops and punish the peasants severely for that kind of activity."

"From Kazan, Sire, they write that they've found a lot of oil and copper ore."

"Put that in," said Peter. "Let them know that Russia is a rich place, it abounds with wealth, so much it hasn't even all been counted."

Peter sat and listened. Then he took up the papers. He made a red cross on those to be included, the rest he placed aside.

Polikarpov announced more and more material. How the Indian ruler, for example, had sent the Muscovite tsar an elephant, how in Moscow in one month 386 births had been registered, and much else.

"Oh yes," said Peter, "write about the schools, and write good things so that everybody sees the good that can come out of them."

After an interval of a few days the newspaper was printed up. It was called *Vedomosti* (The Record). It was small, the print fine, hard to read, lacking in margins and the paper itself grey. Neither here nor there, in sum. But Peter was pleased, it was the first. He grabbed the newspaper and ran into the court. He showed it to whomever he ran into.

"Look," he said, "a newspaper, our own, the first Russian newspaper!"

Peter ran into prince Golovin. The latter was reputed to be a knowledgeable person who had travelled abroad and knew foreign languages.

Golovin looked at the paper, sneered and said:

"You call this a newspaper, Sire! I was in the German town of Hamburg, now there you'll find a real newspaper."

Peter's face dropped. He frowned and turned gloomy.

"You're really something," he uttered, "you're about as smart as a jackass. And you call yourself a prince. It's no wonder you say 'in the German town of Hamburg'! I know very well that theirs is better, but it's not our own. I'm sure that their beginnings were humble too. Give us some time. Be satisfied with small pickings at first, more will come later."

DANILA

Danila was known for miles around as a wise peasant. He had his own opinions on the world.

After Narva, the only subject of conversation in his village was about the Swedes, king Carl, tsar Peter and military affairs in general.

"Those Swedes are strong," said the peasants, "we're no match for them. Why do we need the sea anyway! We've always done without and we can do without now."

"You're all wrong," said Danila. "It's not that the Swedes are strong, we're simply weak. As to the sea, you're off track. Russia can't get along without the sea. We need to fish, to carry on trade, to name just a few things."

When the bells were taken away, the countryside was astir again for a few days.

"The end of the world is coming," the parish priest shouted and tore at his hair.

The women cried, crossed themselves and the peasant men wore gloomy expressions. Everyone expected calamity. But in this matter as in others Danila had his own mind.

"It has to be," he said. "The state needs the bells more than we do. God wouldn't condemn us for this kind of thing."

The priest called him a blasphemer and from that time bore a grudge against him.

To add to the situation, Peter soon instituted new taxes. The peasants moaned and brought out their last possessions for the tax collector, tightening the belts around their waists.

"Well, how do you like that?" they asked Danila. "This new order? Are you still ready to defend it?"

"No," said Danila. "I have some differences with the tsar."

"Listen to that!" snarled the peasants. "He and the tsar! He's found a friend. The tsar's not about to look upon your face!"

"It makes no difference what the tsar will do. It's not forbidden to think whatever you wish," answered Danila. "We owe Peter thanks for bringing glory to the state, but sometime he'll have to answer for the fact that he's taking the last ounce of bread from the peasant."

The peasants nodded their heads in agreement with Danila. One, however, suddenly shouted out:

"Well, why don't you tell it to the tsar."

"I will," answered Danila.

In fact he did. But it didn't happen right away, rather in the following manner.

Somebody informed the officials about Danila's speeches, the priest maybe, or perhaps someone else. Soldiers arrived in the village, bound Danila and dragged him off to Moscow to the authorities, to prince Romodanovsky himself.

They twisted his arms, put him on the rack and began to torture him.

"Who taught you to say all this about the tsar?" prince Romodanovsky asked him.

"What I said doesn't matter, it's long past," answered Danila.

"What?" shouted Romodanovsky. "For that kind of talk we can put you on the stake, vile inciter!"

"Put me where you want," said Danila. "To a peasant it's all the same where he ends up. It might even be better on the stake than slaving for the boyars."

Prince Romodanovsky lost his temper, grabbed a switch which was white hot from the fire and began to lash the naked body of Danila. Danila began to feel faint and bent over like a birch in the wind.

At this point Peter walked in.

"What's this fellow on the rack for?"

"He's a rebel," said Prince Romodanovsky. "He's been spreading bad rumours about the authorities."

Peter approached Danila. The latter's eyes opened a slit, before him was the tsar. Danila gathered together his strength and said:

"Sire, you've undertaken great things, but the common person is on his last rope. You've squeezed everything from the people, like a highway robber. Don't you forget, Sire, the people don't have many good words for such actions."

Danila's eyes closed once again, his head drooped down to his hairy chest. But Peter acted as if something had exploded inside him. He swung his head to the left, to the right and cast a furious glance at Danila.

"Hang him!" he roared, as if stung and stamped out.

CITY ON THE SEA

Peter the Great soon initiated a new war against the Swedes. The Russian troops gained their first victories and reached the Gulf of Finland at the mouth of the Neva River.

The banks of the Neva were pure wilderness: forests, marshland, thickets. The going was difficult and there was no place to pitch camp. All the same it was an important spot: it looked upon the sea.

After a few days Peter took Menshikov, sat in a boat and set out towards the sea. At the very mouth of the Neva there was an island. Peter scrambled out of the boat and began to scout the island. It was long and as even as the palm of the hand. Sickly-looking bushes stuck out in tuft-like fashion and underfoot all was moss and moisture.

"What a place, Sire!" Menshikov uttered.

"What do you mean? It's like anywhere else," Peter answered. "Most important, we've got the sea here."

They went on further. Suddenly Menshikov sank to his knees in the swamp. He yanked his feet out, moving on all fours and crawled his way to dry land. When he stood up he was caked with mud. When he looked at his feet he was short one of his boots.

"Fine work, Alexashka, you're doing just swell!" laughed Peter.

"This damned place!" the offended Menshikov exclaimed. "Sire, let's head back. There's no way to get across these swamps."

"Why backwards? Go on ahead, Danilych. After all, we came here as rulers, not guests," said Peter and continued towards the sea.

Menshikov unenthusiastically followed.

"Now take a look," Peter turned to Menshikov. "They say there's no life here, but what's this if not life?"

Peter went up to a hummock, cautiously pushed aside a bush and Menshikov caught sight of a nest. There sat a bird which looked with surprise upon the intruders but did not fly away.

"Hey, you," said Menshikov, "you're no coward, are you!"

The bird suddenly flapped its wings, flew into the air and proceeded to fly circles about the bush.

Peter and Menshikov finally arrived at the sea. Immense, gloomy, its waves rolled along in huge camel humps, tossed against the shore and smashed against the pebbles.

Peter stood, flexed his shoulder muscles and breathed deeply into his lungs. The sea wind fluttered the flaps of his **caftan,** first revealing the outer, green side, then the inner, red one. Peter gazed into the distance. There, hundreds of miles to the west were other countries, other shores.

Menshikov sat on a rock and took off his boots.

"Danilych!" suddenly said Peter.

Either Peter spoke softly or Menshikov pretended not to hear. In any case no answer was forthcoming.

"Danilych!" once again said Peter.

Menshikov pricked up his ears.

"Here at the sea," Peter made a sweeping gesture, "here at the sea we're going to build a city."

Menshikov's boot fell from his hand.

"A city?" he queried. "Here, on this swamp, a city?"

"That's right," said Peter, stepping along the shore.

Menshikov hung on to his boot and watched the receding figure of Peter, lost in admiration.

For the task of building the city on the Neva River craftsmen from all over Russia were gathered up: carpenters, joiners, bricklayers. Thousands of peasants were driven to the spot as well.

Little Nikita and his father, Silanti Dymov, were among these peasants. Dymov was given a place along with the other workers in a wet dug-out. Nikita settled in with his father on a bunk.

Morning. Four o'clock. The signal-cannon fired over the work camp. The workers got up, among them the father of Nikita. They spent the whole day digging in the mud in swamp, digging canals, cutting down trees and dragging heavy logs.

All day Nikita was left alone. He was a curious chap. He was excited by the multitude of soldiers and the swarms of workers. He was fascinated by the nearby sea. He had never seen so much water! It was even a little terrifying. He raced down to the harbour and was amazed at the ships there. He wandered around the brand-new city. He watched them cut out clearings in the woods and then begin to build homes along these clearings. The workers became used to having Nikita around. Looking at him reminded them of their own homes and families. They became very fond of him. "Nikita, bring some water," they asked and he ran to fulfill the request. "Nikita, do tell, how did you steal tobacco from the soldiers?" And he told.

Until autumn Nikita had a gay life. But then, however, the rains fell. Nikita started growing bored. He had to sit alone in the dug-out all day, with water up to the knees. Nikita was indeed bored.

About this time Silanti carved a toy for his son out of a piece of wood: a soldier with his weapon.

Nikita was overjoyed.

"Stand!" he gave the command.

The soldier stood up without moving an eyelid.

"Lie down!" cried out Nikita and surreptitiously gave him a little shove.

When Nikita got tired of playing with the soldier he would begin to bail water out of the hut. He would drag the water out into the street, return after a short breather, and the water had returned to its previous level. It could make you want to cry!

Hunger soon began to stalk the city. Food hadn't been stockpiled for the autumn and the roads were impassable. Disease began to spread. People began to die like flies.

Nikita too fell ill. His father returned from work one day and found Nikita with a fever. He tossed about on the bunk in a constant thirst. All evening Silanti stayed by his son's side. In the morning he stayed away from work. But during the day an officer and some soldiers burst into the dug-out.

"Don't you know the rules?!" shouted the officer.

"This is my son here. He's sick. My little son is dying..."

The officer didn't bother to listen. He gave a command, the soldiers bound Silanti's arms and drove him to work. When he returned his son's body was already cold.

"Nikita, Nikita!" Silanti shook his son.

Nikita lay still, without budging. His toy forgotten on the ground: the soldier holding his weapon. Nikita was dead.

No coffin was made for Nikita. He was buried like all the rest, in a common hole.

Silanti didn't long outlive his son. By the first frost they brought him to the cemetery. Many others died at that time. The bones of many a peasant were put to rest in the swamps and marshes.

The city which Nikita's father helped to build was Petersburg.

After an interval of a few years it became the capital of the Russian state.

FOR THE GLORY OF RUSSIA

In 1704 Russian troops for the second time approached the city of Narva. A fierce battle ended in complete victory for the Russians.

Peter and Menshikov, riding on steeds, were moving away from the fortress. After them, at some distance, Russian generals left in a group. Stooping his shoulders Peter sat heavily in the saddle, casting a tired gaze upon the rusty coloured withers of his horse. Menshikov, standing up in the stirrups, now and then would turn his head from side to side and cheerfully wave in greeting to the soldiers and officers.

They moved along in silence.

"Sire," Menshikov suddenly said, "Peter Alekseyevich, take a look," and pointed to the bank of the Narova.

Peter followed his gaze. On the bank of the river, its barrel pointed to the sky, stood a cannon. Soldiers crowded about the cannon on all sides. A sergeant had scrambled up the gun-carriage, holding a ladle in his hand. He reached the ladle into the barrel of the cannon, scooped out something and passed it on to the soldiers.

"Sire, take a look," said Menshikov. "Look how they've decided to drink. How did they ever dream that one up?! They've poured wine into the cannon

barrel! Those are our artillery, the eagles of our force, our heroes!"

Peter smiled. He stopped his horse. The voices of the soldiers could be heard.

"What shall we drink for?" asked the sergeant and looked expectantly at the soldiers.

"For Tsar Peter!" the response poured forth.

"For Narva!"

"For the splendid city of Saint-Petersburg!"

Peter and Menshikov continued along, but the sound still carried along to them.

"For the artillery!"

"For our brothers who lay down their lives!"

"Danilych," said Peter, "let's go to the sea."

In an hour's time they stood at the water's edge. Waves licked the soles of Peter's enormous jack-boots. He stood with his arms crossed looking into the distance. Menshikov kept a slight distance from him.

"Danilych," said Peter to Menshikov, "do you remember our conversation then, in Novgorod?"

"I remember."

"You recall Narva?"

"Of course."

"Well, that's how we stand. It turns out that it wasn't for nothing that we kept coming here, that we spilled so much Russian sweat and blood."

"That's right, Sire, it wasn't in vain."

"And the bells. As it turns out, we were justified in taking them. And the factories we built. And the schools..."

"That's right, that's right," affirmed Menshikov.

"Danilych, in that case it wouldn't be a sin for us to drink a bit now? No sin, eh, Danilych?"

"Absolutely correct."

"What should we drink for?"

"For His Majesty Peter Alekseyevich!" ejaculated Menshikov.

"Fool!" Peter cut him short. "We must drink to the sea, to the glory of Russia."

PETRUS ALEXEWITZ

Czaar et Magnus Dux Moscoviæ

1

2

1. Tsar Peter I (the Great) (contemporary engraving). 2. The Preobrazhenski Regiment returning from the Sea of Azov (contemporary peasant woodcut). 3. Gunners in Peter's army. 4. A rank-and-file grenadier, Preobrazhenski Regiment. 5. Dragoon in Peter's army. 6. Fusil (a light flint-lock musket) from the time of Peter. A fusilier. 7. The uniform of a colonel of the Preobrazhenski Regiment, belonging to Peter I. 8. Cannon from the time of Peter.

3

4

5

6

7

8

9

10

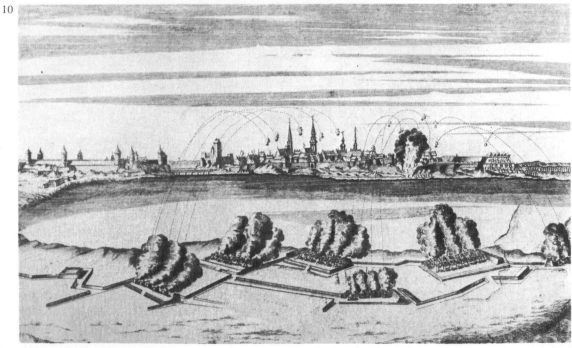

11

12

14

13

9. "Window to Europe". Peter the Great's first naval victory over the Swedes, May 7, 1703. 10. Storming and capture of the Narva Fortress, August 9, 1704 (an 18th century engraving). 11. The city of Tula—here under Peter I were established the first weapons factories. 12. "Beard tokens", given to those who had paid the tax for wearing a beard: Peter forced the **boyars** to shave their faces in order to expose them to "European culture". 13. Bells from Russian churches. 14. Iron collar used to punish delinquent workers at Peter's factories.

15

15. Alexander Menshikov, companion and retainer of Peter I, elevated to the highest government posts from humble beginnings.

17

16

16. Saint-Petersburg under Peter I (contemporary engraving). 17. Painting by Valentin Serov entitled "Peter the First". The tsar is depicted during the construction of the Northern capital.

18

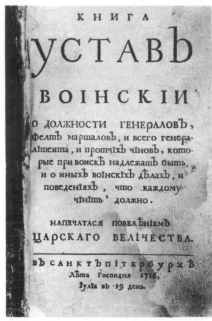

19

20

21

22

23

18. The Sukharev tower in Moscow, housing a school for sailors, artillery men and engineers (an 18th century engraving). 19. "Military Manual", 1716. 20. The first Russian newspaper, Vedomosti (The Record), August 31, 1720. The first number was dated 1703. 21. The Arithmetic of Magnitski, 1703—one of the first Russian textbooks. 22. Captain Martinovich with Russian students, sent in 1697 to Italy to study navigation. 23. ABC book with Peter's corrections.

SUVOROV
AND THE RUSSIAN ARMY

THE PACKAGE

For disobedience to the Emperor Suvorov had been drummed out of the army. The Field Marshal lived in the village of Konchanskoye. He played at knucklebones with the local children and helped to ring the bells in the church belfry. On holy days he sang in the church choir.

At this time the Russian army embarked on a new campaign. There was no one in Russia who had the stature of Suvorov. But soon the village of Konchanskoye was to come into the limelight.

A young officer came on a troika to see Suvorov, carrying with him a package sealed with five official stamps, from the Emperor Paul I himself.

Suvorov glanced at the package and read aloud:

"To be delivered personally to Count Alexander Suvorov."

The Field Marshal turned the package about in his hands and gave it back to the officer.

"It's not for me," he said. "Not for me."

"What do you mean, not for you!" said the astonished officer. "I was ordered to deliver it to you personally."

"Not for me. It's not me that it's for," repeated Suvorov. "Don't delay me. I've promised to go for mushrooms and berries with the children."

With these words he prepared to leave.

The officer stared at the package—all was as fit as it should be: both "To the Count" and "Alexander Suvorov".

"Alexander Vassilyevich!" he shouted. "Your Honour!"

"Well, what now?" Suvorov paused.

"The package..."

"I've already told you, it's not for me," Suvorov said. "Apparently it's for some other Suvorov."

Thus, the messenger was forced to leave mission unaccomplished.

Several days passed and then the young officer once again arrived in Konchanskoye on the troika. Once again he carried a package from the Emperor with five seals.

Suvorov glanced at the package and read:

"To the Russian Field Marshal Alexander Suvorov."

"This one is for me," he explained and unsealed the package.

FIGHT, DON'T MAKE TALLIES!

When Suvorov first entered battle he was a very young officer. Russia was at that time engaged in war with Prussia. The troops of both armies were deployed over a long front. The armies were preparing for a heavy battle but for the time being contented themselves with brief forays to gather information.

Suvorov was given a Cossack squadron and instructed to keep an eye on their opponents.

The Prussian town of Landsberg was located some forty versts from the corps in which Suvorov was serving. It was a small but important town for it straddled major cross-roads. The town was guarded by a heavily armed detachment of Prussian hussars.

Suvorov participated in several scouting expeditions with his Cossacks, covered the whole region, but, as if in spite, they didn't succeed in laying eyes on even one Prussian.

What kind of war is it when you can't even catch a glimpse of your enemy?

At this point the young officer decided to take a gamble, to tempt fate by taking Landsberg. He was young and proud, that Suvorov.

He woke up his Cossacks in the dead of night and ordered them to saddle up their horses.

"Where are we going?" the Cossack lieutenant anxiously inquired.

"Forward!" was all Suvorov offered in answer.

Suvorov's Cossack squadron covered all forty versts before dawn and turned up at the bank of a deep river, just opposite the Prussian town.

Suvorov looked all about—there was no bridge. The Prussians had burned it as a precautionary measure. They didn't want to be caught in a surprise attack.

Suvorov stood on the bank gathering his thoughts. Suddenly he commanded:

"Into the water! After me!" and was the first to push forward into the water.

The Cossacks came out of the water on the opposite shore at the very walls of the enemy town.

"It's our town! Forward!" Suvorov shouted.

"There are Prussian hussars there," objected the Cossack lieutenant.

"Well, dear God! That's just what we want!" answered Suvorov. "It's them we're looking for, isn't it?!"

At this point the Cossack lieutenant understood that there was no stopping Suvorov.

"Alexander Vassilyevich," he said, "why don't we at least find out how many of them there are?"

"What for?" exclaimed Suvorov. "We came to fight, not to make tallies, didn't we?!"

The Cossacks broke into the town and routed the enemy.

BOLDNESS

War was being waged against the Turks. Suvorov was by this time already a general.

In the battle which took place near Focsani the Turks had disposed their troops in such a fashion that their rear was exposed only to areas of swampland.

As for their cannons, one couldn't ask for better positioning. The enemy couldn't attack from the rear and their flanks were unassailable. The Turks were confident.

Suvorov, however, was not afraid of the swamp. His heroic troops pushed their way through the marshes and, like thunder from a clear blue sky, attacked the Turk artillery from the rear. They managed to seize the cannons of the Turks.

The Turks, Austrians and Russians all considered this manoeuvre of Suvorov's to be risky and bold.

It's all well and good that they made their way through the swamp, but what if they hadn't succeeded?!

"Let them call it boldness," grinned Suvorov. "Boldness is no sin when it comes to warfare."

Few knew, however, that before committing his troops to cross the swamp Suvorov had assigned some of his most experienced soldiers to cover the whole area of the swamp and pick out the most auspicious route for their comrades to follow. Suvorov valued his soldiers and acted accordingly.

A month after the incident, during another battle with the Turks, a certain Colonel Illovaisky decided to repeat the bold manoeuvre of Suvorov's.

The circumstances were very similar—once again Turkish cannons and swampland.

"Suvorov succeeded," said Illovaisky. "Am I a lesser man? It'll work for me too."

Unfortunately, it didn't work this time. Illovaisky led his troops through unfamiliar terrain. The soldiers bogged down in the swamp. They began to drown. A commotion ensued, shouts and cries broke the silence.

The Turks understood what was going on. They turned their cannons about and butchered the Russian troops.

Many many died. Illovaisky, however, survived.

Suvorov was infuriated by the incident. He cursed and shouted himself hoarse.

"I wanted to be like you and make a bold move," Illovaisky defended himself.

"Boldness!" roared Suvorov. "Boldness there was, but where was the skill?!"

For this senseless loss of soldiers' lives Suvorov demoted the colonel to the rank of common soldier and sent him to work in logistics.

"It's impossible to trust him with human lives," said Suvorov, "he'll be less dangerous around horses."

IZMAIL

Izmail, a Turkish fortress, was considered unassailable: it stood on the bank of a wide river, the Danube, and had a force of some forty thousand soldiers and two hundred cannon. In addition, it was surrounded by a deep moat and high ramparts. The outer wall surrounding Izmail had a circumference of six versts.

The Russian generals were unable to take this Turkish fortress.

It was bruited about that Suvorov was on his way to Izmail. It was true, he soon appeared. He arrived and called a gathering.

"How are we going to handle this?" he asked.

The situation was complicated by the fact that it was already late autumn.

"We'd better turn back," his generals started to say. "We should go home to our winter quarters."

"'To our winter quarters!'" Suvorov mockingly echoed them. "'Home!' Not on your lives! The road home for the Russian soldier runs directly through Izmail. There is no other way out of this place for the Russian soldier."

A very peculiar life took form near Izmail after this decision. Suvorov ordered that ramparts be built to replicate those which surrounded the Izmail fortress and he began to instruct the soldiers. During the day they learned how to attack with bayonets, but in the evening, under cover from the Turks, he ordered them to climb the rampart. As they approached the rampart he shouted:

"Hold it! Start again. It won't do to run like a herd of rams."

Thus the soldiers rehearsed, first forward, then back, and then over again. When they had learned how to approach in a more scattered formation Suvorov began to show them how to scale the ramparts.

"Here," he said, "you want to be together. Everyone go up at the same time, numbers are important. You all hit the rampart at the same moment."

Suvorov worked with the soldiers for a few days and then sent an emissary to the Turkish general, proposing that the latter surrender. The general proudly answered:

"The sun will set in the East before the Russians take Izmail."

At that point Suvorov gave the order to storm the fortress. The soldiers faithfully executed the manoeuvres which Suvorov had taught: they crossed the moat, scaled the rampart. Using scaling ladders they raced up the walls.

The Turks fought feverishly but could not hold back the Russians. Suvorov's troops broke through into Izmail, and took the entire Turkish army prisoner.

Only one Turk escaped unharmed from the fortress. Trembling from fear he raced to the Turkish capital and related the newest feat accomplished by the Russian soldiers and the newest victory won by General Suvorov.

THE MEDAL

During the battle at the Rimnik River the young, inexperienced soldier, Kuzma Shapkin, took fright and spent the whole day hiding in the bushes.

Shapkin wasn't aware of the fact that Suvorov had caught sight of him.

Many awards and decorations were given out among Suvorov's troops in commemoration of this victory over the Turks. The officers called their regiments and companies to form ranks. Suvorov appeared before the troops and began to distribute awards.

Shapkin stood in the ranks with all the rest and waited impatiently for the whole business to end. He was ashamed of himself.

And suddenly... Shapkin shuddered, he couldn't believe his ears.

"Grenadier Shapkin, front and centre!" ordered Suvorov.

The soldier stood as if his feet were rooted to the ground, not budging an inch.

"Grenadier Shapkin, front and centre!" repeated Suvorov.

"Get moving, get moving," the soldiers prodded him.

Shapkin moved forward with downcast eyes and blushing. In the blink of an eye Suvorov had pinned a medal on his chest.

In the evening the soldiers were each given a cup of wine. They settled down near their tents and began to recollect the details of the battle, to figure out to whom and for what reason the medals had been awarded. One had received an award for thinking up a means of driving the Turks out of a trench. Another for seizing the Turkish standard. A third—for not taking fright in the face of ten Turks and for not falling prisoner despite suffering severe wounds.

"And you, what did you do to win the medal?" the soldiers asked Shapkin.

He only remained silent in response.

Shapkin wore the medal but he could find no peace of mind. He felt oppressed and avoided his companions. He was silent for entire days on end.

"What's the matter with you? Is the medal weighing your tongue down?" the soldiers joked to him.

A week passed: the soldier's conscience was eating him up inside. Shapkin couldn't stand it any longer and went to see Suvorov. He entered the tent and gave back the medal.

"For Heaven's sake!" Suvorov exclaimed. "Turning a medal back in!"

Shapkin's head drooped low in shame. He poured out his heart to Suvorov, confessing all.

"Well," he thought, "it's off with my head."

Suvorov laughed and then embraced the unfortunate hero.

"You've done a fine turn!" he said. "I know everything, fellow, without your confession. I wanted to test you. You're a good soldier. A good one, do you hear? Remember, heroes are not born, you have to develop the qualities within yourself. Run along now. As to the medal, alright, let it remain with me for the time being. But mind you, the medal's yours. It's for you to earn and then to wear."

Suvorov had seen clearly.

In the very next battle Shapkin was the first to break into the Turkish fortress, earning the medal and well-deserved fame.

BRIDGES

The Russians were fighting in Italy. French generals had been pitched against Suvorov. The French had carefully chosen their positions, apparently with the object in mind of destroying Suvorov. They had withdrawn to the river Adda, moved to the far side and burned the bridges behind them. "Here," they decided, "at this crossing we will knock out Suvorov."

The French generals conducted dissembling manoeuvres to try to convince Suvorov that they were moving further on. All day they moved their troops away from the river only to return them in the evening to hide in the bushes and ravines.

Suvorov moved up to the river and halted. He ordered that bridges be built. The soldiers rolled up their sleeves, took up axes and began to work. Two bridges were begun. The soldiers working on each competed to be first to complete the job.

French scouts observed the work carefully and made hourly progress reports to their generals.

The French generals were pleased. All was going according to their plans. They had tricked Suvorov.

The French were indeed clever. However, as it turned out Suvorov was one step ahead of them.

When the bridges were near completion he suddenly took his troops and began to move downstream along the bank of the Adda in the dead of night.

"But what about the bridges, Your Honour?" the sapper officers asked him disconcertedly.

"Hush," Suvorov put his finger to his lips. "Keep building the bridges. Have them make more noise with the axes."

The sound of the axes carried over the river, but at the same time the Field Marshal led his army downstream and forded the crossing, making no use of the bridges leading to the enemy shore.

The French generals were resting peacefully. They knew that the bridges were not yet completed. The sound of the axes over the river relaxed them. They had nothing to worry about.

And suddenly Suvorov appeared from the rear. The bayonets flashed, as they were bared.

"Hurray! Follow me, my heroes!"

The generals saw what was going on, but it was too late. They hadn't expected the Russians. They trembled in hesitation, then ran. Of officers alone more than two hundred fell into Suvorov's hands.

In the end the bridges were completed. After all they were necessary, for an army consists not only of soldier-heroes but also of carts and artillery.

IN THE FRONT AND IN THE REAR LINES

During the night before the storming of Turin Suvorov accompanied by two officers, Major Pronin and Captain Zabelin, went on a scouting expedition. The Field Marshal wanted to get a look for himself at the accesses to the city and ordered the officers to bring along paper to sketch out maps of the localities.

The night was still and bright: the stars and moon shone clearly. The region was picturesque, marked by small copses and tall poplars.

Suvorov took in the scenery as he went along.

They came to the very approaches to the city and stopped on a small hillock.

The officers dismounted from their horses and took up their paper. Major Pronin was a daring fellow—he moved closer and closer to the city. Captain Zabelin was quite the opposite—he stayed behind Suvorov.

Twenty minutes passed when suddenly a fierce cannonade erupted. Either the French noticed the Russians or they simply decided to begin firing up the road. In any case cannon balls landed right on the hillock, at the feet of Suvorov, tearing up the ground around the Field Marshal.

Suvorov sat quietly on his horse, not moving. He looked—Major Pronin continued his work unfrightened by the cannon fire, sketching out his maps of the area. But Zabelin was nowhere to be seen. He had disappeared from view.

The Russian troops, hearing the fierce cannonade, became apprehensive about Suvorov. A Cossack expedition rushed off in the direction of Turin.

"Your Honour!" cried the Cossack lieutenant. "Move away, get away from here! It's too dangerous here!"

"No, Lieutenant," replied Suvorov, "it's a marvellous spot. Look about," he pointed to the tall poplars, "we have no need of anything better. Tomorrow we'll begin our attack from this spot."

The cannonade ended. Suvorov got ready to turn back. He cried out to Pronin and to Zabelin.

Pronin returned, his sheet of paper filled up with indicators marking ravines, hillocks and all that was necessary for their information. But Zabelin was still missing. They began to search for the captain. They found him about two hundred metres to the rear of Suvorov. He lay with his head smashed by a true shot from the enemy. His empty piece of paper lay next to him.

Suvorov glanced at Pronin and then at Zabelin. He said:

"The brave are always in the front, the cowards are always killed in the rear lines."

SOUP AND KASHA

Suvorov's army was in the completing stages of a forced march. Stopping to camp in the woods on a small incline at the edge of a small river, the soldiers built camp-fires and began to cook up soup and **kasha**.

When the food was prepared they all set upon their meal with a healthy appetite. The generals, however, were wandering about their own tents waiting for Lushka. Lushka was the special cook for the generals. He had somehow fallen behind during the march, and the generals were now awaiting his arrival anxiously.

"Well, there's no sense waiting," said Suvorov, "let's go over and join the soldiers at their camp-fires, generals."

"No, that won't do at all," answered the generals, "we'll wait. Lushka will be here soon."

Suvorov knew that the generals would turn their noses up at the food the common soldier ate.

KASHA — thick porridge

"Well, as you like."

He made a beeline for the nearest light from a camp-fire.

The soldiers squeezed more closely together around the fire and offered Suvorov the best place. They handed him a tureen and spoon.

Suvorov made himself comfortable and began to eat. The Field Marshal was used to the common fare of the soldier. He wasn't squeamish about either soup or **kasha**. He ate and filled himself to his heart's content.

"Hey, this is really fine soup, delicious in fact!" Suvorov praised.

The soldiers broke into smiles. They knew that the Field Marshal was something of an expert about soups. It meant that the soup really must be quite tasty.

Suvorov ate his fill of the soup, then began on the **kasha**.

"Not bad, in fact it's really delicious **kasha**."

Suvorov satisfied his hunger, thanked the soldiers and returned to his generals. He lay down to sleep, and slept deeply and peacefully. But his generals could not drop off. They tossed about from side to side in their beds, still hungry. They were waiting for their Lushka.

Lushka, however, had still not arrived by morning.

Suvorov got his troops up and on the march again. The generals moved dispiritedly, their stomachs grumbling. They were famished. But they had to suffer until the next halt was called. This time when the troops stopped the generals were right on Suvorov's heels when he approached the soldiers' camp-fires. They weren't about to starve to death. They found places around the camp-fires and could hardly wait for the soldiers' fare to be finished cooking.

Suvorov grinned. He decided to ladle out the soup and **kasha** to the generals himself. As he dished out a portion to each of them he added:

"Eat heartily, go ahead, take it. And from now on, don't be so squeamish about the soldier's way of life. The soldier is a human being after all. The common soldier is dearer to me than my own life."

PROSHKA

When Proshka was assigned the job of being orderly to Suvorov he was overjoyed. "I've lucked out!" he thought. "I won't have to get up early in the morning. None of the usual duties, no particular regime of any sort. Nothing to complain about!"

But Proshka was in for a very big surprise. On the very first day, at four in the morning, somebody shook Proshka awake.

He opened his eyes and looked—it was Suvorov.

"Get up, young fellow," he said. "Our Russian heroes aren't fond of oversleeping."

As luck would have it, Suvorov was the very first in the army to wake up mornings.

Proshka got up and immediately encountered another unpleasantry. The Field Marshal ordered him to bring in a bucket of cold water and he began to pour it over himself.

Suvorov bathed his chest, neck, back and arms. Proshka watched him, eyes wide-open in wonder. This was really something to behold!

"Well, what's with you?" barked Suvorov and ordered Proshka to follow suit with the freezing cold water.

The soldier huddled up and screeched from the unaccustomed shock of the water. But Suvorov laughed.

"A sound mind in a sound body!" and continued to laugh.

After the dousing Suvorov led Proshka out into a meadow.

"Catch me!" he shouted to the soldier as he ran.

The soldier pursued the Field Marshal for a half hour. He was terribly winded, his side ached. Suvorov, though older, looked as if he'd just returned from a stroll. He stood there and once again burst into laughter.

Thus, for Proshka not the easy life but rather a series of tortures had begun. Either Suvorov would decide to conduct a review of all the defensive positions and Proshka would have to bounce around in the saddle all day or he would make checks on the night patrols and Proshka would go without sleep.

To add to his misery Suvorov began to study Turkish and ordered Proshka to study it as well.

"Why in the world do I need to know how the infernal Turks speak," the soldier objected.

"What kind of a statement is that?" Suvorov said in an irritated manner. "The Turks are preparing for war, we're going to be fighting them."

Proshka had to resign himself to the inevitable. He picked up a primer in Turkish and began to grind away miserably.

Proshka dreamed about a quiet place to relax—but it didn't help. He thought about asking to be reassigned to his old company. But then he became accustomed and attached to the Field Marshal and to the end of his days faithfully and honestly served Suvorov.

A TRUE SOLDIER

Suvorov once approached a soldier and began firing questions at him:

"How far is it from the Earth to the Moon?"

"The length of two of Suvorov's forced marches!" was the soldier's riposte.

The Field Marshal gasped in amazement. Here was an answer! Here was a soldier!

Suvorov loved it when soldiers were resourceful in their answers, when they didn't hesitate. Thus he appreciated this fellow, and liked the answer but was vexed at his own position.

"Well, can it be true that I, Suvorov, can't beat this fellow in a game of wits?"

After an interval of a few days he again ran into this resourceful fellow and immediately took to the attack:

"How many stars are there in the sky?"

"Just a minute, Your Honour," answered the soldier, "I'll count for you," and stared up into the sky.

Suvorov waited and waited, chilled by the cold wind, but the soldier unhurriedly counted away.

Suvorov spat in irritation and left. "What a soldier!" he thought once again. "Well, I'll make sure that the third time we meet I'll catch him flat on his feet."

He encountered the soldier a third time and had another question ready:

"Well, my fine fellow, what was the name of my great grandmother?"

Suvorov was quite satisfied with the question. How in the world could a simple soldier know the name of such an obscure person? He rubbed his hands in pleasure and was about to say: "Well, fellow, you've fallen for it!" when the soldier suddenly came to attention and shouted:

"Victoria, Your Honour!"

Suvorov was delighted: "No, no, it wasn't Victoria."

"Victoria, Victoria," the soldier repeated. "How could it be that our Field Marshal had no Victoria somewhere in his background?"

Suvorov was astonished. What an answer! I certainly have run into a clever fellow, this soldier.

"Well, since you're so clever," said Suvorov, "tell me, what is the difference between your company commander and myself?"

"The difference is," the soldier replied without hesitation, "that even if my commander wanted to promote me to sergeant there's nothing he could do, whereas if the thought even crossed your mind, I'd be..."

What could Suvorov do? He had to promote him to the rank of sergeant. He returned to his tent and spoke highly of the young soldier:

"My God, how he made a dunce of me! That's for sure! Here's a real soldier for you! A Russian!"

GET OUT OF THE WAY!

Suvorov loved to travel at breakneck speed. Whether on horseback or in a sleigh he loved it when the wind lashed his face and he had to catch his breath.

They were in the North. One day he got into his sleigh and, together with Proshka, set out to inspect the network of fortresses. At this very time a courier was rushing on his way from Petersburg with important papers to be delivered to Suvorov. The officer reined in his sweating horses at the headquarters and shouted out:

"Where is Field Marshal Suvorov? I have urgent business for him!"

"He left," it was explained to the courier.

"Where to?"

"To the Ozernaya Fortress."

The officer rushed off to Ozernaya Fortress.

"Is Suvorov here?"

"He's already gone."

"Where to?"

"To Likola Fortress."

He rushed to Likola.

"Is Suvorov here?"

"He's left for Kyumen-Grad Fortress."

He raced to Kyumen-Grad.

"Is Suvorov here?"

"He left..."

Suvorov had managed this point as well, but he'd got stuck on the road. One of his horses picked up a limp and it became necessary to turn back. They crawled along barely moving. Proshka sat in the coach-box lost in thought. Suvorov fretted away, now and then poking the orderly in the back to insist that he prod the horses on.

"It's impossible, Your Honour, the horse is injured," was the persistent reply from Proshka.

Suvorov quieted down, waited a bit and then Proshka would receive another poke. The Field Marshal couldn't sit still, he didn't have enough patience to move at such a slow clip.

They proceeded about two versts when Suvorov spotted a troika coming in their direction. The steeds fairly flew across the field. The snow spewed up from under their hooves. The steam rose up from their nostrils in streams.

Suvorov virtually jumped up in delight. He looked: instead of a coachman on the driver's seat sat a young officer, reins in hand, whip at his belt, wearing a **papakha** over his ears, his curls whipped by the wind.

PAPAKHA — a tall Caucasian hat, usually of sheepskin

"What a daredevil, what a daredevil!" Suvorov couldn't restrain his admiration.

"A courier, Your Honour," said Proshka, "not from these parts, by the looks of him from Petersbourg."

Suvorov watched the courier with admiration. The winter road was narrow and unpacked. The going was difficult. But the horses approached rapidly. The snort of the horses and screaching of the sleigh-runners were already audible.

"Out of the way!" shouted the officer.

Proshka hesitated: he wasn't used to making way for others.

"Out of the way!" repeated the officer as the sleigh hurtled down upon Suvorov's... Smash!

Suvorov and Proshka tumbled out into the snow and sunk in up to their waists.

The courier raced by: he whistled as he galloped into the distance.

Proshka picked himself up, shook the snow off his clothes and cursed as his eyes followed the receding figure of the courier.

"Keep quiet!" Suvorov snapped at him. Once again he feasted his eyes upon the sleigh: "Daredevil, my word, what a bold fellow!"

For three days the officer rushed about the Russian Northern border. Finally he found Suvorov.

Suvorov received the papers, glanced at the courier and taking the ring off his finger, he suddenly handed it to the officer.

"What's this for, Your Honour?" the courier said in amazement.

"For boldness!"

The officer stood there, not comprehending a thing. Suvorov continued:

"Take it, take it. Accept it from me! For daring. For the Russian soul."

BAYONET

Suvorov once visited a friend of his in Novgorod province. In the evenings the friends stayed home, recollecting old friends, battles and marches. But during the day Suvorov set out to wander in the woods and take a look at the area. Here in the woods, near an old oak he met a little boy called Sanka Vydrin.

"Are you a soldier?" Sanka asked Suvorov.

"That's right," the Field Marshal answered.

"Where are you coming from?"

"From the war."

"Tell me about Suvorov."

The Field Marshal squinted his eyes and looked mischievously at the little boy:

"Who's this Suvorov you're talking about? Suvorov you say?"

"You don't know? He's the one who fought against the Turks. Who took Izmail. The Field Marshal."

"No," said Suvorov, "I don't know."

"What kind of a soldier are you anyway," Sanka grinned, "if you don't know of Suvorov!" The little boy grabbed a stick and shouted in the manner of Suvorov: "Hurray! Follow me! Forward, my heroes!"

Sanka raced around the Field Marshal, making a grand effort to stab Suvorov in the stomach with the stick.

"Hey, you're quite some fellow!" thought the astonished Suvorov. Still it pleased him to know that his name and his feats were known even to children.

Finally Sanka quieted down, stuck the stick in his belt and said:

"Mister, give me your bayonet."

"What do you need that for?"

"To play war. To attack the enemy."

"My word!" exclaimed Suvorov. "Uh, you see, I don't have a bayonet."

"Don't fib, don't fib," said Sanka. "It can't be, a soldier without a bayonet."

"I mean it, I have none," Suvorov assured him and gave a sweeping gesture with his arms.

"Well, bring one to me," Sanka relentlessly pursued him.

He pestered him to the point at which there was nothing left for Suvorov to do but to promise him a bayonet.

On the very next day Sanka raced to the old oak in the woods and waited there until evening, but the "soldier" didn't appear again.

"Liar!" Sanka cursed. "Good-for-nothing, that soldier."

After a few days, however, a man on horseback rode up to the hut in which Sanka lived, summoned the little boy and gave him a package.

"From Field Marshal Suvorov," he announced.

Sanka's mouth dropped wide open in astonishment and remained in that state. He stood dumbly looking at the package, not believing his eyes or ears. Could it really be that the Field Marshal himself had sent him, Sanka, a package?

Peasant men and women ran to the Vydrin hut, the children gathered in a flock, even the invalid Kachkin limped his way over.

"Open it up, open it up!" the peasants shouted.

With trembling hands Sanka undid the package—it was a bayonet.

"An invincible Suvorov bayonet!" shouted Kachkin.

"My God, a real bayonet!" the women crossed themselves.

"Show us, show us!" implored the children.

At about this point Sanka began to come to his senses. He could finally close his mouth and his hands finally stopped trembling. He had figured it all out. He related the story of his meeting in the woods to his mother and father, to Kachkin, to the other children and to all the peasants in the village.

For years Sanka continued to tell this story in all its detail.

As to the bayonet?

Sanka treasured this bayonet more than anything else in the world. He wouldn't sleep without the bayonet next to him, he polished it, had a special case sewn, and carried it around like a precious gift. When Sanka grew up and became a soldier he went to war with this bayonet and used it in battle in a manner to make Suvorov proud.

POWDER ISN'T GUNPOWDER

The Emperor Paul I set about to reorganise the army. He didn't like the way Russians did things but preferred anything foreign, and especially German. Thus he decided to rebuild the Russian army in a Prussian, that is to say, German, manner.

He forced the soldiers to wear long braids, to set felt curls on their temples and to powder their hair with flour. Looking at such a soldier you'd think it was a dummy and not a Russian soldier.

The soldiers began to study parade formations. They learned how to turn smartly on the heels and how to march precisely in step in place of how to handle weapons and how to thrust properly with a bayonet.

Suvorov found the new system extremely distasteful and often made his opinion known.

"Russians have always beaten the Prussians, why do we have to imitate them?" the Field Marshal would ask.

Once Paul I invited Suvorov to attend a parade. The much praised Russian regiments marched past him in formation. Suvorov couldn't recognise his former heroes. The boldness and heroism was absent. They marched like wind-up toys. The clacking of heels against the cobblestones, the swishing of braids on the soldiers' backs... The Emperor was content.

"Just take a look, a little more work and we'll be a match for the Prussians," he said to Suvorov.

Suvorov's face contorted at these words and he involuntarily shuddered.

"I don't see what's so wonderful about that, Your Majesty. Russians have always beaten the Prussians, why should we make a lot of it now?"

The Emperor fell silent, simply casting a wrathful glance upon Suvorov. He stood in silence for a bit and then turned once again to Suvorov:

"Look, just you look! What dandy braids! What fine curls!"

"Curls, indeed," growled the Field Marshal.

The Emperor could no longer restrain himself. Turning to the Field Marshal, he poked him in his old-style uniform and shouted:

"Change it! Without delay! I order you!"

Here Suvorov uttered his famous phrase:

"Powder isn't gunpowder, curls aren't cannons, braids aren't broadswords, and I'm not a German, Your Majesty, but a full-blooded Russian!" and left the parade.

Paul, in a fit of anger, sent the stubborn old man into exile to the village of Konchanskoye.

FAT

The Alps are towering mountains marked by abrupt precipices and bottomless abysses. There are inaccessible cliffs and thundering waterfalls. The peaks of the mountains are covered with snow and swept perpetually by an icy wind.

On his last expedition Suvorov and his heroic soldiers made their way through the gorges and rapids of the Alps.

Blizzards ... avalanches ... frost. It was a long journey and the way was uncharted. The soldiers slipped, lost their footing and fell into the gorges. They had to drag heavy cannons and carry their ill and frostbitten comrades. They were surrounded by the enemy. Every interval of a mile brought a new battle.

Still the Russian army kept going, through the mountains and despite the enemy. They were determined to push through the Alps.

Food rations were scarce. The rusks had been soaked and ruined by the weather. Swiss villages were few and far between and had little to offer. The soldiers ate horsemeat and dug up roots in the ravines. When these were finished they began to eat the hides of the horses.

The soldiers lost weight until they were completely emaciated. They fastened their belts on the very last holes. They sighed as they marched along, conjuring up the fragrant smells of cabbage soup and the sensation of hot **kasha** melting in their mouths.

"If only we had even one loaf of bread, just one piece of pork fat!" sighed the soldiers.

To their surprise they soon procured a chunk of real fat from a remote cottage in the hills. It was a small chunk, the size perhaps of a palm. The soldiers surrounded it, their eyes sparkling, their nostrils distended.

The soldiers had decided to divide up the fat when suddenly they realised—how in the world could they divide up a portion which scarcely sufficed for one man?

The soldiers raised their voices in disagreement.

"Let's cast lots," suggested one.

"Let the person who found it eat it," objected another.

"No, we must do it so that everyone receives a share," piped in a third.

The argument went on and on.

Suddenly someone suggested:

"Brothers, here's what I suggest: let's give the chunk of fat to Suvorov."

"Now he's talking! Suvorov! Suvorov!" came from a chorus of voices.

The soldiers contacted Suvorov's orderly Proshka, gave him the chunk and ordered him to hand it to Suvorov.

The soldiers were content and Proshka was happy as well. He began to estimate how long the fat would last. He decided that if he cut off each day a piece the width of a finger, the whole chunk would last exactly a week.

Proshka broached the matter to Suvorov.

"Fat?" the latter said, astonished. "Where did it come from?"

Proshka related the incident with the soldiers. In a word, it was a present from the soldiers.

"Those men, my heroes!" Suvorov exclaimed with tears in his eyes. Suddenly he spun upon Proshka and barked at him: "How could you accept it! What a nerve! The soldiers get horsehide and I fat!..."

"Well, they're only common soldiers," Proshka said.

"Soldiers, eh," continued Suvorov. "Soldiers who mean more to me than my own life. Turn right around and hustle over to them. Give them back the chunk with my thanks. Give them my deepest regards."

"But they themselves sent it along," insisted Proshka. "What possible good can a palmful of fat do them. For them it's a drop in the bucket. But for one person..."

Suvorov glanced at the fat. There was reason in what Proshka said, the piece was small.

"Alright," he agreed, "go over to the hospital tent and give it to the wounded."

Once again Proshka objected:

"To the wounded?! That's like throwing it away. They're going to die anyway."

"You're absolutely shameless!" Suvorov roared and reached for his whip.

At this point Proshka realised that if he persisted any further matters could get serious. He grabbed the fat and hastened to the hospital tent.

The next day the soldiers encountered Proshka.

"Well, what about the fat?" they asked. "Did the Field Marshal eat it?"

No sooner had Proshka opened his mouth to speak when Suvorov appeared next to him.

"My comrades-in-arms!" he said. "My heroes! Excellent fat. I haven't tasted such since childhood. Please accept thanks from this old man here!" and bowed lowly to the soldiers.

Proshka's eyes popped in astonishment. But the soldiers broke into wide grins, paid their respects to the Field Marshal, turned about and returned to their company.

"He liked it," they whispered amongst themselves along the way. "Did you see how he thanked us! Fat, it's a delicacy even for a Field Marshal."

"I SEE IT!"

Having completed a rear-guard skirmish with the enemy and having gathered up the wounded, the company headed by Captain Lukov set out to catch up with the troops.

They moved along a narrow footpath on the very edge of a yawning precipice moving in a fine stretching almost the length of a verst.

"Don't lag behind, don't fall back!" shouted Lukov. "The wounded up front!"

They dragged the wounded up.

The company covered some two versts in distance. It grew dark and the wind began to pick up. Snow began to fall. A storm was clearly in the making.

The soldiers travelled for one hour, then a second and a third. Captain Lukov peered ahead trying to catch a glimpse of the camp-fires of the troops. They were surrounded by pitch darkness. The mounting blizzard cut off all vision, the stubborn wind tousling the soldiers' frock-coats and capes. Needles of snow were blown by the wind under the collars and sleeves, into their shirts, their faces and hands froze. The soldiers stumbled and slid along in the darkness. It was an effort to keep moving their stiffening legs. The pace became slower and slower.

"Don't fall behind! Don't drop back!" shouted Lukov.

Another hour dragged by. Finally the soldiers' strength simply gave out. They stopped in their tracks and dropped their exhausted bodies upon the nearest rocks in view.

"Forward! Keep moving!" the captain cried in a strained voice. The problem was, the soldiers simply had no strength left to keep marching forward. Lukov, himself exhausted, peered once again into the darkness—there were no fires to be seen—and himself dropped down upon a rock.

Suddenly:

"I see it! I see it!"

The captain and soldiers roused themselves and moved. They looked: a wounded soldier, Ivan Kozhin, had sat up on his stretcher and was pointing his finger forward.

"He sees it, the fire!" the group shouted, one after another.

Somehow the soldiers mustered up strength and jumped up from the rocks. They grabbed their weapons and hit the road again. Their spirits were lifted. That Kozhin! What an eagle-eye!

The soldiers trudged another verst or so, but no fires came into sight. Those closest to Kozhin began to mutter:

"So where's your fire? Were you lying to us?"

"I see it! I see it!" he repeated his cries and pointed his finger ahead.

The soldiers peered ahead intently but couldn't make out a thing. Nevertheless they kept on moving forward. Who knows, perhaps Kozhin really did have better eyesight than they.

Yet another verst was covered with still no camp-fire in view. Again the soldiers began to grumble:

"We won't go any further!"

"Don't believe him!"

"Brothers!" Kozhin cried out. "I see it! Believe me I do! It's not far now. A few more steps. Look how it's blazing away!" and again his finger pointed the direction.

The soldiers cursed and grumbled but kept on moving.

The path wound around a jut in the cliffs. The soldiers completed the turn when suddenly below, a few paces away, they glimpsed a fire through the blinding snow.

The soldiers stopped in their tracks, not believing their eyes.

"Do you see it?" they asked each other repeatedly.

"I see it!"

"I do too."

"And I also!"

"That Kozhin! What an eagle-eye! What a chap!" shouted the soldiers. "He saw it first. Three cheers for him!"

They raced from the spot in which they were standing and trotted down to the camp-fire, to the warmth, to their comrades.

They dragged along the stretcher with Kozhin in it.

"Bring him up to the fire," they shouted. "Let him warm up. He certainly deserves it! He led us all!"

The flames lit up Kozhin's face. The soldiers looked and froze in their tracks. His face was burned, his eyebrows seared. His eyes...

"Brothers! He's blind!" someone whispered.

The soldiers stared. Kozhin's eye-sockets were empty. A grenade had torn out his eyes the day before in the skirmish against the French.

THE GENERAL OF GENERALS

For his march through the Alps Suvorov was made Generalissimo of the Russian Army.

Returning with a group of soldiers to his native land, the Field Marshal stopped to rest at an inn on the border. He entered the cottage and ordered some cold veal, a tureen of buckwheat **kasha** and a glass of wine.

"Now this is **kasha**," Suvorov praised. "I haven't eaten so heartily in a long time. And the wine is first rate. It's no sin to drink such wine for the glory of Russian soldiers."

The soldiers all found places near the cottage and also ordered **kasha** and wine.

"Not bad, this wine," the soldiers exclaimed. "It's strong. It's no sin to drink for the Field Marshal with the likes of this."

Proshka alone cared for the horses, and was soon surrounded by the local peasants.

"How do you explain the rank that your lord now has?" they inquired of the orderly. "We've never heard of it before."

"What's so difficult about understanding it?" answered Proshka. "It's all very simple. A generalissimo is simply the general of generals. The most important of the important."

"Just look at that, will you!" piped in a puny little peasant in tattered **lapti**.

"He earned it," agreed a peasant with a beard.

Suvorov had been standing on the porch during this exchange and overheard everything.

"Not I! Not I!" he interjected from the threshold of the porch. "Not I," he repeated, approaching the peasants. "Proshka here, he was most important. And this one," he turned to a lanky pock-marked soldier. "And him," he pointed to a stocky corporal with a grey moustache. "And them," he made a sweeping gesture toward the remaining soldiers. He got into his cabriolet and ordered his driver to set off.

The soldiers got up and set out on the road. The dust curled up in wreaths. The sound of soldiers' songs burst forth.

The peasants remained standing along the road. They stood and looked with puzzled expressions upon the receding figures.

"He was pulling our leg, the lord was," the youth finally broke the silence.

"It sure was a little odd," uttered the puny one.

"Oafs!" the bearded peasant spat out. "The Field Marshal was telling the truth. A general without an army is useless. In the common folk, that's where Russia's strength lies. The people. Here you have the real general of generals."

GLORY

The general and prince Barokhvostov was envious of the glory Suvorov had won. Once he approached a soldier and asked him:

"Tell me, friend, why do the soldiers love Suvorov so much?"

"Because, Your Honour," answered the soldier, "Suvorov eats the common fare of the soldier."

Barokhvostov, in imitation of Suvorov, also began to eat cabbage soup and **kasha**. He made a wry face but persisted. He wanted, apparently, the glory that had been heaped upon Suvorov.

A few days passed, but no chorus of praise rose for Barokhvostov. Once again he asked the soldier:

"Why isn't the praise for me increasing?"

"Because, Your Honour," answered the soldier, "Suvorov not only eats cabbage soup and **kasha** but also sleeps like the common soldier."

Barokhvostov also began to sleep as the common soldier did—upon hard straw in a simple tent. He rubbed his delicate side in agony, froze from the cold, but persevered. After all, he really wanted the praise that Suvorov had.

A few more days passed, but no outpouring of praise was in evidence. Once again he summoned the soldier:

"Tell me, what's Suvorov's secret?"

"The fact," the soldier answered, "that Suvorov respects his troops."

Prince Barokhvostov began to make an effort to respect his subordinates and to address his soldiers gently.

Even now the general's reputation didn't seem to be improving. The soldiers would look at him and laugh amongst themselves. That and nothing more.

The general began to lose his temper. Again he summoned his soldier-confidant.

"How is it," he asked angrily, "that I eat cabbage soup and **kasha,** sleep on the straw, speak politely to my soldiers—and yet no one praises me?"

"Because, Your Honour," answered the soldier, "that's not all there is to it."

"What more could there be? What other secrets does Suvorov have?"

"Well, there's the fact," replied the soldier, "that Suvorov knows how to conquer the enemy in Suvorov fashion."

Somehow Barokhvostov couldn't quite master this last secret. For that reason he saw no glory and died in obscurity. But Suvorov's glory has outlived the centuries. Everyone knows of Suvorov.

1. Alexander Suvorov (engraving by Utkin, 1818). 2. 3. 4. 5. Soldiers from Suvorov's time.

6

8 9

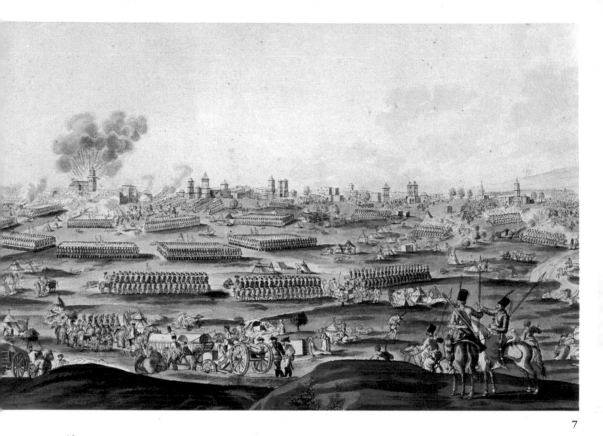

12

НАУКА ПОБѢЖДАТЬ.

Твореніе

Препрославившагося въ Свѣ-
тѣ всегдашними побѣдами

Генералиссимуса Россійскихъ
армій, Князя Италійскаго,
Графа Суворова-Рымник-
скаго,

Съ письмами,

собственноручно имъ писанными, и
открывающими наиболѣе въ немъ
величайшія свойства его души и
таковыя же знанія военнаго искус-
ства, сердца человѣческаго, духа
Россіанъ и выгодъ обществен-
ныхъ.

ВТОРОЕ ИЗДАНІЕ.

ВЪ САНКТПЕТЕРБУРГѢ.
при Сенатской типографіи 1809 года.

10

6. The flight of Friedrich II after defeat at the hands of the Russian army at Kunersdorf, August 1, 1759 (an 18th century engraving). 7. Battle at Focsani, July 21, 1789, in which Suvorov's army crushed the thirty-thousand-men-strong Turkish army (contemporary engraving). 8. A grenadier of the Schlüsselburg Musketeer Regiment. 9. A rank-and-file chasseur of the second half of the 18th century. 10, 11. An officer's broadsword and rapier of the time of Suvorov. 12. Title page to the second edition of **The Science of Victory**, written by Suvorov.

13

14

15

16

17

18

13. 14. Weapons from the time of Suvorov.
15. Military headgear of a grenadier. 16. Medal
commemorating Suvorov. 17. Foreign medals
honouring Suvorov. 18. Suvorov's defeat of the
Turkish army at Rimnik, September 11, 1789
(contemporary engraving).

19

22

21

19. The storming of Izmail, December 11, 1790 (contemporary engraving). 21. Monument to Suvorov in the town of Izmail. 22. The battle at Devil's Bridge (engraving from the 18th century).

20. Plan for the storming of the Iz-mail Fortress drawn up by Suvorov. 23. Painting by Vassili Surikov "Suvorov crossing the Alps".

MARTIAL GLORY

SOLDIERS PASSING ALONG THE BRIDGE

The year was 1812. Summer. The place: a bridge over the river Niemen. The frontier of Russia. Column after column, regiment after regiment, soldiers passed over the bridge. The sound of strange tongues buzzed in the air. French, Austrians, Prussians, Saxons, Italians and Swiss. The residents of Hamburg, of Bremen; Dutch, Belgians, Italians, and Spaniards. Soldiers passing over the bridge.

"Vive l'Empereur!"

"Vive la France!"

"Glory, glory, glory!" resounded from all directions.

Napoleon, riding upon a stately Arabian steed, observed the crossing. The Emperor of all Frenchmen was lost in thought. His three-cornered cap was pushed forward over his forehead, his uniform buttoned to the neck. A frown was gathering on his face.

Behind him, forming a semi-circle, his retinue waited in respectful silence. The buzz of bumble-bees work could be heard in the morning air.

Napoleon abruptly turned to one of his retinue, General Caulaincourt.

"You're not a Frenchman!" he cried out.

Caulaincourt maintained silence.

"You're not a Frenchman!" shouted Napoleon vituperatively.

Caulaincourt had made some bold statements the previous evening during a meeting of the military council. He was the only person among all the marshals and generals opposed to a march into Russia:

"It's the road to hell," were his words.

"There are Russians, Russians in my camp!" sputtered Napoleon, pointing at Caulaincourt.

Thus, on the next day he was unable to bear the sight of the general:

"Grow out that Russian beard of yours," Napoleon mocked. "Put on your **armyak** and **lapti!**"

The sun peeked over the neighbouring woods.

Napoleon rose up in his stirrups:

"There it is, the sun of Austerlitz!"

"Vive l'Empereur!"

"Glory to the Emperor!"

"Vive la France!"

"Vive, vive, vive!" resounded from all directions.

Red, yellow, blue—the uniforms flashed dazzlingly about the eye.

The soldiers were passing over the bridge. One hour, two, three. The first day, a second and then a third. The soldiers passed over the bridge. They marched to their doom.

THE TALE OF AN OLD CORPORAL

Verst after verst the Russians gave ground, retreated.

There were two Russian armies engaged. One commanded by General Barclay de Tolly retreated first to Vilnius, then on to Drissa and Polozk. The second, commanded by General Bagration, headed to the South, from Grodno to Slutsk and Bobruisk.

Napoleon's forces were almost three times as large as the combined troops of Barclay and Bagration. The French didn't give the Russian forces the opportunity to unite, for they wished to destroy them separately.

The Russian generals understood that for the time being their forces were inadequate to resist the onslaught of the enemy. They conserved their strength by withdrawing their men in regiments.

"My God, what are they cooking up anyway?!" the soldiers complained.

"This is an insult to our honour as soldiers!"

An old corporal, marching along with the rest, looked at his comrades:

"Do you want me to tell you a tale?"

"Go ahead, tell it."

During a halt the soldiers settled about in a circle and all grew quiet.

ARMYAK — a peasant cloth cloak

AUSTERLITZ — city in Austria near which Napoleon won one of his most important victories

"Whether or not this happened long ago," began the corporal, "it doesn't really matter. Anyway, at one time or another in the woods a grey wolf encountered a yearling elk.

"'Yearling, yearling, I'm going to make a feast of you.'

"'Wait a bit, grey wolf,' said the elk, 'I've just come into the world. Let me fill out a bit first.'

"The forest bandit agreed. Let the calf alone a bit, let him put some meat on his bones.

"How much time went by, it doesn't really matter. Anyway, once again the grey wolf encountered the elk. He stared—the calf had grown a bit in the interval. His horns were shooting out. His hooves had taken shape. It was no longer a calf standing before the wolf, but rather a partially grown elk. The wolf licked its chops.

"'Elk, elk, I'm going to make a feast of you.'

"'Alright, grey wolf,' answered the elk. 'Only give me a little time to say farewell to my native land.'

"'Well, say good-bye,' the wolf replied.

"The young elk wandered about his native land, through the fields and woods and into the oak groves. As he travelled his home soil his strength grew in him. And the wolf followed in his tracks. He grew worn out on the road: his wool began to fall off, his tongue hung out over his jaws, his ribs stuck through.

"'Hold it, stop!' the wolf complained.

"Whether or not a lot of time passed, it doesn't really matter. The point is that the elk finally came to a halt. It turned to meet the wolf. The latter looked and before him was not just an elk, but a bull-elk. The wolf bared its teeth:

"'Elk, elk, I'm going to make a feast of you.'

"The majestic elk laughed.

"'Come on over here.'

"The wolf hurtled forward. Only his strength wasn't what it used to be. The elk reared up on its hind legs, struck the wolf with its heavy hooves, lifted him on its antlers and smashed him to the ground—crash! The grey was dead."

The corporal fell into silence.

The soldiers reflected deeply upon the tale.

"You might say, that calf was a clever sort."

"It grew into a bull-elk!"

"Wait a minute. You know there's a point to that story."

"To the retreat! On the move!" rang out the command.

The soldiers jumped up and formed ranks. They lifted their heads high. They moved over fields, through woods and into oak groves. It was their native land they were travelling in, not that of a foreigner.

"WHERE ARE THEY, THE HEROES?"

The Russian armies linked up near Smolensk and pitched into battle.

For two days the French stormed the city.

Wave of attack followed wave of attack.

The soldiers pressed forward into battle against the French. There was no fear in the soldiers' hearts. One man would fall upon a whole company of the French. Two—upon a whole regiment.

The regiments fought side by side: the Simbirsky, Volynsky, Ufimsky.

Other regiments and companies fought as well. No one took second place in terms of heroism.

Egor Pinayev, a Simbirsky soldier, was wounded in the collarbone by a bayonet thrust. The blood spurted over his body. He didn't even feel the wound:

"To the attack! To the attack!"

A grenade tore off the ear of Peter Zanoza, a Volynsky soldier. He wiped away the blood and entertained the others with a joke:

"A fly is not a bird, a sheep is not a wolf, an ear is not a head!"

Rassada, a soldier from Ufimsky Regiment, was struck in the leg by buckshot. He collapsed to the ground. He had to aim lying down, but still kept firing:

"Forward, brothers!"

The soldiers struggled fiercely. The blood flowed in rivers.

Towards evening on the second day Smolensk caught fire after a fearful cannonade from the enemy.

Walls of flame roared and rushed furiously about, spreading to the Smolensk hills.

The Simbirsky, Volynsky and Ufimsky regiments continued to fight. They stood side by side with other regiments and companies. They didn't know the meaning of fear, these heroes. Replacements for the French kept pouring in. Barclay de Tolly could see that the Russians couldn't hold back the French. In the night he gave the order to withdraw to the troops.

The regiments withdrew from their positions and quietly moved behind the Dnieper River. They counted off still more versts.

Pinayev marched with the troops. Zanoza marched as well. Rassada was carried on a stretcher.

The Simbirsky, Volynsky and Ufimsky regiments moved along the road, along with the other companies and regiments.

General Barclay de Tolly pulled up astride the troops.

"All praise to the heroes!"

The soldiers exchanged glances: "Who's that Barclay de Tolly's crying out greetings to?"

"It must be to the men from the Volynsky Regiment," decided the Simbirsky soldiers.

"It must be to the men from the Ufimsky," decided the Volynsky soldiers.

"It must be to the men from the Simbirsky," decided the soldiers from the Ufimsky Regiment.

The soldiers looked about in all directions.

"Where are they, the heroes?"

A MILITARY MANOEUVRE

Kutuzov's life was not an easy one. Difficult, yet glorious.

In 1812 Mikhail Illarionovich Kutuzov was 67 years of age.

There was much to look back to. He had survived countless battles and marches. The Crimea and the Danube, the fields of Austria and the threatening walls of Izmail, the battle at Alushta, the siege of Ochakov and the protracted battle at Kagul.

Kutuzov had been seriously wounded three times. Twice he had been hit in the head and once in the cheek. He had lost his right eye in yet another battle.

It was high time to retire to the peace of the aged. But the time had not come—the people remembered the name Kutuzov. Like an old steed called back into service, Kutuzov went to the troops. He became the new Commander-in-Chief.

The soldiers were overjoyed. "Kutuzov has come to drive out the French," the word passed through the ranks of the soldiers.

On his way to the troops Kutuzov tossed matters over in his mind: "Our situation is bad. It's not a good thing when an army retreats. Such actions are contrary to the nature of the Russian soldier ... eagles that they are! To be sure, our strength is not up to par for the time being. We have to safeguard our forces. Without an army the Russian state itself would be in deadly peril. But we have to take the soldiers' morale into account. We must understand the Russian soul."

Kutuzov arrived where his troops were situated.

"Hurray!" the troops shouted to their commander. "Lead us into battle, sir! We're ready, eager to go!"

"We're talking the same language," replied Kutuzov. "It's time to take care of this enemy on our soil."

The soldiers exchanged knowing glances and winked: now they had a real, dauntless general.

"What are we anyway, if not Russian?" continued Kutuzov. "Did God really deprive us of the strength to fight? Are we really short on courage? How long can we retreat anyway?"

"Now that's hard talking for you!"

"Hurray for General Kutuzov!" the soldiers exclaimed their pleasure: "Well, brothers—it's not another step backwards. The decisive battle will be soon, for sure!"

The soldiers slept peacefully that night. They woke the next morning to receive their first order from Kutuzov. There it was, clear as a bell—continue to retreat!

The soldiers grumbled:

"But what about the battle! What are we supposed to make of this?" they shrugged their shoulders.

"Maybe it's just a left-over order from the last command."

The soldiers caught sight of Kutuzov.

"Your Excellency, what's the story, are we really going to retreat again?"

Kutuzov peered at the soldiers and mischievously squinted his remaining eye:

"Who said retreat? This is just a military manoeuvre!"

A NEW DUTY

Kutuzov was reading a letter:

"To His Excellency, the Venerable Mikhail Illarionovich!..."

The letter was from an old friend and general who had by this date already stepped into retirement. The general recalled his long service with Kutuzov and the marches they had participated in together. He congratulated him with his recent appointment to the position of Commander-in-Chief and wished him success. But the central point of the letter came only at the very end. The matter concerned the son of the general, a young officer named Grishenka. The general asked Kutuzov, in the name of their long-standing friendship, to find a cozy niche for Grishenka, to take him into headquarters, or, best of all, to take him on as an adjutant.

"Indeed," sighed Kutuzov. "That's not how we began. Apparently the younger generation isn't quite what ours was. They spend all their time looking for a cozy spot where life is most peaceful. Everybody wants a place at headquarters, but heaven forbid that they should go into battle."

But, after all, friendship is friendship. The general had been a worthy soldier. Kutuzov held him in esteem and decided to honour his request as a father.

A few days later Grishenka arrived.

Kutuzov looked—before him stood a fledgling of a youth. No officer—a little boy, in fact. In height he hardly reached Kutuzov's shoulders. The fellow was as thin as a reed. His cheeks boasted only of a layer of unshaven goose-down.

The situation was even a little humorous for Kutuzov. "Yes, our youth isn't what it used to be, our officer corps is slipping. Frailty in mind and body, that's the word!"

Kutuzov inquired of Grishenka's mother and father and then:

"Well, alright, step to it. I've carried out the request of Peter Nikodimych, your father. Now, go get an adjutant's uniform."

The officer, however, didn't move.

"Your Excellency!"

Kutuzov frowned. He knew that the officer was about to thank him:

"On your way! On your way!"

"Your Excellency!..." Grishenka once again began.

Kutuzov grimaced: "What a pest."

"Well, what now?"

"Mikhail Illarionovich, I'd rather be in the regiment... I'd rather be in the army under Prince Peter Bagration," Grishenka bubbled.

This struck Kutuzov as very funny. He looked at the diminutive officer, at his budding moustache. "A child, he's still a child." Suddenly he was very sorry for the boy. How could he send such a fledgling to face the bullets?

"I can't do it, I simply can't," he said. "I promised your father."

The officer's lips trembled with agitation. It looked as if he were about to break out into tears.

"I can't do it," Kutuzov repeated. "Where would you fit in the regiment anyway? The soldiers wouldn't even notice you on the battlefield."

The officer took insult at this last statement:

"Well, Suvorov was no giant himself."

Kutuzov lifted his eyebrows in surprise. He saw that Grishenka was not one of those who hide behind the coat-tails of their fathers. Kutuzov went up to the officer and embraced him.

"Alright, enough. Your father, now, was quite a..." Kutuzov didn't finish: tears appeared in the old man's eyes.

He paused for a moment.

"Away with you," Kutuzov finally said. "Let it be, you beat your own trail through the woods, wherever it may lead."

Grishenka snapped to attention, turned smartly on his heels and exited. Kutuzov lingered quite a while, however, and watched the retreating figure of the youth.

Then he demanded a piece of paper and began to write a letter to his friend, the old general.

"Your Excellency, the Venerable Peter Nikodimovich! The gods have sent me great joy. Your Grishenka has arrived. And it seemed to me that this is not a new generation, but our own youth returning. Many thanks for such a surprise. I deeply hope to see him among our heroes..."

Then he thought for a bit and added:

"Your request has been fulfilled. From this point on Grishenka will be with me in the most conspicuous spot—near my heart as an adjutant."

After receiving the letter, the old general spent much time picking his brains: "'near my heart'—what could this mean? Well, I guess I've just been away from military affairs too long. Apparently they've instituted some new position at headquarters."

THE TATAR

One time, the soldiers were preparing to bury their fallen comrades near the city of Gzhatsk. They had chosen a spot between three pine trees up on a hill; there they dug a large grave.

If one looked to the left from this spot, a sparkling river made a sharp bend before the eyes. To the right the road stretched towards the horizon. Directly ahead were field after field, the vast expanses of Russia.

The heroes had found a peaceful resting-place.

The soldiers carried their deceased comrades up the hill and placed them at the edge of the grave. They awaited the arrival of the army chaplain to read the funeral service.

The dead soldiers lay as if in formation, the only difference being their closed eyes. Each had his hands placed on his chest. There were different types: young and old, thin, heavy-set, moustached and with the goose-down of an adolescent, with thick and with thin eyebrows... and here was a wide-cheeked fellow completely without eyebrows.

"Hey, that fellow's a Tatar!"

The soldiers peered, what could they do with the fellow—after all, a Tatar was not a Christian, he belonged to a different faith. What kind of service should they give him? How could they arrange things such that God wouldn't punish them for performing rites for this Tatar?

The soldiers crowded together and began to whisper amongst themselves.

"Of course it's not strictly correct. But then he fought side by side with the rest. He gave his life for Russia. Although his blood isn't Christian, it's the blood of a soldier. No, it just wouldn't be right to cast him aside and bury him in a separate grave. Let him remain with all the rest."

The priest appeared, pulled out his censer, smoothed down his flowing beard and prepared for the ceremony. He was just beginning to recite the service when his eyes fell upon the Tatar.

He frowned deeply.

"Get him out of there!"

The soldiers didn't budge.

"Remove him," the priest repeated.

"Your Reverence," stammered the soldiers, "let him remain. He is a soldier after all. God won't condemn it."

The face of the priest contorted in revulsion at these words. His jaw muscles twitched and his mouth hung open in astonishment.

"Blasphemers!" he roared out. "Befoulers of the word of the Lord! Confess, confess your sin to the holy saints!"

The soldiers exchanged glances: this wasn't a speech, it was thunder! They wanted to swallow their words. Still something held them back. The commonality they felt as soldiers was very strong.

At this very time Kutuzov was riding in that vicinity and passed by the three pines. He caught sight of the priest, the graves and the rows of corpses. He removed his cap, dismounted and made the sign of the cross.

"What's the problem, Your Reverence?"

The priest explained the situation. Kutuzov cast a glance on the deceased soldiers—on the Tatar—and on the living ones. Finally he turned to the priest:

"Couldn't we possibly do what the soldiers ask?"

"Your Excellency, revere the Lord, have fear! ..."

"Alright, alright," frowned the Commander-in-Chief. He glanced once again at the soldiers and pointed to the censer.

"Give me that thing."

The priest completely lost his composure but gave over the censer.

Kutuzov took it and himself swung the censer over the bodies.

THE SILENCE
WAS SWALLOWED UP

If you climb to the belfry of the church which stands in the very centre of the village of Borodino you'll catch a view of the nearby fields.

It was here, on an immense field pock-marked by ravines, that the immortal battle broke out on the 7th of September, 1812. It was here that the great future glory of Russia was insured. Our distant ancestors on this spot protected the inheritance that was to pass to us. Pay your respects to this great field. Pay your respects to the valour it witnessed.

Learn about, know well and never forget it!

Before the break of dawn, when it was still dark, Kutuzov, without a word to anyone, mounted his horse and travelled just short of the 1.5 versts necessary to reach Borodino, stopping on a hill near the little settlement of Gorki. He had already selected this spot the previous evening. Kutuzov's headquarters were to be established on this spot.

Off to the right a bit the Kolocha River flowed, branching away from the Moskva. Here the right flank of the Russian position had formed. From here the line of Russian regiments was to cut across the new Smolensk road and extended just short of seven versts to the left where, just behind a stream and the village of Semenovskoye, was located the village of Utitsa.

The Russian batteries were situated on several elevated positions in the vicinity. One of these batteries, called the Kurganovaya, was destined to become pivotal in the battle of Borodino.

This was the renowned battery under Raevsky. To the left of it, behind Semenovskoye, flèches—trenches dug at angles to the enemy—had been dug out. These were the famous Bagration flèches.

The right flank of the Russian troops was under the command of Barclay de Tolly. The left was commanded by Bagration.

A few versts away from the basic concentration of forces reserve regiments, Cossacks and cavalry had been hidden in copses and low-lying areas.

Kutuzov sat silently on his horse in the darkness. He couldn't see clearly, but nevertheless apprehended by the glow of the nearly-extinguished fires the position of the enemy. He relied more upon the fifth sense of an experienced soldier than upon his hearing to catch the signs of movement in the enemy camp.

Kutuzov laboriously dismounted from his horse. It was no easy task for him without help. He was old, his body felt the burden of years. His youth was far in the past.

Groaning, the Commander-in-Chief got down on his knees, bent over and put his ear to the ground. He tried to verify what he felt was happening. The earth was a resonating board in the night stillness. With the ear of a musician Kutuzov flawlessly identified the slightest sounds.

Then he stood up and again mounted his horse. Once again he peered endlessly into the night horizons.

The first ribbons of the dawn appeared in the east. The rooks began to sound off in the white willows. Kutuzov's steed began to dig up the grass with his hooves and softly whinnied. Frantic adjutants, generals from Kutuzov's suite and officers from headquarters rushed up to Kutuzov and surrounded him.

The east grew steadily brighter. From the hill the environs seemed the size of one's palm. All life quieted and then was still. The troops remained immobile. There was a deafening silence over the fields. Only the clouds stole cat-like over the forests.

Suddenly ... the thunder-clap of cannon. The silence was swallowed up. The hour of the Borodino battle had struck.

WHERE SHOULD ONE LOOK FOR BAGRATION?

Positioning his troops before the battle, Kutuzov had placed Bagration's army on the left flank. This was the most dangerous spot for it was most widely exposed. Kutuzov knew that the French would open their assault here.

"Isn't Prince Peter a little short on manpower?" one of his staff officers anxiously inquired.

"But Bagration's there," Kutuzov answered, "and that doubles their strength."

Just as Kutuzov thought Napoleon did first strike on the left flank. Overrun Bagration's flèches—and from there throw his forces directly into the centre—such were the Emperor's plans.

Some 130 French cannon opened fire. Three cavalry corps hurtled towards the flèches. Dozens of infantry regiments converged on a small spot. The best French Marshals, Ney, Davout and Murat, personally led the attack.

"So many Marshals for one General," the Russian troops joked.

"They could threw five against him for all the difference it would make!"

"Hang on, don't be afraid, brothers!"

Wave upon wave of assault followed. The French were absolutely fearless. New heroes moved in to replace their fallen comrades and continue the assault.

"Bravo! Bravo!" shouted Bagration, unable to hold back his praise for the heroes.

But the Russians proved to have just as much back-bone. Their courage matched that of the French. Two walls of steel clashed. Hero fell upon hero, courage met with courage. It was like a scythe meeting with stone. The Russians didn't retreat a step, the French didn't move forward. Mounds of corpses piled up on the field.

The battle at the flèches went on and on. The sun was already high in the sky, yet the stubborn defences had not yielded.

Napoleon was dissatisfied, his plans had been upset.

He sent into the fray two hundred, three hundred, four hundred cannon. He ordered threateningly:

"All forces to the left flank!"

New reserves threw themselves into the battle.

"Well, how's it going? Has Bagration retreated?"

"No, Your Excellency."

Messengers raced from Kutuzov to Bagration. They carried orders, instructions and injunctions but it was difficult to find the general in the heat of the battle. Bagration just didn't stay in one place.

"I'm not a general, I'm just the first soldier," he loved to quip.

The couriers looked and looked for Prince Peter.

"He must be here," they'd decide.

"The general went off in that direction," the couriers were sent scurrying off in another direction.

They'd reach that place only to find out:

"Yes, he was here, but he's already left."

The couriers once again would dash off. And once again to no avail. They were wasting valuable time, though the sweat on their horses continued to gather.

One officer alone, a certain Voyeikov, as soon as he received an order from Kutuzov, immediately found Bagration.

The other messengers were envious. "What a lucky fellow, that Voyeikov," they murmured. They tried to elicit from him how he unerringly could locate the general.

"It's very simple," answered Voyeikov. "Prince Peter Bagration himself helps me out."

The officers took offense. They understood that Voyeikov was joking:

"Don't try to turn our heads. Don't think we're stupid. Let us in on your secret."

Voyeikov broke into laughter.

"Secret? Here it is, my secret," pointing in the direction of Bagration's army.

The couriers' eyes followed his finger. They saw nothing there of the unusual. The army as it always was, the battle going on as earlier, shooting, smoke, bayonet attacks. The ground quaked under the attack.

"Look harder, look harder!" shouted Voyeikov. "Where is the hottest spot?"

The officers located it.

"Over there," they pointed with their fingers.

"Well, just head in that direction," answered Voyeikov. "That's my secret. Bagration goes right into the inferno. You look there and you'll always find him."

HERCULEAN STRENGTH

The battery under the charge of Lieutenant Zhabrin had to alter its position in short notice. The soldiers harnessed the horses and rushed to the new spot. The regiment under General Miloradovich had mounted an attack and was in need of immediate help.

"Step along, faster!" Zhabrin commanded. "Hey, on the move! Don't you hear me? Faster!"

The road crossed the scene of a recent attack. The horses dipped down into a low lying area. The whole field was strewn with corpses. Russians and French lay one on top of another. It looked as if someone had carelessly tossed flour bags all over the field. The soldiers stopped in their tracks.

"Oh God, what a sight!"

Zhabrin glanced first to the left, then to the right. There was no free passage. There was no time to make a circuit. The lieutenant crossed himself.

"Straight ahead! The dead can't harm the living."

One soldier named Epifanov lagged slightly behind the rest. Seized by fear he closed his eyes.

If only they could get through this terrifying spot quicker. The cannon rolled along as if over pits and bumps. Chills ran up the soldier's spine. Suddenly he heard a soft protracted groan. He opened his eyes and saw, directly under the wheel of the cannon, a grey-moustached corporal move slightly. The soldier broke out in sweat.

"Whoa!" Epifanov shouted at his horses. He jumped to the ground.

The corporal lay in a state of delirium. His side was one bloody mess. His shako lay by his side. However he held his weapon tightly under his arm.

Epifanov ran up to the corporal. He strained to pull him out from under the wheel. The corporal was heavy, his own weight increased by the pressure of other bodies.

The corporal moved, looked at the sky, at Epifanov and at the cannon:

"Where are you from?"

"We're with the artillery," began Epifanov. "We're moving from the left to the right flank. We got an urgent request for help. Listen, can you hear the firing all about? General Miloradovich has moved to the attack."

"He's our general, ours!" shouted the corporal. "Raise my head up a bit, will you?"

The corporal looked. There on the hill an avalanche of soldiers moved forward. The old battle horse heard the familiar sounds. It was as if he'd heard a call from his comrades. A smile broke out on the face of the corporal:

"Give me a hand, eh!"

Epifanov helped the corporal up from the ground.

"Now put my shako on me."

Epifanov put the shako on the grey head.

He straightened up as if about to fall into rank and prepared his weapon, as if for the attack. A step forward with his left foot, and then one with his right. From a walk he broke into a run.

Epifanov was astonished. Blood was gushing from the corporal's wounds.

"Hurray!" the sound carried victoriously from the hill.

"Hurray!" the corporal answered.

He managed to run perhaps ten to fifteen metres when suddenly, like a huge oak after the felling stroke of a lumberman, he collapsed to the ground.

Epifanov flew to the side of the hero. The corporal didn't moan; he wasn't breathing. The warrior's career had ended.

Epifanov caught up with his own men. Zhabrin fell upon him:

"Where'd you disappeared to? You coward!"

The soldier explained the reason for the delay. He couldn't quite come to his senses. He told about the old corporal, jumbling his phrases as he spoke.

Zhabrin fell silent and the soldiers followed suit.

"What was his name? What was he called?"

Epifanov shrugged his shoulders.

"A corporal, you know, an old fellow with moustaches. He didn't have any strength left at all."

The soldiers took off their caps.

"He didn't have any strength?! Fool! He had Herculean strength in him!"

THE HEART OF A SOLDIER

They became friends during the campaigns: a greenhorn and an old war-horse—Klim Duga and Matvei Borodulin. Together they retreated from the Niemen. They fought side by side at Vitebsk and almost perished together at the walls of Smolensk. They arrived together one more time at the fields of Borodino.

Matvei Borodulin was like a second father to Klim Duga. He taught him the fundamentals of military knowledge: how to keep powder dry, to sharpen a bayonet, to march in such a fashion that as little energy was expended as possible. During halts Borodulin gave up his place nearer the fire to the young soldier.

Duga resisted:

"What am I anyway, a baby?"

"Lie down, lie down!" the soldier returned. "I'm used to it. I even sleep better in cold spots."

When the **kasha** was ladled out Borodulin also thought of the other fellow. He poured a goodly portion from his tureen to that of the younger soldier.

"Matvei," protested Klim, "what am I? A swine that has to be overfed?"

"Eat it! Eat it! You're a growing boy, you need it."

The soldiers fought together at Borodino. Klim—the young hero, Borodulin—the wiry old man. Duga was covering for the old soldier, nevertheless the latter was suddenly hit and wounded. Matvei Borodulin collapsed to the ground, melting like a snow-drift before the sun.

"Matvei, dear Matvei!" shouted Duga. He dropped to his knees and shook Borodulin. He placed his ear to Matvei's chest. "Matvei, oh please!"

Borodulin opened his eyes slightly and glanced at the younger soldier.

"Water," he gave a moan and once again lost consciousness.

The soldiers searched for a flask, but those they found were all empty. The battle had lasted almost ten hours. Not a drop of water was left to be consumed.

There was no water. There were no streams in the vicinity. The nearest stream was in the hands of the French.

Duga bolted up and looked all about with a distracted air. And then he acted as if an electric current had just hit him. He seized an empty flask, stuck his hand in the air and raced point blank at the French, towards the bayonets and weapons which were between him and the stream in the ravine.

The nearby soldiers, observing, gasped.

"My God, it's sure death for him."

"Insanity!"

"He'll be caught by the French."

The Russian soldiers anxiously watched his journey. The French also looked curiously upon the racing figure.

"Mes amis," shouted Duga. "Matvei is dying! He wants water! All the flasks are empty," and he waved his flask like an entry permit.

"Water! Water!" the sound carried over the field.

The French, though they were the enemy, were also human beings. They couldn't understand a word of Russian, but they understood human emotions. Not for nothing would a fellow run into the lap of the enemy!

The French moved aside and cleared a path for him to the stream. There was silence on the battlefield, neither side firing. There was no sound except:

"Matvei is dying!" the soldier's words cut through the air.

Duga ran to the ravine. He scooped up a flask of ice-cold water, turned about and raced back along the corridor of French soldiers.

He rushed back to Matvei, again fell on his knees, lifted up the old man's head and raised the flask to his mouth. He moistened his forehead and temples.

Borodulin again opened his eyes and slowly came back to consciousness. He recognised his young friend:

"Where in the world did you get this water, dear friend?"

Where?

It came from the heart of the soldier.

THE BIRD OF GLORY

A soldier named Izyumov, though he dreamed of glory, failed to win distinction for himself until the battle of Borodino. At the very beginning of the war he had the following conversation with another soldier.

"What is glory, anyway?" Izyumov asked.

"Glory is a bird," the soldier answered. "It always circles over the battlefield. Whoever catches this bird wins glory."

Whether the soldier was joking or himself believed something of this nature, Izyumov from this time on lost all his sense of internal calm. He couldn't take his thoughts off this miraculous bird.

He thought about it at Vitebsk. Other soldiers fell to the attack and soundly drubbed the enemy. But

Izyumov kept his eyes fixed on the sky, afraid of letting the bird pass by unnoticed, which in fact it did. Other soldiers won the glory.

The same thing happened during the battle near Smolensk. The soldier once again failed to win glory.

Izyumov was extremely distraught. He complained to his friends about his lack of success.

The soldiers laughed:

"You can't catch glory, it finds the brave of its own accord. It really is like a bird, but it's better not to think about it. You might just scare it away."

In point of fact at Borodino the soldier really did forget about glory. To be sure not right away but gradually, imperceptibly he forgot.

The battle drew to a close. The French strove to grab victory. **Uhlan** and **cuirassier** regiments were thrown against the Russian infantry. The cavalry galloped at lightning speed; such a mass could sweep anything from the road. Izyumov looked and froze in his tracks. Mesmerized, he forgot about glory. He thought only about how to withstand the mounted attack.

The horses loomed larger and larger. He pictured them trampling the soldiers as broadswords and sabres descend upon Russian heads. He even huddled up a bit in fear for he stood in the very first row.

"Ready arms! Aim! Wait until they come into range!" It's difficult to say what exactly happened after that.

One would have to be at a distance to see clearly.

Izyumov stood rooted in place for a second, then suddenly raised his weapon in readiness for a bayonet attack and rushed to meet the cavalry assault.

The other soldiers followed suit. As it turned out the infantry actually attacked the cavalry.

"Hurray!" shouted Izyumov.

"Hurray!" the soldiers shouted in unison.

The French **cuirassier** and **uhlan** regiments were thunderstruck. They had never seen the likes of this. And although, of course, they didn't halt their own attack, the cavalry did waive and hesitate for a second. In war this second is crucial. The enthusiasm drained out of their spirits.

The soldiers rushed up to the French and began to put their bayonets to work like pitchforks. A miracle

UHLAN regiment — light cavalry unit armed with lances

CUIRASSIER regiment — horse-soldiers wearing cuirass, a piece of close-fitting armour for protecting the breast and back

took place on the field, infantry were striking down cavalry. The ardour of the soldiers flamed up.

"Brothers, beat the French with your rifle-butts if your bayonets break!" Izyumov shouted in a state of intoxication.

The French lost all semblance of control. Their sabres flashed more and more rarely now, their blows more and more feeble. The French weakened and lost all will to fight. They turned their horses about.

That would seem to have ended things. Victory had been won. But it wasn't the end.

"Brothers, to the pursuit!" shouted Izyumov.

The soldiers raced off in pursuit of the French. Infantry chased cavalry across the field. It was a rare sight to behold.

Of course horses are swifter than men. Nevertheless, more than a few French were overtaken and despatched with bayonet thrusts.

Even having fallen behind the soldiers continued to throw their bayoneted weapons, like spears, after the French.

The French galloped away. The soldiers gathered up their weapons and began to return to their troops.

Soldier meeting soldier said in greeting:

"Glory to the heroes!"

"Glory to Izyumov!"

"Honour and esteem to the brave!"

The soldiers were utterly exhausted from the battle. They walked on as if in a fog, seeing and hearing nothing. The soldiers didn't see anything. But we can see very clearly: over them circled the bird of glory.

FILI

The little village of Fili just on the outskirts of Moscow. A peasant hut. An oak table. An icon and lamp in the corner.

In this hut Russian generals were gathered around the table: a council of war was in session. It was necessary to decide whether to give up Moscow without a fight or to engage the enemy in battle at the very walls of the city.

The words didn't come easy—abandon Moscow. The phrase was a dagger in the heart of a Russian. The generals were in favour of fighting.

It wasn't an easy hour for Kutuzov. He had just been promoted. For his part in the battle of Borodino he had been awarded the title of Field Marshal. As the highest in rank, as Commander-in-Chief, as Field Marshal his was the deciding word: yes or no.

The French hadn't succeeded in overpowering the Russians at Borodino. But neither had the Russians smashed the French. In a word, it had been a draw. It was a draw, but it depended on how you looked at it. For the first time Napoleon had not emerged with a clear victory. The Russians were the first in the world not to concede defeat before Napoleon. For the Russians, then, it was indeed a victory. The same could not be said for the French.

The generals were thirsting for a new battle. The soldiers wanted to fight. What was there left for Kutuzov to decide?

Kutuzov was battle-seasoned and wise in the ways of war. He knew that troops were rushing from Vitebsk and Smolensk to the aid of Napoleon. Though the French were down, they were not yet through. As before they commanded superior weight in numbers.

A new battle—a decisive battle. "Look before you leap" was the order of the day. The army was the most precious quantity. It was most important to preserve the troops. If the army remained intact the time would come to destroy the enemy.

Everyone was waiting for Kutuzov to voice his opinion. The Field Marshal stood up from his oak chair and looked at the generals.

They waited.

Kutuzov looked at the icon and its lamp, out of the window at a patch of grey sky and then down at his feet.

The generals waited. Russia was waiting.

"With the loss of Moscow," Kutuzov quietly began, "we still haven't lost Russia. But if our army is destroyed, then Moscow and Russia will perish."

Kutuzov paused. A fly tapped against the window. The floorboards creaked under the Field Marshal's heavy body. A deep sigh cut the silence. Kutuzov raised his head of grey. He saw the face of the ataman Platov. A tell-tale tear was sliding down the cheek of this old warrior. At this point Kutuzov understood what was necessary: not just words but a command. He finished briefly and firmly:

"By the power ordained me by the tsar and homeland I order... I order," repeated Kutuzov, "to withdraw from Moscow."

...Thus the troops abandoned Moscow. Yauza bridge. The dejected soldiers were crossing. Kutuzov rode up. He looked upon the troops. The soldiers noticed him. Noticed him, but pretended not to. For the first time they did not greet him with cheers.

AN OCEAN OF FLAME

The Russian army was positioned to the south of Moscow, in the village of Tarutino.

Kutuzov without delay began to look after practical matters. The army was in rags—he had to find uniforms. Autumn had set in, it was time to find warm clothing. Supplies were low—the reserves of grain had to be replenished.

Kutuzov had many things on his mind.

As for Napoleon, then in Moscow, his burdens were no lighter. The expectations of the French had not been justified. The residents had left and taken all with them. There was no bread or meat to be found in Moscow. There was no feed for the horses. The only thing available in plenty was wine. The soldiers drank themselves silly and then began to plunder. And where there was plunder, fire followed on its heels. It was a dry autumn. Fire spread rapidly. Kitai Gorod went up in flames... then Gostiny Dvor... then Krestny Row. Okhotny Row was the site of a fire. Beyond the Moskva River Balchug burned. The night was lit up like the day. Napoleon sat in the Moscow Kremlin. From all vantage points all he could see was fire. The city was engulfed in an ocean of flame.

"Your Majesty," Napoleon's marshals and generals anxiously said, "it's dangerous! Fire is lapping at the Kremlin."

Napoleon didn't want to leave the Kremlin. It would be awkward and shameful. To have just occupied the Kremlin and then to skitter out! He delayed.

"Your Majesty! Save yourself! Let's get nearer to the river," his generals implored him.

Napoleon delayed.

"Your Majesty!"

Now the Emperor reluctantly donned his frock-coat.

The flames rushed closer.

Napoleon hastened down the wide Kremlin staircase. "This is the road to hell," he recalled the words of Caulaincourt. He bit his lips in fury.

The fire raged for four days.

On the fifth day Moscow was in ashes.

The French no longer controlled a city but rather a heap of ruins.

At Tarutino the Russian troops were doing well. Provisions were being carted in, the soldiers receiving new outfits, the cavalry was being replenished with horses. The soldiers were getting a breathing spell.

Things weren't going so well for the French in Moscow.

Napoleon had something to think about: "Am I the victor or not?"

"Why don't the Russians sue for peace?"

Three interminable, exhausting weeks passed. Napoleon was indignant:

"Peace, immediate peace with Russia!"

The Emperor didn't wait to hear from the Russian emissaries. He summoned his general-adjutant, the marquis Lauriston:

"Go to Tarutino, to the old fox... on your way, march!"

TARUTINO

Kutuzov understood after Lauriston's visit that the French were doing poorly. He decided to give battle near Tarutino.

Once again the cannon thundered. Bayonets and sabres crossed. Army advanced against army.

This time the French lost: 36 cannon were seized by the Russians.

Four days after the battle an ensign named Yazykov was out on a scouting expedition with a detachment of Cossacks. The Cossacks became headstrong and pushed right up to the edge of Moscow.

They stood gazing at the scorched town.

"There she is ... a martyr."

Although it was warm and windless droplets of light autumn rain splattered about. The bark of a dog could be heard in the distance.

"Hear that? They said that they ate all the dogs."

"That clever beggar escaped away, it seems."

"Just look, our beautiful Moscow is destroyed..."

"Fool, don't weep about what's past. Moscow isn't dead, it'll be rebuilt."

The Cossacks whispered on among themselves. Suddenly they heard a strange rumble and explosion from the city. The Don Cossacks exchanged glances and looked askew at their commander. Curiosity pulled at them. They exchanged glances once more and then rushed towards the city.

"Hey, let's chance it. You have to take chances sometime! That's what a scouting expedition is all about!"

They flew along the empty streets of the city. Not a sign of life, either French or Russian. The ruins lay in silence. Only the beat of the horses' hooves broke the tomblike silence. The horsemen headed towards the centre. They galloped right up to the Ordynka Street near the Kremlin. The French were nowhere to be seen.

They ran into an old man.

"Hey, old fellow, where did the barbarians go?"

"They left, the French left Moscow. They left in the morning, friends."

Napoleon had been more than a month in Moscow. He'd waited for proposals for peace from the Russian emissaries. No emissaries had appeared before him, however. Then he'd sent Lauriston, but he came back empty-handed. And then there had been that battle near Tarutino. Soon it would be winter. Famine already stalked the troops. It made no sense to remain, like mice caught in a trap, in Moscow. No, while they had the strength, while there was still time, they decided to head home. The French left with no laurels, like shadows, from Moscow.

Having learned the unprecedented news the Cossacks forgot about the rumble and explosion, turned their horses about and shot off like arrows to carry the long-awaited news to Kutuzov.

At a later date they learned about the explosion. Napoleon was a vindictive one, he decided to take revenge for his failures. He ordered, upon leaving, that the Kremlin be mercilessly blown up. Fortunately, very little suffered. Rain fell and extinguished the wicks to the explosives.

Kutuzov listened to Yazykov's report, then made the sign of the cross.

"It's happened. Now it's inevitable. Russia is saved from this date."

He swung about and faced the village:

"My thanks to you, Tarutino!"

TISHKA AND MINKA

Leaving Moscow behind, Napoleon pressed towards Kaluga. The city, undamaged by the war, was a potential source of supplies for the French. From there they could turn towards Smolensk, to Vilno and then out of Russia.

Kutuzov understood the calculations of his opponent and placed his army across the path of the French. At the city of Maloyaroslavets a new battle flared up. Once again, as at Borodino, the fighting lasted from morning until evening. Both the French and the Russians fought with the stubbornness born of desperation. The French drove the Russians out of Maloyaroslavets. The Russians began a counterattack.

The Russians drove the French out of Maloyaroslavets. The French began a counterattack.

This happened eight times. The city passed back and forth from hand to hand. Two twin brothers from the city, Tishka and Minka, had taken shelter in a cellar when the first French assault began. A little window from this cellar looked out into the street. The boys pressed their faces to the window. Though frightened they were interested by the events around them.

With the approach of the French almost all of the residents had quit the city, among them the parents of Tishka and Minka. They took their children with them as well, but these children had got separated in the crowd and returned to the city. They were excited about the prospect of watching a real battle.

Thus, they were at the window when the battle broke. Everything was new and interesting to them: how the soldiers attacked, how the commanders shouted out orders and how the smoke from weapons floated up into the air.

At first, when the French attacked, the battle raged somewhere off in the distance. The children could hear terrifying cries, but little else. Then, when the Russians broke into the town, one of the clashes occurred on the street where Tishka and Minka were. The Russian detachment was commanded by a young officer. He was handsome and smartly dressed.

The boys followed the officer with their eyes.

"A general," whispered Minka.

"He's too young to be a general, perhaps he's a lieutenant," Tishka corrected him.

Right next to the window a bitter clash took place. Each side attacked with bayonets.

"Men," shouted the officer, "your bayonets will grow rusty from inaction. A soldier's no soldier without victory. Forward!" The lieutenant was first to move.

In a minute the bayonets were stained crimson. Uniforms were covered with blood. A puddle of blood formed in the spot of the action. French and Russian blood merged on the ground.

The children jumped away from the window.

"Are you frightened?" Tishka asked his brother.

"No," answered Minka.

He said no, but his hands were trembling. He was not alone in this. The hands of both boys shook uncontrollably.

When they approached the window again the battle in this spot had already ended. All was quiet. The dead were strewn about. Closest to them lay the young officer. The boys could see that the officer had been wounded by a bayonet. He lay quietly, moaning in a drawn-out voice. The youths looked at each other.

"He'd be better off in the cellar," Tishka said cautiously.

"Yes, that's right," agreed Minka.

But fearing to go out on the street, they paused and gathered up their courage. Stealthily they went outside, grabbed the officer under the arms and dragged him off.

"He's heavy," Minka whispered ever so quietly.

"It's from all that good officers' food," Tishka agreed.

They dragged the officer into the cellar. Just in time. On the street another battle had got underway. This time the boys didn't go near the window, they bustled about the officer, pouring water over his head. Tishka made rags out of the cleaner parts of his undershirt and applied them to the wound in the officer's side.

The officer tossed about in a fever. He would shout something, quiet down and then begin once again.

This lasted until the evening and then into the night. The boys were exhausted from taking care of him. In the immediate neighbourhood houses went up in flame. Smoke poured into the cellar. They were fortunate that the house in which they were hidden was built of stone. This saved them from being engulfed in flames.

But the most frightening episode of all was just beginning. Maloyaroslavets remained in the hands of the French and some soldiers occupied the home. The boys feared that they would at some point make their way into the cellar.

"Quiet, Your Honour, quiet!" they pleaded.

As if he understood them he fell silent, but then again began to toss and cry out in delirium.

Fortunately all ended well.

During the night the boys fell into a deep sleep. When they woke up the sun was already high in the sky. Silence surrounded them. They ran to the window but no one was on the streets. There were no French to be seen.

This is what happened. Although Maloyaroslavets remained in the hands of the French Napoleon realised that he couldn't make way to Kaluga. For the first time in his life the Emperor didn't dare to undertake another battle. He gave the order for his troops to withdraw.

The boys crawled out of the cellar and entered the street. They looked, Russians were entering the town. The residents were pressing in by the side of the soldiers. Among them were the parents of Tishka and Minka. The father spotted his sons:

"Ah, you, bandits! You mangy curs!"

Tishka and Minka stood frozen in one spot. Their father took off his belt and, right there on the street, began to thrash the children.

The twins had to suffer it out. Their father was a strict man and they had known what to expect.

Finally he grew weary and stopped to catch his breath.

"Pa," Tishka interrupted him, "there's a wounded man down there," he said, pointing his finger at the window jutting out of the ground.

"It's an officer," Minka added.

The father went down into the cellar. He soon discovered that the boys were telling the truth. He looked and soon caught sight of a young colonel.

"Wow!"

The father hurried off to report to the authorities. Orderlies came and took the colonel away. Then the father again took off his belt and renewed his beating. To be sure, this time there wasn't quite so much force behind the blows, and he grumbled rather than cursed.

"You could have at least felt pity for your mother. Blast you!..."

A few days passed when suddenly the father was summoned before the city administration and awarded a medal. To the medal was attached an order in which was explained that the resident of the city Maloyaroslavets Ivan Mikhailovich Kudinov, that is to say the father of Tishka and Minka, had been awarded the medal for saving the life of a Russian officer.

The father was dumbfounded. He was about to say that it wasn't really he, but rather Tishka and Minka, who had saved the officer, but the members of the board didn't wait to hear his explanation.

"Whoever saved him, you figure it all out. You

received the medal, now run along, we've got a lot to do."

The father returned home. He didn't know what in the world to do with the medal. How could he divide it in two so the boys each received one?

"Here's your medal. One for the two of you," he told the children.

Tishka and Minka gazed at the medal. Their eyes burned, their arms almost involuntarily reached towards it. Wouldn't that be something to hang on your chest! However their father was a strict one. He took the medal and hid it in a small chest.

"This isn't a toy, you know," he announced sternly.

And that's where the medal remained.

However twice a year, at Christmas and on Easter, when the whole Kudinov family went to church, the father dug out the medal for the children.

On the way to church Tishka wore the medal. On the way back home it flashed on the chest of Minka.

MAJOR CONSEQUENCES

One day, at some point before the outbreak of the battle of Borodino and when the Russian troops were still withdrawing, a lieutenant-colonel of the Akhtyrskyi **hussars** regiment, a certain Denis Davydov, approached Prince Peter Bagration.

Bagration had known Davydov for a long time—at one point the latter had served as his adjutant—and received his call immediately and with warm greetings.

"Well, tell me what's on your mind. Don't hold back. Did your superiors offend you?"

"No," answered Davydov.

"Did you miss out on an award that was coming to you? Do you need a leave for a vacation?"

"No," replied Davydov.

Bagration was somewhat taken aback. He waited to hear what the officer would say.

"This is what's on my mind..." began Davydov.

He began to talk about the French army. Wasn't it true that they were dispersed over a length of hundreds of versts? Didn't lines of support run through Russia all the way back to the very Niemen River? Didn't

HUSSAR — soldier of light cavalry regiment

all supply, wagons, powder, reinforcements and cannon balls have to be dragged from that point?

"That's all true," answered Bagration.

"Their messengers are constantly racing up and down these extended lines of communications."

"True, true," said Prince Peter. "This is no news to me."

"Well, what's new about it," Davydov suddenly interjected, "is the need to place mounted detachments of our men to the rear of their forces. Let them harrass small convoys and formations. It would be a real thorn in the enemy's side. I ask you for some Cossacks and **hussars,** and I'll show you how it can be done."

As Davydov had been talking, Bagration's face had grown brighter and brighter and even broken into a smile. "What a fine lad! Let's embrace." They embraced. "Just wait a bit."

At this point Bagration paid a call on Kutuzov.

He began by reciting Davydov's arguments. After all, wasn't the French army dispersed over several hundred versts... then he restated word for word the request of Denis Davydov.

Kutuzov heard Bagration out.

"Such wild fantasies..."

Kutuzov had just taken command, was preparing for battle, and was jealously protecting every detachment of soldiers.

"Your Excellency," said Bagration, insulted (for he did lose his temper on occasion), "the fantasy lies more in the fact that we often don't even see what is really to our advantage!" Then, somewhat more calmly: "This suggestion makes a lot of sense. It could lead to some major consequences."

"Well, alright, my friend, have it your way. I've already concluded as much. Is this lieutenant-colonel a reliable fellow? What did you say, from the **hussars?** They know how to con their superiors, you must be careful."

"He's reliable, Your Excellency. He was an adjutant for me for five years."

Kutuzov paused and thought:

"Alright. Maybe this operation really will turn into something significant, as you say."

Kutuzov signed an order providing Davydov with 50 **hussars** and 80 Cossacks. Thus the first partisan detachment came into existence. The Russian army retreated further, but Denis Davydov took to the woods.

The damage which the partisans wrought upon the French was significant. The Field Marshal soon came to appreciate the wisdom of Davydov's suggestion and himself began to send out detachments of soldiers to harrass the enemies rear lines.

As the process snowballed, more and more peasants joined up with the soldiers. They also created their own units. Hundreds and thousands of peasant detachments began to strike at the enemy.

Just as during flood-time a river overflows its banks and inundates the area about, here the peasants' rage appeared in the midst of the people's war. After an interval of two months, when the Russian army had already moved to the offensive, Kutuzov sent out an order to summon Davydov to his headquarters.

He stared long and intently at the **hussar**. Finally he said:

"You know, when Prince Peter was still alive I said in front of his face that your idea for a manoeuvre was crazy, a fantasy. You must forgive an old man. Only don't think that I'm about to take those words back. What you've accomplished truly has to be called fantastic!" Then, just as Bagration had done, he went up to Denis Davydov and embraced him warmly.

A ROUND TRIP

Rumours about the marvellous feats accomplished by partisan hero Denis Davydov were rampant in the Russian army. These rumours followed in quick succession. First he'd seized a convoy of gunpowder, then he'd dispersed a whole artillery unit in transit, then he'd intercepted a courier with extremely valuable papers. Finally, it was said that Davydov had distinguished himself in battle by killing with his sabre, and seemingly without effort, four French.

A young **cornet** named Vassilchikov began to dream of the possibility of falling in with the partisans. He asked the commander of his squadron:

CORNET — soldier of the lowest rank, flag bearer for his troop

"Let me go to join Davydov!"

He ran to the regimental command:

"Let me go to fight with Davydov!"

His superiors, however, refused. The **cornet** fretted and hesitated, then suddenly went absent without leave. To be sure, he left a note so no one would call him a deserter. He wrote that he couldn't resist, he'd left to join the partisans.

He began to make his way to Gzhatsk district, the area where Davydov was reputed to be.

As he went along he thought about Davydov. He pictured the partisan commander as a real **hussar,** complete with dress jacket, the laces, the cap and extravagant plume of the **hussar.**

The **cornet** managed to make his way successfully to Gzhatsk and to find the partisan detachment. More accurately speaking, he was seized by partisans in the area and led to Davydov's camp.

He looked expectantly upon Denis Davydov. But where were the **hussar**'s jacket, plume and galloon?!

Instead he was faced by a real down-to-earth peasant. The beard, the caftan, and even the belt typical of the peasant. Vassilchikov was distraught. He even forgot to introduce himself. Davydov laughed:

"Allow me the honour. I'm Lieutenant-Colonel Davydov. I'm at your service, **cornet.**"

"Vassilchikov," the **cornet** squeaked out.

He was exhausted from his journey and looked about for a place to sleep. He was given a place on an overcoat under a pine. His partisan existence had begun.

The next morning Davydov began to instruct him:

"What's most important for the partisan?"

The **cornet** shrugged his shoulders in ignorance.

"Surprise," answered Davydov. "What position is the best?" and again answered: "Constant motion. What's the partisan's best weapon? Skill, not numbers."

Then it began—marches, marches, crossings, nights in the woods. They were inundated by downpours, frozen by the frost, then chilled by evenings spent on the wet ground.

Battles fought without plans, without any rules, a

skirmish in the morning, an unexpected battle in the evening, a sudden alarm during the night—this was the life of the partisan.

The **cornet** was not prepared for such. He began to regret that he had left his unit. He lasted for a week, then picked up and left the partisan detachment. This time he didn't even leave behind a note.

Vassilchikov returned to the ranks. When he had left his unit it had caused quite a stir. Unwarranted absence was a serious offense for an officer. His departure had been reported to Kutuzov. Now his return was also reported.

Kutuzov listened to the news and ordered:

"Punish him for absence without leave." Then he paused and added sternly: "And for the fact that he returned, punish him doubly."

HIS EXCELLENCY,
THE PEASANT SOLDIER

A soldier of the **dragoon** regiment, by the name of Ermolai Chetvertakov, fell into captivity after his horse had been wounded in battle. He was taken to Gzhatsk but soon escaped.

Chetvertakov found himself in an area occupied by the French. The dragoon came across a village named Basmany. He could tell that the peasants were boiling with rage and ready to fight: a reference to the French would bring out a string of curses.

At this point the idea crossed Chetvertakov's mind of arousing the peasants to fight the French by creating a partisan detachment. He began to suggest the idea.

But at this point the peasants faltered. After all, who knew anything about the soldier? Where did he come from? Who knew where such a suggestion would lead. Only one pock-marked youth joined the dragoon.

They set off together to another village—Zadkovo— to recruit peasants. On the road they met with two French soldiers and killed them. Then they encountered two more who soon suffered the same fate.

"Wow! Two of you—took care of four of them!" said the astonished peasants in Basmany.

DRAGOON — cavalryman

"If there were four, that would mean eight!"

"And if eight, then sixteen?!"

The peasants in Basmany were in a state of great agitation. What if the lads in Zadkovo got together a detachment before they did.

"Let's get the dragoon back here!"

"Let's get our own detachment together!"

The dragoon responded and returned to Basmany. The villagers asked his forgiveness.

"Don't take offense. We wanted to test you," the peasants said cleverly, "to see if you were a true soldier."

At that point more than 200 peasants agreed to participate in the detachment. This was the beginning. Within a short amount of time more than four thousand peasants had gathered under the command of Chetvertakov.

Chetvertakov was a true commander. He maintained military discipline in his ranks: patrols, guard-duty and even studies. He made sure that the peasants held their heads high and that they remained in good trim physically.

"What are you, a colonel?" laughed the peasants. Secretly they were pleased that their commander maintained a firm hand.

"What do you mean colonel—he's a general! His Excellency!"

The peasants continued to live in their villages. They moved to action by a given signal when the need arose...

...A French detachment was travelling along a Russian road. It was a convoy under heavy guard. It was bringing powder for the army. Up in front the horses were dragging cannon, to frighten the peasants but also, of course, to bolster French morale.

From church belfries in the area the ringing of many bells sounded forth. First they shouted as if in an alarm, then pealed soothingly, then flowed out in crisp, distinct tones.

It was pleasant for the French to hear these bells.

Then the bells fell silent. As the French came around a hillock the sound struck them once again from left and right. The bells were singing from village to village. Such beautiful sounds...

The French continued along their way. Little did they know that listening to the charming music they were hearing not simply tonalities but voices singing a funeral dirge for them.

Chetvertakov used the church bells as a system of signals for his troops. They were not merely alarm networks, each modulation contained a command. By listening carefully one could tell where to go and where to gather forces.

The French continued along their path. By this time detachments were already leaving from several villages in the region. The order was to gather today at the stream at the Egoryevskaya gorge.

The French approached this stream, by now surrounded by peasants. Their numbers were legion. A horseman stood out among the sea of **caftans**—surely the commander. The horseman gave an order. The troops fell upon the French convoy. The soldiers in charge of the cannon were frantic—which direction should they fire in? There were peasants everywhere. They fired at the mounted rider, for he was clearly the superior in rank. Fortunately they gauged poorly and shot over the target.

That round was their first and last. The French didn't get another chance to reload. The peasants' legs were swift, their hands agile and very tenacious. The cannon, carts, horses and soldiers—within a moment all was in their hands.

The partisans returned home from their courageous exploit. On the steed rode the soldier, Chetvertakov, Ermolai... What is your second name? Well, we can do without the second name. Ermolai Chetvertakov... peasant general. Your Excellency the Peasant Soldier!

LASSO

Peasants in the village of Lokotka had become quite skilful at catching the French with lassoes. They would hide in the bushes on a road through the forest and wait in hopes that a detachment would pass by. When infantry or cavalry did come through, they would lie in ambush for the straggler and then... a loop around his neck. He would be pulled to them and gagged before he could utter a cry in protest. And, we wish you well, monsieur! You've fallen, hook, line and sinker!

Once the peasants took up their rewarding positions for yet another ambush. The French approached the spot where the peasants lay in ambush. The lasso went up. The rider flew from his horse and was promptly gagged. The peasants dragged the Frenchman to their village. Along their way they had to clout him, for he had turned out to be very volatile and kicked the peasants at every opportunity.

They placed the prisoner in a pigsty, brought over some water and doused him. They pulled out the gag, having decided to bring him to the district centre, Sychevka, where prisoners were held.

When the Frenchman stood up he began to shout:

"Muddleheaded yokels! Bull-headed fools! I hope the plague gets you all!"

The peasants stood mouths agape. They began to giggle nervously.

As it turned out the fellow was no Frenchman at all, but a Don Cossack from Denis Davydov's detachment. The Cossacks had intentionally disguised themselves as French, they were either on a scouting expedition or some other related mission.

The peasants, though stunned, did of course begin to come to their senses and to find words:

"Well, how in the world were we to know?"

"It wasn't written on your forehead, you know."

"You should be thankful we didn't cut your throat right away."

"Oakheads! Stupid oafs!" the Cossack wasn't convinced. "What's this?!" he pointed to his Cossack forelock.

Of course the French didn't have forelocks. But who would have noticed such a thing at that moment?!

"Alright," finally the Cossack quieted down. "Do you at least have a glass of wine for me?"

"We can find that."

The Cossack drank up and straightened up his shoulders:

"Well, my buddies, farewell! Thanks for the hospitality!"

For a few days the peasants didn't dare go out on the road.

"What if the same thing happens—we catch one of our own?"

But then, they went back into operation. Now, however, they watched their step. If they seized a Frenchman, first of all they looked at his forehead— was there a forelock to be seen?

TOSSING THE HAT

Having heard countless stories about the heroic actions of peasant detachments, Kutuzov decided to take a look at the heroes. He summoned the peasants to meet him near the city of Yukhnov. They were a colourful group: young and old, portly and simple. Some had battle scars, one had even lost his right eye, like Kutuzov.

The peasants piled into the cottage. Kutuzov passed around tea. The peasants drank cautiously, without haste, holding their sugar, rural style, between their teeth. As they drank the tea the conversation began, and quite naturally turned to the French.

"The French are a heroic people," the peasants declared, "but they're lacking in spirit. Napoleon made a blunder. Did he really think he could take Russia by fear?!"

"Wasn't it Nevsky who said," recalled the peasant with one eye, "you come bearing a sword and you'll perish from the sword!"

"That's right!" the other peasants responded.

The conversation then turned to Moscow.

"Of course it's sad. It's a great city, the pride of our nation for centuries. But is Moscow really the whole of Russia? The city will be rebuilt. The most important thing is that the State survives."

Kutuzov then praised the peasants for their courageous encounters with the French.

"It's nothing, we don't get the brunt of their forces. It's the army that does the real work."

Kutuzov could see that these fellows weren't stupid by a long shot. He enjoyed the conversation.

"Have you heard of Denis Davydov?"

"Heard of him?! His detachments are in our own district. He's a bold, daring commander. He's done some great things."

"They say that there's a woman partisan in Smolensk?"

"That must be Kozhina," the peasants answered. "Vasilisa, the wife of the village elder. A real fighting woman! The fiber of a man!"

They recalled Chetvertakov as well:

"A natural-born commander. He should be an officer by all rights."

Then the conversation almost unnoticeably drifted to other topics. The peasants discussed the winter and spring plantings, the crop failure in Smolensk region, the landowners and then suddenly: "Mikhail Illarionovich, Your Honour, what about our freedom? Is it true that after victory we'll all be given our freedom?"

Kutuzov wasn't expecting this question. What could he tell the peasants about freedom, anyway? Of course it was scandalous, the situation in Russia. If it were up to him he knew the answer. But he was only commander in military affairs. He had no say over the question of their freedom.

He didn't know what to say in reply. For the first time the Field Marshal was at a loss for words.

It was clear to the peasants that they'd put him in a difficult spot. Not wanting to embarrass Kutuzov, they turned the conversation back to the war. But now the conversation didn't really stick together, something was lacking. Kutuzov let them all go.

The peasants returned to the village, talking along the way.

"Well, it's clear. He doesn't forecast much in that line for us."

"And the land, just like before, will remain in the hands of the nobility."

One youth suddenly slowed down and forcefully tossed his hat against the ground.

"Well then why are we fighting against the French? What are we risking our lives for?"

"Quiet down, you young buck!" shouted the one-eyed man. "We're comparing two different things. The nobility is the nobility. Russia is Russia!"

THE PICTURE FRAME

Georges Michelet, a French soldier, came to Russia with high hopes: "Russia's a rich country. I'll bring home a nice bundle of treasures." He wasn't alone in this thought for most of his compatriots had the same expectations. The Emperor himself had promised as much.

Michelet began his collection in Smolensk, where he picked up an ermine coat. In Vyazma he found some expensive candle-holders, in Gzhatsk—a rug of Pamir wool. In Moscow in one of the large churches he plundered an icon in a silver frame. Michelet was satisfied. He would have taken more but the weight would have been too much of an encumbrance. "Well," Michelet opined, "now the Russians can ask for peace... I'm about ready to go home."

But the Russians didn't ask for peace. With every passing day the situation of the French grew worse. Moscow became a dread name for them.

After that the French began to make tracks home. If only they could make it out of Russia!

Michelet got his things together hastily. He packed his Pamir rug in a bag, the candle-holders in his knapsack and wore the ermine coat over his uniform. But what could he do with the frame. He decided to carry it about his neck. The face of the marauder, sticking out of the frame, now took on a holy cast!

The Russians pursued the French. The army struck, partisans made forays from the woods, peasants ambushed along the road. The French moved at a forced clip. Michelet sweated under his burden.

Carrying such a treasure required no little effort. The knapsack rubbed against his shoulders. The frame was heavy: it contained a good eight kilograms of silver and bent his head to the ground like a supple branch in the wind. The ermine coat was long and its folds dragged along the ground. All in all, it was no easy task. The French army retreated. It was constantly under fear of the Cossacks. Kutuzov was chopping them up on the battlefield.

The French had more and more stragglers dropping behind. Michelet wove unevenly along the road, also falling behind. His strength was draining from him. He had to part with some of his treasure.

They made it to Gzhatsk, where, coming in, Michelet had picked up his rug. The Frenchman, remembering those bright days, broke into tears. He tossed aside the Pamir rug.

They trudged in Vyazma, where he had found the candle-holders. He looked fondly at them, wiped away the tears and threw them away. When they reached Smolensk he parted with the coat.

It was difficult—to the point of tears—for Michelet to part with his spoils. He tossed off his knapsack, dropped his weapon along the road, but stubbornly clung to the frame.

"For God's sake, throw away that stupid frame!" his comrades shouted at the stubborn soldier.

He would have been glad to rid himself of it, but he simply didn't have the strength. He had been promised riches, perhaps his whole reason for going to Russia was just to find that silver frame.

The last ounce of strength parted from the soldier. Beyond Smolensk he dropped behind, lost his way and died on the road. A frame lay in the drainage ditch along the road. The face of a marauder stuck through it like the face on an icon.

THE WEDDING

In a small village near Smorgon Kutuzov came upon a peasant wedding.

He was invited to join in and didn't refuse.

A cottage. Tables and benches in a long row. A clearing for dancing. Guests in bright costumes. The groom in a peasant shirt the colour of the sky, the bride in pink ribbons. The young people, accompanied by Kutuzov, sat at the table.

Now here was a sight for the Russian village. A wedding not with any old general, but with the Field Marshal himself! The whole village gathered about the cottage. The merrymaking got into full swing. Toasts were offered for the bride.

"To the health of the groom!"

The cups were filled to overflowing.

"To the prosperity of the bride and groom!"

"To the health of the father of the bride!"

"To the parents of the groom!"

"To the mothers!" And suddenly:

"To his Excellency, Field Marshal and Prince Kutuzov!"

Kutuzov got up from his position of honour:

"Enough, enough! I'm not the groom, I'll propose my own toast. To our Mother Russia. To the heroic people!"

"To Russia!" shouted the peasants.

Kutuzov returned to his headquarters. His generals surrounded him.

"Your Excellency, it's not good for your health to take part in peasant weddings." They added in reproach to the peasants: "War is raging around us and they want to carouse at a wedding. Somehow it isn't fitting."

"It's fitting and proper," Kutuzov answered. "The peasants love a peaceful way of life. The war is on the wane. Peace—not war, life—not death; that's what's dear to the soul of the Russian."

YET ANOTHER MARCH

1812. December. The Niemen. The borderline of Russia. The same bridge that we saw in the summer half a year ago.

Soldiers were passing over the bridge, but in the opposite direction. This time their steps were not measured, no drums rolled out the beat. The fifes weren't playing, no banners unfurled over the soldiers. A handful of tortured souls, a little band of ragged men, miraculously still alive, the French left the Russian bank of the river. The pitiful remnants of a once great force. Proof of the strength of another.

The Russians emerged at the bank of the Niemen. Here it was, the end of their campaign.

"Well, it looks like Russia has pulled through!"

"Alive," a grey-moustached corporal added.

The soldiers glanced at the latter—a familiar face.

"Hey, isn't it you who told us that tale a while ago?"

The soldier answered in the affirmative.

"You might say that the calf grew into a bull-elk," laughed the soldiers. "It smashed the old wolf to death with its hooves!"

"It does seem that way, doesn't it?"

The soldiers' hearts were gay—they had carried out their mission. They stood on the banks of the river and reminisced about the past. The battle of Vitebsk, the battle near Smolensk, the bitter fighting at Borodino, the fire of Moscow... No doubt, the path to victory was no easy one. Would their descendants remember those days... A lot of Russian blood had been spilled. There were many new graves in Russia.

The soldiers' voices were tinged with sadness as they recalled their comrades. The day was both joyous and sad. At this point Kutuzov and his retinue appeared at the very same spot on the river.

"Hurray!" shouted the soldiers.

"Glory to the saviour of our homeland!"

"Glory to the Field Marshal!"

"Hurray!"

Kutuzov bowed to the soldiers:

"Glory to the heroes of Mother Russia! Glory to the Russian soldier!"

Then he moved closer to the soldiers:

"Exhausted?"

"Exhausted," the soldiers confessed. "But it's all over now."

"No, it's not," said Kutuzov. "There's yet another march to make."

The soldiers were confused. What was the Field Marshal hinting at here? But they replied:

"Glad to try!" the answer the Army Rules and Regulations would suggest.

Kutuzov moved to a spot where he could see all his troops and ranged his eye over them. In a stentorian voice (what happened to the old man's rasp?) he proclaimed:

"Heroes of Vitebsk, heroes of Smolensk, eagles of Tarutino and Yaroslavets, of the field of Borodino— immortal sons of Russia!" Kutuzov stood up in the saddle. "Those who died and those who have survived— fall into rank! You heroes have one more march to accomplish—into the pages of history!"

1. The initiation of Napoleon's Russian Campaign—the French army crosses the Nieman on June 12, 1812 (engraving from the beginning of the nineteenth century). 2. Pillage—the first sign of the disintegration of an army. "French Soldiers in Byelorussia", this was the name given by Faber du For to his "nature-painting".

3

4

5

3. Barclay de Tolly, general of the Russian army under Kutuzov, hero of the War of 1812 (engraving by Dow). 4. Bagration, legendary military commander during the War of 1812 (engraving by Cardeli). 5. Napoleon and his army near Smolensk (engraving by Martinet). 6. Prince Mikhail Golenishchev-Kutuzov.

7

8

9

10

11

7. 8. 9. Kutuzov's generals, heroes of the War of 1812, Matvei Platov, Nikolai Raevski, Mikhail Miloradovich. 10. The Battle of Borodino. The eighth attack is hurled back at the Semenovski flèches. Bagration was wounded in this battle (engraving by Gess). 11. The Battle of Borodino. The French attack on the battery under General Raevski. 12, 13, 14, 16, 17, 18. Representatives of the various arms of the service under the Russian command. 15. A. Kivshenko "Council in Fili".

2

14

5

6

18

17

19

20

21

19. Painting by Vassili Vereshchagin. "Execution of Muscovites by the French Soldiers".
20. Painting by Vereshchagin. "Peace at Any Cost". Adjutant General Lauriston brings the fearful news to Napoleon: Kutuzov rejects the peace offer. 21. Moscow burns (water-colour by Gaberman "The Kremlin Embankment").
22. Russian militia. 23. The remnants of the Napoleonic army are driven from Moscow (contemporary engraving).

2

23

4

25

26

27

французы голодныя крысы. Въ командѣ у старостихи Василисы.

24. Gerasim Kurin, peasant partisan. 25. Denis Vassilyevich Davydov (drawing by Alexander Orlovski). 26. Vasilisa Kozhina, peasant woman and leader of a partisan detachment. 27. Woodcut by Terbenev "Peasant partisans in the Patriotic War of 1812". Under the woodcut is the inscription: "The French are like hungry rats, when captured by the Elder Vasilisa" (Kozhina).

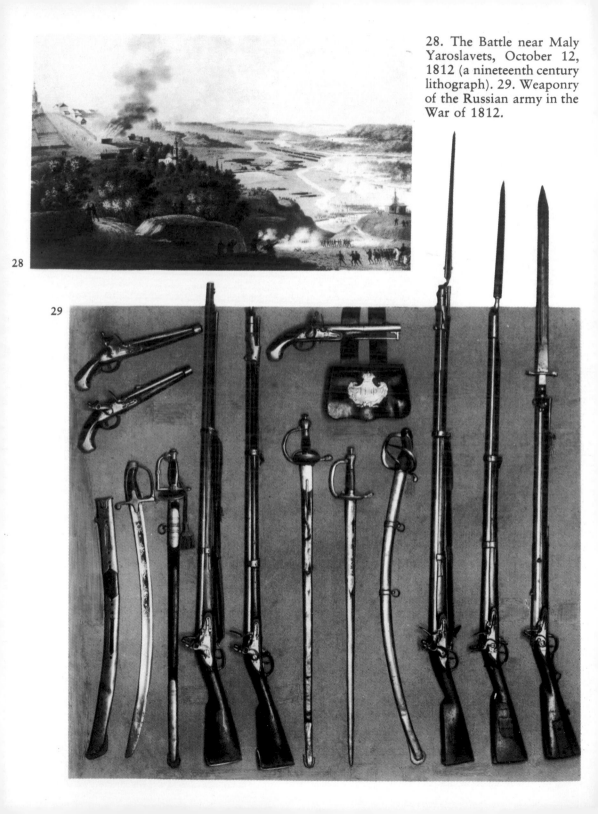

28. The Battle near Maly Yaroslavets, October 12, 1812 (a nineteenth century lithograph). 29. Weaponry of the Russian army in the War of 1812.

28

29

30. Painting by Vereshchagin, "On the Highroad". The "invincible" Napoleonic army thus departed Russia. 31. Painting by Pryanishnikov, "1812".

32. Russian soldier with medal, received for participation in the War of 1812 (lithograph by P. Zhukovski). 33. Cannon from the early nineteenth century. 34. One of the monuments to the Russian soldier erected on Borodino Field.

32

33

34

THE RED BANNER OF LABOUR

IN THE WOODS
NEAR EMELYANOVKA

The village of Emelyanovka was situated at a distance from the thoroughfare, about three versts from Petersburg. Behind the village was a forest which in turn ended abruptly on the shores of the Gulf of Finland.

Emelyanovka was a commonplace little village, boasting only of a small and peaceful population. Its history was undistinguished for little had happened there of note. The woods were typical for the region: pines and birches, prickly raspberry bushes and thickets of hazel-nuts. Passers-by rarely wandered here from the road. But one day...

A local boy named Sanka Lapin was playing near the woods one day when he spotted two unfamiliar figures. They made their way across a field, looking in all directions, and hid in some hazel thickets.

"Who could it be?" Sanka wondered. "They're young and strong looking. Maybe they're bandits."

The boy wanted to sneak up to the hazel bush but couldn't muster up the courage. He passed by at a distance, ran down to the gulf and there encountered another surprise: one, two, three boats hugging the shore... People were disembarking, also casting glances to all sides and heading for the woods.

Sanka raced back to the village to find his friend Pashka Dudarov.

"Pashka, Pashka," he whispered. "Strangers, two hundred of them!"

"Stop telling fibs!"

"I swear it's the truth!"

The two friends rushed down to the gulf. Pashka looked—there really were boats!

They hastened into the woods, then made their way stealthily from bush to bush. They came to the clearing —a crowd of people! The crowd stood in a semi-circle around a broad-shouldered man who unfurled a red banner and began to speak.

The boys, stupefied, lay down quietly behind the bushes to observe.

"Workers of Petersburg! We're gathered here to-day..." the words of the orator drifted over to the boys. "We are only a few today but the day of the awakening of the masses is near..."

The speaker continued for quite a while, then ended with the words:

"Long live our proletarian holiday!"

Sanka prodded Pashka:

"What's he talking about?"

Pashka shrugged his shoulders.

After the first speaker several others got up in turn to speak. They spoke of the difficult lot of the worker, about the need to struggle for a new life and once again about the holiday.

The boys lay under the bush for two hours until the gathering came to a close. The workers began to disperse in small groups. After waiting for a short while the boys also got up. As they walked along they tried to guess who these people in the woods had been and what holiday they had been talking about.

The boys returned to Emelyanovka and decided to find out from the grown-ups.

Sanka approached his father and told him about the gathering and the banner.

"You sure you didn't make this up?" his father asked him with doubt in his voice.

"Make it up? We saw them with our own eyes. We hid behind the bushes."

His father shrugged his shoulders. He himself couldn't explain the matter.

The boys asked their mothers, they ran to Aunt · Marya and then to Uncle Yegor. Nobody, however, seemed to know anything about a workers' holiday.

The two finally went to see Old Onuchkin. He was the oldest in the village; surely he must know something. Onuchkin began to explain that there are all kinds of holidays: Christmas, Easter, the tsar's birthday, the tsarina's birthday...

"Not those, not those!" the boys interrupted him. "What about a workers' holiday?"

"Workers'?!" The old man paused to think. He scratched the back of his head, then made a despairing gesture with his hands. "I've never heard of any such holiday."

Thus, as it turned out, the two friends remained in the dark about the holiday.

This is what really happened near the village of Emelyanovka: Russian workers for the first time celebrated the First of May. It was 1891, a long time ago.

It was a long time, however, before Sanka and Pashka learned about the May 1 holiday and why it is celebrated. They found out only after they grew up and themselves became workers.

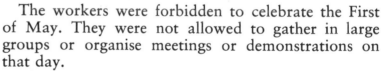

THE FUNERAL SERMON

The workers were forbidden to celebrate the First of May. They were not allowed to gather in large groups or organise meetings or demonstrations on that day.

They had to resort to various subterfuges. For example, the workers from one of the districts of Moscow decided to gather in the cemetery.

They made a coffin and hired a priest. Six fellows carried the coffin, the rest fell in behind. The procession moved in the direction of the cemetery. The priest walked up front, pompously swinging the censer.

Under these circumstances no one would drive the workers away. Even the police respectfully stepped aside as they passed.

A liturgy was sung for the "deceased" in the church in the cemetery. The priest waved his censer and droned:

"For the tranquillity of the soul of this servant of God. What was his name?" he asked the workers.

"Nicholas."

"For the tranquillity of the soul of the servant of the Lord, Nicholas," the priest iterated.

Having finished the service and received his previously arranged five rubles, the priest went his way. The workers, however, gathered in the furthest corner of the cemetery and held a meeting. In subdued voices they sang out revolutionary songs and read proclamations which had been written for the occasion.

That evening the night watchman for the cemetery, a man named Tyatkin, while making his rounds stumbled upon a coffin lying above the ground. The astonished Tyatkin opened the lid, looked in and saw a sight too horrible for words.

The watchman raced to the local inspector.

"Well, what's it with you?"

"A coffin, sir."

"So what's new?"

"In the coffin was..." Tyatkin began to stammer.

"Well, what was in the coffin, anyway?"

"His Excellency, the Tsar Nicholas the Second," Tyatkin uttered.

"Have you gone mad?!"

"In no fashion!" the night-watchman crossed himself earnestly. "It was the tsar himself. Excuse me for saying as much."

The inspector set off to the cemetery. He looked into the coffin and there... well if not the tsar at least the tsar's portrait: full-scale, in his military uniform and decorations.

An investigation was begun into the matter.

Tyatkin couldn't add any new information.

They looked up the priest.

"Did you perform the service?" queried the investigator.

"I performed it."

"For whom?"

"For Nicholas, servant of God."

"Idiot!" shouted the investigator.

The priest at first didn't understand the cause for these harsh words or why he, a personage of the church, had been dragged to the district police. What was he guilty of?

But when he realised he began to shake like a leaf in the autumn wind. He trembled, made the sign of the cross and blinked his eyes which bulged in fear.

"Who was at the gathering?" the inspector persisted.

The priest tried to recall but failed.

"Uh, various people...about forty. There were tall ones and thin ones, young and old. One of them even sang the Alleluia quite heartily."

"Alleluia!" the inspector mocked him. "Well then, who hired you? Who paid out the money?"

"A fellow with broad shoulders," the priest said enthusiastically. "With a moustache. And his hands were calloused."

A search began. There were too many workers with broad shoulders and moustache, however. Indeed there were few without callouses on their hands. Thus, the search was futile.

The inspector once again dressed down the priest and Tyatkin and the matter ended with that.

The workers were satisfied. It would only be partially in jest if one were to say that they managed to both observe the First of May holiday and to say the last rites for the tsar.

GRISHA LOZNYAK

Grisha Loznyak was serving out his time in solitary confinement. He was thin and slight, his shoulders narrow. Judging by externals he was nobody special. He conducted himself modestly as well. He didn't begin fights with the wardens and obeyed the prison rules. During walks he remained silent. The prison guards looked at him and thought: "He must have done something silly to end up here. There must have been a misunderstanding."

Once a week his sister brought him a package—always the same thing: a loaf of bread, a bottle of milk and a quarter of a pound of cheap confectionery each wrapped in a piece of paper.

Her name was Liza. She resembled her brother in that she was thin, slight and very young.

Liza patiently waited her turn, mildly handed over the package and left.

"She seems to be as timid as a mouse," the guards observed.

Appearances were deceiving, however.

It was no accident that Grisha was in prison. He was a member of the Bolshevik Party, a printer arrested during a raid on an underground press.

Liza was by no means the sister of Grisha. She was also in the Bolshevik Party and was carrying out instructions from the party. Not for nothing was she bringing in bread, milk and candies, for the candy wrappers contained letters from his comrades still at freedom. Although Grisha was in prison he remained abreast of the news outside.

Grisha made ink-wells from his bread, poured milk in them and with this milk wrote answering letters to his comrades. If in the process one of the guards approached Grisha's cell he would simply swallow both the "ink" and "ink-well". You perhaps know that this is how Vladimir Ilyich Lenin wrote his prison letters.

The First of May was approaching.

Grisha had taken part in many of the previous May Day activities. He decided to observe the workers' holiday in prison as well. He communicated this to his neighbours—other prisoners confined in nearby wards. He communicated by tapping out a special code. At first he tapped on the right side of the wall and then on the left. His comrades understood, supported the idea, and in turn passed it on to their neighbours.

In a short time all the political prisoners knew of Grisha Loznyak's proposal.

On the very next day shreds of red material began to find their way into the prison: one was baked into the bread, another made up the filling for a pie and a third was stuck into the back of a book.

During the daily walk the prisoners surreptitiously handed the rags to Grisha, and during the night he sewed them into a red flag.

May 1 arrived. As usual the prisoners were led out for a walk in the morning. The courtyard of the prison was small and the prisoners moved about in a circle.

Ten circles—thirty minutes. Thirty minutes—that was the entirety of their walk.

The prisoners completed one circle, a second, and suddenly a banner unfurled over the heads of the incarcerated. The crimson fluttered in the breeze and stretched out towards the sky and sun.

> Boldly, my friends, never losing
> Courage in unequal fight.*

Grisha Loznyak began to sing.

> Shield your dear land, ever choosing
> Honour and freedom and right!

the others joined in.

The guards ran up, agitated.

"Shut up!" they shouted. "Shut up!"

The prisoners paid no attention:

> What though they cast us in prison,
> What though they test us in fire,
> What though to mines we are driven,
> What though the noose threatens dire!

The supervisor of the prison arrived. The guards surrounded the prisoners on all sides and began to beat them fiercely with their rifle butts, after which they drove them down to the putrid, underground punishment cells.

The demonstrators spent two weeks in the punishment cell, then were dispersed to separate prisons in other cities. Grisha Loznyak was sent out along with the rest.

He was brought to a new prison and placed in solitary confinement.

A week passed, then Grisha received an "ink-well" and some "ink" once again. Once again he began to receive letters from his friends outside...

Grisha was thin and slight of build. He was modest. Judging by externals he was nobody special...

* Here and elsewhere the verse has been translated by Walter May.

THE CANNON

In the morning of the First of May the colonel of the gendarmes, Golova-Kachanov, was handed a letter. He unsealed it and inside the envelope found a leaflet which read: "Long live the First of May! Down with the autocracy!"

Golova-Kachanov turned pale, grabbed the leaflet and rushed into the office of the gendarmerie. He gathered his subordinates only to learn that a captain named Galkin, a lieutenant named Kuteikin and two police officers named Tupikov and Nosorogov had all received identical letters. And this was only a partial list! Golova-Kachanov's telephone began to ring as various notable citizens reported that they too had received letters: the factory-owner Rublev called, the merchant Sobakin called, the retired general Atakin called, and on and on...

Golova-Kachanov clutched his head in despair. To add to his misery, his gendarme officer Nosorogov suddenly piped in:

"Your Honour, do you think that the workers are planning a riot?"

"To your posts!" Golova-Kachanov shouted. "Machine-guns on the street! Cannon!"

The gendarmes rushed to carry out his order. They set up machine-guns at street intersections. A cannon was placed in front of the gendarmerie building. Police spies hastened out into the town. However all was quiet in the city—no disorders of any sort. The only thing that happened was that little boys began to crowd around the cannon placed in front of the gendarme administration. It was an interesting sight for the boys: for many it was the first cannon they had ever seen. They pressed to get closer and closer. The bravest even touched the wheels and the barrel.

"Away, away!" a soldier shouted at the boys.

The boys backed away, then returned.

"Fire it," they asked the soldier.

By the middle of the day Colonel Golova-Kachanov calmed down, his mood improved. But then Nosorogov rushed into the office and showed the colonel a sheet of paper.

"Yo... You..." he stammered, "Yo-your Honour, please take a look. It was just pulled off the cannon."

The colonel glanced—a leaflet: "Long live the First of May! Down with the autocracy!"

Once again Golova-Kachanov blanched. Again he clutched at his head. And Nosorogov started in again:

"Your Honour, there's no doubt, there'll be an uprising!"

Once again the gendarmes and spies raced about the town. The machine-guns were readied another time. Golova-Kachanov ordered that the cannon fire a blank charge every two hours. He wanted to serve warning that the authorities were on the alert.

Every now and then a gendarme or officer would appear before the colonel only to report that all was calm. A gendarme named Tupikov arrived:

"Your Honour, everything's in order."

"Good man. That's all, move along."

Lieutenant Kuteikin arrived to report:

"Everything's quite in order, Your Honour."

Nosorogov showed up as well:

"Your Honour, no disturbances of the peace have been reported. Everything's quiet."

"Fine. Run along now."

Nosorogov turned to leave, exposed a back, upon which had been pasted a leaflet: "Long live the First of May! Down with the autocracy!"

"Idiot!" Golova-Kachanov roared. "You're under arrest! To the guard-house with you!"

For a third time the gendarmes and spies rushed around the city. For a third time the police moved the machine-guns into position. Once again the cannon fired.

During the day the workers gathered in a grove of trees outside the town and quietly celebrated the First of May.

WILL THEY OR WON'T THEY?

In the middle of April a group of Belgian workers arrived at the Polisadov factory. Some machinery had been imported from Belgium and they had come along to install it.

May 1 was approaching. The Russian workers had agreed not to show up for work on that day. Now the question was: what about the Belgians?

Some said:

"They'll go to work."

"No, they won't," others objected.

The same question occupied the minds of the children of the factory workers. Kolka Zudov thought that the first viewpoint expressed was the correct one. Lyonka Kosichkin, on the other hand, was sure that the Belgians wouldn't work.

"They're not our blood, Belgians won't support Russian workers," Kolka declared.

"You watch, they'll support us," Lyonka insisted.

They argued and argued, finally deciding that the loser would get ten cuts across the brow.

The eve of May 1 was an anxious one for Lyonka. What if Kolka was right and the Belgians did show up for work? Kolka's fingers were stronger than his. His raps could be extremely painful!

Kolka didn't sleep well either. What if Lyonka were right after all! Although he didn't much fear the pain that might ensue he didn't want to be embarrassed in front of the other boys. Kolka loved to be right all the time.

Early the next morning the boys raced to the factory. Kolka was there, Lyonka showed up, then Lyonka's sister—Katka the red-head—then another dozen or so children. There was a lively interest in the outcome of this argument!

At seven o'clock the Belgians showed up at the factory gate. First five showed up, then another five, and finally the rest arrived.

The children counted carefully: they were all there—twenty one of them.

"Well, what did I tell you?!" Kolka shouted triumphantly.

The children descended into a ravine which protected them from the wind, where Kolka rolled up his sleeves.

"Once," he counted out, "twice, three times, four..."

He hit soundly. Lyonka's face contorted, he bit his tongue from the pain.

"Five, six..."

Lyonka held his ground, but tears appeared in his eyes.

"Seven, eight, nine, ten."

Kolka had just struck the tenth blow when they noticed Lyonka's sister, red-headed Katka, rushing down the ravine and crying out:

"The Belgians have left, they've left the factory."

"What do you mean—left?"

"Just what I said. They've left!"

The children climbed out of the ravine and looked. Katka was right, the Belgians were indeed leaving. At first five left, then another five, and the rest followed behind. The children counted carefully—twenty one of them.

Lyonka pounced upon Kolka with his fists:

"What did I tell you, what did I say! Get ready, it's my turn!"

"Why should I," Kolka began to object. "Maybe they'll return."

This time the children supported Lyonka:

"They won't return. Not a chance. They saw that ours weren't around, so they got up and left."

"Turn your forehead!" Lyonka demanded a second time.

Kolka submitted, turning towards him...

The two youths returned home with swollen brows. When they met their fathers in the workers' settlement questions were asked:

"Who did that to you?" Kolka's father asked him.

"Tsk, tsk," Lyonka's surprised father uttered.

"It's because of the Belgians," Katka the red-head slipped out.

"What do you mean, because of the Belgians?"

The little girl related the incident.

The workers had a good laugh.

"You say they're not our blood. That's where you're wrong. All of us have proletarian blood and that's what counts."

THE NEW SHIRT

Nikolka's father had promised to buy him a new shirt by the First of May.

Sometimes during the evening his mother, father and his sister Klava would sit about and discuss the kind of shirt to buy him.

"A white one with a belt would be best kind you wear over the trousers," Klava suggested.

"It would get dirty too quickly, a blue one would be best," his mother objected.

"Why a blue one," his father objected. "We'll buy him a bright red one, the colour of poppies."

Nikolka's heart was bursting, his eyes burning with excitement.

"So what kind do you want?" his father asked.

"I'd like a shirt with pockets, a red one."

Nikolka boasted about the shirt to all his friends and acquaintances. Even the children began to argue about which shirt was best for him.

"You'd do better with a sailor's shirt," Zoika Noskova declared.

"Pick one with an embroidered collar," Pashka Soldatov advised him.

"With a button, one on the chest!" Kuzya Vodichkin lisped.

Nikolka raced about the factory barracks and told whomever he ran into about the shirt.

He encountered a worker named Stepan Shiroky:

"They're going to buy me a new shirt!"

"You don't say!"

"That's right!"

He saw Tikhon Gromov, a metal craftsman:

"My father promised to buy me a new shirt for the First of May, you know!"

"Just think about that. It seems your father's a good man."

"He's good, that's for sure!" Nikolka laughed.

He met old Kashkin, the lathe operator:

"Papa's going to buy me a new shirt for May!"

"Isn't that something!"

"A new one. With pockets and buttons. Poppy-red," the child boasted.

In a few days there wasn't a person in the whole workers' settlement who hadn't heard of the shirt.

Nikolka's father had some business to take care of in the city of Ivanovo.

"Well, Nikolka," his father said in farewell, "obey your mother. There'll be a shirt for you."

The father left, but didn't return. He'd run into trouble: the police in Ivanovo had arrested and held him in custody.

Things changed in Nikolka's home: the house seemed empty and cold.

"Mommy, mommy," Nikolka insisted, "why doesn't papa return?"

Nikolka's mother embraced him but remained silent.

The boy cried and cried for his father.

"Hush, hush," Klava comforted her brother. "Father will return soon. He won't forget us."

Not long before the First of May the workers organised a meeting. They talked about the holiday, about mutual aid and about solidarity. Old Kashkin was there, Tikhon Gromov, the metal craftsman was there, Stepan Shiroky was present as were many others. They thought about Nikolka's father and remembered that he'd promised his son a shirt for the May Day holiday.

"Let's buy him one," the workers decided.

May 1 came around. Nikolka woke up and could not believe the sight before his eyes—a shirt on the nearby chair. New! With pockets! With buttons on the chest! Poppy-red!

"Papa, papa's returned!" shouted Nikolka.

His mother came to his side. She was at a loss for words.

"No, papa hasn't returned," she answered. "He won't be soon."

Nikolka stared at his mother and tried to imagine where the shirt could be from in that case.

"I know, I know!" he yelled. "Papa sent it!"

His mother stared at him and wondered whether or not to tell the truth about the shirt. He was little and silly. How could he understand the meaning of workers' solidarity? She decided not to say anything.

Nikolka put on his new shirt, raced into the street and began to boast about his new shirt to everyone he could find.

He met the young worker Stepan Shiroky:

"Papa sent me a new shirt!"

"Isn't that wonderful?" the youth replied.

"He sent it, he sent it. He didn't forget!" Nikolka shouted and ran down the street.

He saw Tikhon Gromov, the metal craftsman:

"Look, papa sent me a shirt!"

"Just look at that!" Gromov smiled. "It seems your father's a good man, he remembered."

"A good man, a swell man!" Nikolka laughed.

He chased down old Kashkin, the lathe operator:

"Look at the shirt papa sent me!"

"You don't say," said Kashkin. "That's the truth. And what a shirt!"

"It's new, it's new," Nikolka couldn't restrain himself. "He didn't forget about the pockets either, or about the buttons or even about the poppy-red."

Kashkin embraced Nikolka and caressed his head as tears came to the eyes of the old man.

Nikolka looked up:

"So what are you crying about?"

"Oh, that's the way I am," the old man said hastily. "Run along and play. It's May now ... the workers' holiday."

THE STUBBORN ICE-FLOE

Spring came late that year. The river was swollen but the ice didn't budge. It finally broke up on the very eve of May 1st. From early morning on people gathered along the shore to watch.

One after the other the huge ice-floes moved down the river, grinding, gnashing, turning up on their edges and, showering spray into the air, once again coming to rest in the water.

The crowd was highly engaged by the spectacle.

The river-bank was the beat assigned to Okhapkin, one of the town policemen. He was walking his beat when, noticing that a crowd had gathered, he thought: "If only they don't start any trouble. If only the workers don't organise a disturbance. It is the First of May! I'll cross my fingers."

No sooner had these thoughts crossed his mind, when an enormous ice-floe floated around the bend. Okhapkin couldn't believe his own eyes: there was a red flag on the ice-floe!

The crowd flocked to the very edge of the river.

"Hurray!" the shout arose behind Okhapkin's back. "Long live the First of May!"

The policeman lost his composure and grabbed his whistle. He blew first in the direction of the crowd and then towards the ice-floe itself.

The people hooted and remained in a crowd on the shore.

"Disperse! Go back! Don't gather together!" Okhapkin shouted at the top of his lungs.

During this time the ice-floe moved closer and closer. Almost as if intentionally, it moved directly towards the bank. The red flag fluttered in the breeze.

The policeman rushed around in circles at a loss for what to do. He halted, breathed deeply and again began to blow his whistle.

He whistled, but the ice-floe was already bumping against the shore. It came to a halt directly in front of Okhapkin and floated there, stubborn and mocking.

The flustered gendarme thought: "And what if I just jump on the ice, rip out the flag, and end this whole affair?!"

"Jump!" somebody in the crowd cried out.

Jump he did. He landed and the ice-floe, as if waiting just for that, pushed off from the bank.

"Help!" he wailed. "Save me!"

Okhapkin rushed about on the ice-floe, forgot about his whistle and the flag and almost lost his cap as he waved his arms and begged for help. But no one was anxious to jump into the frigid water to save a gendarme.

"Say hello to the Caspian for us!" they shouted to him.

"Have a nice voyage!"

"May Day greetings!"

The ice-floe struck against another block of ice and the gendarme, losing his balance, fell heavily into the water.

"He-e-lp!" Okhapkin cried once again before he sank to the bottom like a stone.

A group of young men stepped out of the crowd and jumped into the water. They dragged the terrified Okhapkin to the shore.

The gendarme stood shivering and turning various shades of white and blue. To the accompaniment of general laughter from the crowd he made the sign of the cross.

During this time the ice-floe made its way to the middle of the river, turned and moved downstream with the current. The red flag fluttered, played in the spring breeze.

"Long live the First of May!" the shout carried from the shore.

THE RED BANNER OF LABOUR

Three factories decided to observe May Day together. The workers from Nagornaya, Liteinaya, Marshevaya and other streets converged and moved in solid columns to the centre of the city.

In the morning Goshka's father set out with the other workers to his factory.

"I want to go with you," Goshka pestered him.

"You're too small for the time being," his father grinned. "You stay home."

"I want to go too," Goshka persisted. "Look what I made yesterday," and showed his father a little red flag.

"It's a nice flag," his father agreed, but nevertheless left his son at home.

Goshka remained alone. He wandered about his room, clutched the flag to his chest, then moved towards the door.

"Where are you going?" his mother asked him with a tinge of alertness in her voice.

"To see Vanka Seregin."

He ran into the yard, pretended to be heading off towards Vanka's, then flew off like the wind in the direction of Nagornaya.

When he got there a crowd had gathered. A column of workers was heading down the road. In front a red flag unfurled over their heads.

Goshka waited until the workers had passed by, then joined the rear of the column. He had only just reached for his little flag when he heard:

"Home with you! Get a move on! To mother!"

"I'm staying with you. Going to celebrate May Day."

"Right this moment. Along with you!"

There was no alternative but to leave.

Goshka stood for a while thinking, then raced to Liteinaya. When he arrived there another crowd had gathered. Once again a column of workers was marching down the road. Once again a red flag flew over their heads.

Goshka joined the column. He reached for his little flag, but suddenly:

"And what are you doing here?!"

"Uh, well, I..."

"I'll teach you a lesson with my belt! Home!"

Goshka fell behind. He thought for a moment then raced off towards Marshevaya.

Here also a crowd had gathered. The column of workers marched down the street, the red flag unfurled over their heads.

Goshka approached the workers and said cunningly:

"I'm looking for papa. My mother sent me. He's up front."

The workers moved aside and made room for Goshka. He made his way to the very front row. He took a deep breath and looked about. To the right just a bit walked his father. He walked holding the red flag in his hands.

Goshka wanted to slip back into the rear but it was too late.

"Hey, come over here," his father signalled him.

Goshka obeyed.

"What's up with you? Don't you listen to your father and mother?"

"I'm like all the rest. I want to go too. I already made this, see?" Goshka pulled from his bosom the little red flag.

The father smiled with pleasure at his son. The other workers began to laugh.

"Take a look at that—a flag!"

"And a real one at that!"

"Red too."

The father glanced at his big red banner, looked at Goshka's replica, grinned once again and patted him on the head:

"Alright, now, go home to mother."

"Well, I..."

Goshka didn't have a chance to finish. A group of soldiers with rifles emerged from a side street and jumped across the path of the demonstrators.

"Hold it!" the commanding officer shouted to the workers. "Stop!"

The demonstrators slowed down then came to a halt.

"Disperse!"

The workers closed their ranks, surrounding Goshka's father and the banner.

"Ready arms!" commanded the officer.

The soldiers raised their weapons.

"Son..." whispered Goshka's father. "My son, run!" Goshka didn't budge.

"Who do you think I'm talking to, run!" his father shouted and forcefully pushed Goshka away.

Goshka flew out of the column onto the sidewalk. There he stood, a little boy with a dazed look on his face. He looked from the soldiers to the workers, then back again. He watched the officer raise his arm and the soldiers press their rifles to their shoulders. One more second and they'd fire.

Suddenly:

> *Boldly, in step, lads, with me then!*
> *We shall grow stronger in war.*
> *Into the kingdom of freedom*
> *Force your own road to the fore.*

Goshka's father sang out. He waved the red flag and in the same breath the workers moved forward in a body. Moving in unison, as if their actions were those of one man, they moved upon the soldiers.

"Fire!" the officer rasped.

"Papa! Papa!" shouted Goshka and hurtled into the column of demonstrators. He ran up to his father and hid his face in his father's trousers. "Papa! Papa!"

His father bent down, grabbed Goshka and lifted him up on his shoulders.

The little boy looked around: the soldiers were making way for the workers, lowering their weapons and backing off the pavement.

"Fire, fire!" the officer whined.

But nobody listened to him.

Goshka broke into a smile and waved the little flag in greeting to the soldiers.

The workers passed along Marshevaya Street, met others coming down Nagornaya, joined up with the workers from Liteinaya and merged with those coming from other streets and city squares. The crowd became huge. Dozens of red banners fluttered in the May breeze. A song thundered over the city:

> *Age-old repression we'll shatter,*
> *Tyrants our strong arm shall foil.*
> *Over the earth then shall flutter,*
> *Blood-red, the banner of toil!!*

A glimpse of the life endured by workers and peasants under the tsar in pre-revolutionary Russia.
1. Peasant huts. 2. Women barge-haulers on the river Surga (they are pulling a loaded barge). 3. Peasant with a flail—a primitive implement for grain-threshing. 4. A miner in the shaft.

5. The Putilov factory on strike, January 1905. 6. The troops fire on Petersburg workers who are peacefully demonstrating on January 9, 1905. "Bloody Sunday" was the name given to this day by the workers (from a film reconstruction of the events).

5

6

7

8

9

7. Painting by Valentin Serov, depicting the dispersal of the demonstrators by the Cossacks.
8. 9. Revolutionary leaflets from 1905. Leaflet written by the Petersburg Committee of the RSDLP (January 1905) released before "Bloody Sunday" and warning the workers that it was useless to hope for good deeds from the Tsar. Only with weapons in the hand could liberation be achieved. The second is a leaflet from the Moscow Committee of the RSDLP (January 1905) holding up the tsarist butchers to shame after the events of "Bloody Sunday" and calling for struggle.

10. The first issue of the newspaper "Iskra", December 1900. 11. A workers' demonstration on the Neva embankment. October 1905. St. Petersburg.

10

11

12

12. The workers employed a wide variety of forms of struggle. One of them was the printing of proclamations which were then posted in well-frequented places. This was a dangerous business... (Painting by I. Kolochkov "Posting Proclamations").

14

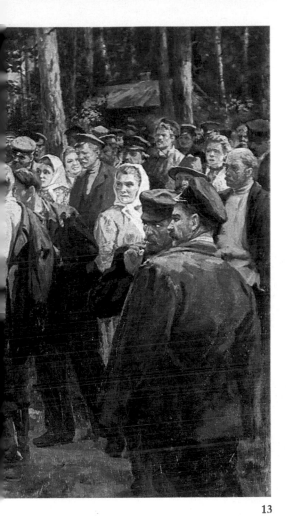

13

15

16

13. One of the centres of the revolutionary movement was the city of Ivanovo-Voznesensk—a textile centre in Russia. The painting by G. Knyazhevski, F. Kulagin and V. Govorov depicts a general strike of the Ivanovo-Voznesensk weavers. 14. The Russian autocracy dealt cruelly with intransigents. In Siberia in 1912 at the Lena Gold Fields workers were mowed down by the tsar's troops. 15. Thousands of revolutionaries were thrown into jail and sent into exile. 16. The clanging of chains resounded throughout the land...

17

17. However no amount of persecution could hold back the people's drive for freedom and justice. The revolutionary movement in Russia expanded. (Painting by M. Klionski "People's Demonstration in Ekaterinoslavl").

THE TSAR IS OVERTHROWN

CITIZEN OF THE RUSSIAN REPUBLIC

Little Danilka lived in the basement of a tall building on Liteiny Prospekt in Petrograd. He was born and grew up in this building; thus he knew all the residents by sight.

The first floor was occupied by Countess Shcherbatskaya. The rooms of the second were taken up by Prince Pirogov-Pishchaev. On the third floor lived the high ranking bureaucrat Gorokhov. On the very top floor lived another bureaucrat named Ardatov, whose rank in the civil service was only slightly lower than that of Gorokhov's. All of the residents, then, were distinguished and titled people.

Events had whirled by in the last few days since the revolution had taken place. Danilka had even ceased being amazed. But what happened on this day ...

Danilka's father brought home a newspaper, opened it up and looked at his son.

"Well," he said, "from now on you're a citizen of the Russian Republic. Vladimir Ulyanov-Lenin himself signed the decree."

Somehow it didn't ring true to Danilka's ears; after all he wasn't even sure exactly what being a citizen of the Russian Republic exactly meant.

"It is more important than the rank of **statski sovetnik**?" (This was Ardatov's rank.)

"More important," his father smiled.

"And more important than that of **taini sovetnik**?" (He remembered Gorokhov's title.)

"More important."

"And higher than a count?"

"Higher."

"Higher than a prince too?"

"Higher, higher," his father laughed.

STATSKI SOVETNIK — 5th in the Table of Ranks in the civil service in tsarist Russia

TAINI SOVETNIK — 3rd in the Table of Ranks

Danilka rushed out into the street and hunted down his friends and acquaintances.

"Do you know that my rank is higher and more important than that of **statski** and even more of **taini sovetnik,** higher than that of count and higher than a prince? I'm a citizen of the Russian Republic. It's written in the newspapers. Vladimir Ulyanov-Lenin himself signed the decree."

Danilka ran into many of his friends that day and he told each and every one of them without fail about this. He finally ran out of energy and sat down to rest near his home. He sat and began to think, and where had this Ulyanov-Lenin heard about him, Danilka. As he was pondering this he suddenly saw red-headed Kyril rushing towards him. Kyril raced up, caught his breath, and the words poured out:

"Do you know who I am?! I'm a citizen of the Russian Republic!"

Danilka was bowled over with astonishment.

"You really think you're a citizen?" he uttered in a mocking tone. "I'm the citizen. They were writing about me in the papers."

"About you," Kyril whistled through his teeth, "they wouldn't waste the paper on you!"

A fight began.

"I'm the citizen..." Danilka tried to drown out the voice of Kyril.

"No, I'm the citizen..." howled the latter.

A young worker was passing along the street at this time and separated the boys. They maintained silence for a long time, refusing to say what the problem was. Finally they confessed. The youth grinned, reached into his pocket and pulled out a newspaper. The children began to read, slowly and with great difficulty.

"Decree on the Abolition of Estates and of Civil Titles," they read out the headline.

Further down it said that all titles, ranks and names of high posts were from that time on, and forever, abolished. No longer would there be nobility, merchants, **tainye** and **statskye sovetniki,** princes or counts. "One title is hereby established for each and every member of the population of Russia—Citizen of the Russian Republic," were the words of the decree.

Below it was signed:

Chairman of the Council of People's Commissars, Vl. Ulyanov (Lenin).

"So, as it turns out, you're both right," declared the youth. "You're a citizen of the Russian Republic," he pointed to Danilka, "and you are," he nodded at Kyril, "and so am I. All are now citizens of the Russian Republic. Vladimir Ilyich Lenin wrote this decree for the common people."

At first, of course, Danilka was offended that the decree had been written for everyone and not only for himself. Soon, however, he came to see that it was all for the best. As it turned out, this way Vladimir Ulyanov-Lenin had forgotten no one: not Danilka's mother or father, nor his friends, nor his acquaintances. He had remembered everyone.

As far as matters concerned, however, Countess Shcherbatskaya, Prince Pirogov-Pishchaev, **taini sovetnik** Gorokhov and **statski sovetnik** Ardatov, it was clear that the decree signed by Lenin didn't please them at all. They left the country, and so much the better, good riddance to the likes of them. New people moved into the tall building on Liteiny, common people like Danilka's father and mother—working people. They became not only citizens, but masters of the entire country.

AN UNDERSTANDING FELLOW

Eremka Bykov tossed about from side to side. It was uncomfortable and hot on the stove-ledge.

His father couldn't sleep either. It was not hard to understand why. First thing in the morning the land of the nobility was to be divided up. It was not every day that such a thing came to pass!

"Go to sleep," his mother scolded.

Thirty minutes passed. No matter how they tried they couldn't fall asleep.

His father said at last:

"I'd better go outside for a breath of fresh air."

"I'll go with you," Eremka added quickly.

"My word, you are restless souls," his mother muttered anew.

She scolded, but in fact she also found it hard to fall asleep. Land and the upcoming events were on her mind as well.

Eremka and his father went out on the street. They passed through the village, then through its outskirts, over a bridge across the river and then ascended a hillock which looked down upon the land of the nobility.

Eremka's father gazed at the field, his eyes brimming with tears.

"What's the matter, pa?" Eremka tugged at his father's hand.

"It's nothing," the latter replied. He rubbed his palms against his eyes: "My mind's on a certain very fine fellow."

"You mean Ulyanov-Lenin and the decree that he signed? He's a good man, wouldn't you say?"

"That's putting it mildly, Eremka. He's an understanding fellow. The peasants can't do without land. We're grateful to Lenin."

They stood gazing at the field until they had had enough fresh air and returned home.

Eremka once again crawled onto the stove. "Oh, I hope I don't oversleep and miss the land distribution. I can't let slip the most important moment."

No sooner had he lain down than he fell asleep.

Eremka then had a remarkable dream. It was as if Lenin himself came to divide up the nobility land. He walked over the field carrying a stick to measure out the land. Lenin said to Eremka:

"Why don't you be my assistant? Tell me who to begin with, how many mouths are there to feed in each home, who should get land, and how much."

Who to begin with? With him, Eremka, of course.

He and his father fell silent, waiting.

"No, that won't do. As a participant in the actual distribution, you must be last in receiving your share," Lenin replied.

They divided up the land of the nobility and all were satisfied. Finally Eremka's turn was next. The boy woke up at this point. He blinked—the sun was high in the sky. His father and mother were both gone.

"It was all just a dream," Eremka realised. "I overslept, overslept. I'd better hurry to the field. But the dream ended just at the most important moment. What part of the land was I going to receive?"

Eremka closed his eyes once again. He was interested in learning what parcel of land he'd receive? If it only could be near the river on a hillock where the old birches stood. He would plant peas there and treat his friends in the summer. He had only just closed his eyes when the door hinges squeaked. His mother and father stood there:

"Wake up, get up, Eremka!"

Eremka was sore: he had slept through the land redistribution and yet not finished his dream. He got up with a gloomy expression on his face.

"What's the matter with you, Eremka?"

His only answer was silence. He dressed and went out on the street. His friends surrounded him, laughing mischievously.

"Sleepy-head, sleepy-head!..."

"You overslept."

"You missed the most important!"

Eremka became more and more offended. He looked at the other children and suddenly said:

"Well, I saw Lenin, Lenin himself. He came to us."

The children's mouths opened wide in astonishment.

"He came, he came," Eremka insisted. "He was with a measuring stick and I was his assistant."

"Sure, you saw it all in a dream."

"No, I didn't, it wasn't a dream. No dream at all. He was really here."

At that time an old man named Prozorov approached the group. Eremka said to him:

"I saw Lenin. With my own eyes. Lenin divided up the land."

The children giggled again. "Old man," they said, "isn't that Eremka quite a liar?"

The old man, however, paused, shifted his feet and looked sternly at the shouting children. He came to the support of Eremka.

"What do you mean? Lenin was after all present."

The children were amazed.

"Well, how come we didn't see him?"

"You didn't look carefully enough. You didn't understand, that's why you didn't see him," answered the old man.

SHKURIN AND KHAPURIN

Once upon a time there lived two men named Shkurin and Khapurin. Each of them owned a factory, Shkurin's made nails and Khapurin's soap.

They looked upon themselves as old acquaintances and friends. Both were rich and both were greedy. What's more, both were covetous of any good that came to others.

Thus it always seemed to Shkurin that the profit which Khapurin accrued from his soap factory exceeded his own, that which he received for his nails. To Khapurin, on the other hand, the opposite seemed to be true.

"Oh, if only I could get my hands on Shkurin's nails," sighed Khapurin.

"Oh, wouldn't it be nice to have Khapurin's soap," dreamed Shkurin.

When they met, conversations of the following type took place:

"Because of your soap, Sil Silych," said Shkurin, "money simply rains down from the sky on your head."

"Don't say such things," answered Khapurin, "it's you, Tit Titych, whose money bags are filling up thanks to your nails."

Envy ate away at their spirits, they thought about the possibility of exchanging factories. The subject even entered their conversations, but words are one thing, actions another. They didn't quite dare.

What if they miscalculated?

While they calculated and tried to make up their minds, 1917 descended upon them. The land, factories and enterprises began to be transferred to the hands of the people.

Shkurin rushed to Khapurin.

"Oh, oh!"

"My, my!"

They felt that their turn was soon to come. Only they didn't know whose factory would be nationalised first. Khapurin thought his soap factory would be the first to go. But it seemed to Shkurin that he would lose his nails first.

They fretted and tried to figure it out. Once again the idea of exchanging factories crossed their minds. Once again the thought was fearful, intimidating.

"Oh, that Khapurin will swindle me, cheat me."

"That Shkurin will swindle me, I'll go bankrupt."

A short time passed, then Shkurin received a packet from the provincial Soviet of Workers' and Peasants' Deputies. He unsealed the package, pulled out the paper and felt his eyes grow dim. There it was, written in black and white, the nail factory would be nationalised.

"Dear God, woe is me!" Shkurin implored. "Why me? Why not Khapurin?" He bowed deeply, cringed before his icons, but all the while thought:

"What if I rush over to Khapurin's and talk him into an exchange while he's still in the dark about this."

However Khapurin had received the very same packet that day. And he began to kneel before his icons and implore the saints. He knelt, all the while thinking: "And what if I rush over to Shkurin's..."

They both cut short their genuflections and raced to find each other. They met at midpoint and, in their haste, almost knocked one another over. They halted, breathing deeply and gasping for breath.

"I was looking for you, my dear Sil Silych," Shkurin finally managed to say.

"And I for you, my friend Tit Titych," pronounced Khapurin.

"Let's trade factories."

"That's fine with me."

They made quick work of the deal. The old friends and acquaintances were well satisfied.

"I took him for a ride," Shkurin judged. "Ha-ha."

"Ha-ha," chuckled Khapurin. "The old chicken fell for it."

They strolled about the city pompously, their noses stuck high in the air. They arrived at their factory offices only to see the new legal owner—the working class.

"Greetings, Shkurin! Greetings, Khapurin! You've arrived, now move aside. You've lost power!"

A NEW SCHOOL

Before the Great October Revolution the city schools were called gymnasia.

Kyril's father was a landlord, Paul's an important tsarist bureaucrat, Natalya's was a general and Rosalia's a factory-owner. As for Modest the blockhead, his father was a gendarme.

Here, on the other hand, was Peter Sorokin.

His was not an easy life. His mother was a laundress. The rich children looked down their noses at Peter.

"Hee-hee," giggled Natalya, catching sight of Peter.

"Hee-hee," Rosalia joined her.

"Ho-ho," Kyril and Paul made faces at the boy.

"Look at the laundress," blockhead Modest laughed wildly.

One time Peter couldn't restrain himself, and soundly thrashed Modest. After that things only got worse for Peter. Modest told his father and the gendarme no longer patronised Peter's mother.

Peter wanted very deeply to study, but where could he go to learn? His mother was, after all, a washerwoman.

Peter would have remained illiterate just like many, many others. But then—the revolution came!

The factory-owners and landlords were driven out, the power of the rich came to an end.

Natalya, Rosalia, Kyril, Paul and even Modest dropped from sight, nobody knew where.

Everything now changed. There were no longer gymnasia. Instead there were schools. Different children attended these schools.

Vassili Lotanov's father was a worker, Tolya's a Soviet professional worker, Olga's a carpenter, Polya's a truck driver and Grisha's a stoker.

And here was Peter Sorokin. He now attended school along with all the rest.

The children walked in groups to the new school, the free school, the Soviet school.

THE ARTEL

The coast of the Sea of Okhotsk is one of the most remote and isolated corners in Russia. The Pacific or Great Ocean kicks up storms just beyond its outer limits. On the shore of the sea stands a fishing settlement isolated by a distance of at least a hundred versts on all sides from other life. People rarely settle in this area.

In the settlement at the time there were thirty fishing families and thirty log cabins. Four long-boats were tied up at the pier. In these boats the fishermen went out into the deep sea and caught fish with their nets.

The Sea of Okhotsk doesn't hoard its wealth. When the fishermen returned home, the water-line would be riding high up on the hull of the long-boats from the weight of their hauls.

Then the fish would be pickled and packed into barrels.

The work community in the village was often called an **artel**. However, the long-boats, the barrels and the whole haul—all belonged to one owner. For every kopek of earnings the fishermen brought home the owner's profit would run into rubles. There were in fact two owners: the merchant Fedor Provorov and the local priest Mefodi. These two divided the lion's share of profit.

So this was an **artel**—a cooperative work enterprise? Some worked and the others counted their profits! That's the way things were run here. Not only in this place, either, but all over Russia.

Fedor Provorov knew what he was doing. Even though the wage the fishermen received was meagre, nevertheless he devised a way of getting most of it back. He opened a store in the settlement where the villagers could make their purchases.

The priest, Father Mefodi, was a clever shark as well. Summoning God to his aid he charged fees for baptisms, for benedictions for the dead, for repairs—so he said—for the church and for new icons...

This was how life stood in that settlement. Provorov traded his wares, Mefodi waved his censer about. The

ARTEL — a cooperative association of workers or craftsmen working together by agreement

fishermen set forth on the stormy sea. The profit went to the wealthy, the crumbs to the poor workers. That was the **artel**.

But Soviet power was established on the remote shores of the Sea of Okhotsk as well.

Fedor Provorov and the local priest, our Mefodi, were deprived of their barrels, long-boats and their profit. Those who catch the fish now in the Sea of Okhotsk divide the profit.

THE AUTOMOBILE

Kolya's ears were ringing with new words: "nationalisation", "expropriation", "property of the Russian Republic" ...

He gathered his friends and acquaintances together and began to explain to them about the new way of life.

"Expropriation," he explained, "is when wealth is taken away from the landlords and capitalists. Nationalisation is when this wealth passes into the hands of the working people. The rich are beasts of prey," Kolya specificied, "their spoils have to be taken by force."

"Do you know the factory-owner Zaikin? Have you seen his Rolls-Royce? Let's expropriate the automobile."

The children froze in their tracks in astonishment.

"We'll learn how to drive," continued Kolya, "then we'll drive everyone about town without charge."

Kolya was right. What better suggestion could one come up with!

The next day the children set up an ambush around Zaikin's home. They waited until the Rolls-Royce had arrived and the owner had got out and gone into his home. They ran up and clung to the automobile on all sides. Kolya climbed into the car and released the brake lever. The children leaned, and the car began to roll.

"Faster, faster!" Kolya shouted.

The children pushed and pushed and the Rolls-Royce moved faster and faster. Kolya sat proudly and contentedly, clatching the wheel with both hands.

The road came to a steep descent. The wheels began to turn faster and faster. The children could hardly keep up.

"Hang on, hang on!" wailed Kolya. It was already too late, the machine had left the children in the dust. Kolya wanted to pull out the brake lever, but lost his bearings from fright and couldn't even remember where it was located. The automobile careened from the left to the right side of the road, hopped onto the sidewalk and smashed into a tree—BOOM! Kolya flew out the door, his face scraping against the cobblestones—OW!

A shout rose in the street. The children understood that things could end badly for them, and in more ways than one. Kolya jumped up, ran as fast as he could away from the automobile.

He returned home, his face all puffed up, one of his eyes swollen and his shirt tattered.

"Good heavens!" his mother clasped her hands in dismay. "You mean you've scrapped with that Grishka Marafetov once again?"

"You've been up to mischief again," his father said angrily.

Kolya didn't reply.

"Well, I'll teach you..."

His father pulled off his belt and doubled it up. Kolya understood that no mercy was forthcoming and decided to confess everything.

Kolya related the story of the expropriation.

His father dropped the belt and burst into laughter.

"He does have to stick his nose into everything," his mother complained. "Punish him, punish him, he has it coming, Mitrofan Afanasyevich."

"I'll give him a good thrashing, alright," the father replied.

However Kolya could tell by the tone of his mother's voice and his father's answer that he wasn't about to be beaten.

And rightly so. Why punish him? After all, Kolya had made the attempt not for himself but for the working people as a whole!

MISSISSIPPI

The children loved to stand on the bank of the Volga and watch the steamboat *Mississippi* cast off. It had two wheels, two smoke-stacks and two decks. When it blew its whistle it was loud enough to rouse the dead from their slumber. Wouldn't it be something to travel on that ship!

But the *Mississippi* was out of their class. Only people from the upper crust filled its decks. The owner himself, the portly, broad-chested merchant Mitridatov greeted his passengers with his flowing beard.

"Dear passengers, we're at your service! At your disposition you'll find individual cabins, restaurants, showers, snack-bars," he recited to each boarder.

Dimka Pukhov, the son of a stoker, once made his way on board the steamboat. Returning, he was full of stories.

"What an engine it has, wow!" he said, waving his arms. "It eats up coal." Standing on tiptoes he continued, "The deck is fancy, what wood! The stairs are carpeted. As for the name, *Mississippi*, it's a river in America."

During the winter of 1917-1918 the steamboat stood idle. When spring came around the nationalisation of all river transport began. The time came for Mitridatov to part with his *Mississippi*.

"It's the end for Mitridatov," Dimka explained to his friends. "The end, and period. From now on the ownership goes to someone else. The working people now own all, and that's that!"

Now the children began to pester Dimka to ask his father, the stoker, to help them arrange a trip on the steamboat.

"My, you've got some ambitions," grinned Dimka. Secretly, however, he also harboured thoughts about such a trip.

"Everything's been arranged," he announced after a short interval.

But that very evening a fierce explosion sounded over the Volga. At daybreak the children rushed to the steep bank and looked below—the *Mississippi* was gone.

Mitridatov didn't want to give the steamboat to the working people. Instead he had blown it up and sunk it.

"So much for our excursion!"

It took a whole summer to salvage the ship from the bottom, repair the damage and then repaint it. When autumn came around the children again began to talk of a trip. Once again Dimka talked with his father and once again declared:

"Everything's arranged."

The children pestered Dimka:

"Will it be soon?"

"Soon."

"Not long now."

"Tomorrow."

At the crack of dawn the children raced to the bank of the Volga and looked below—the *Mississippi* was gone.

The times were tumultuous. The rich hadn't accepted the loss of their land, factories and enterprises, and had organised a White Army which embarked to wage war against the young Soviet Republic.

So the *Mississippi* had gone to war. Cannon and machine-guns had been installed on its decks, it was manned with Red soldiers and set off to fight the Whites.

The children crowded about on the slope of the Volga and discussed the matter:

"It had to be this way."

"We'll wait."

"We're in no hurry. Let the Red troops go to fight and smash the Whites."

"It'll return. Our *Mississippi* will return."

AN UNPLEASANT EPITHET

Uncle Ipat had worked as a doorman in a restaurant on Tverskaya Street. He had thought of finding Lyonka a job as an assistant dishwasher, but his plans had fallen through when the October Revolution had occurred, for the owner had fled and the restaurant had folded. Uncle Ipat himself was left without a job.

"Those were the days, but now, see what we've come to. The times have changed, that's for sure."

Once Uncle Ipat, preparing to set out for the public baths, decided to take Lyonka with him. The bath-house exhaled its soapy breath over the boy, its mirrors gazed at him from the walls, and its patterned strips of carpet tickled his bare feet.

"It's elegant, isn't it," said Uncle Ipat. "Take a good look, I'm sure it's the first time you've ever seen anything like it."

Lyonka gazed about.

Uncle Ipat undressed sedately, taking his time. First he took off his shirt and carefully folded it. He then smoothed out his beard and sat for a long time, dressed only in his drawers, watching the people gathered there. It was a busy day at the bath-house.

Uncle Ipat washed to his heart's content. He splashed, snorted, soaped down his flowing beard and washed untiringly his neck. Then he led Lyonka to the steam room. The boy was soon surrounded by a shroud of steam and found breathing difficult. He looked about—people were reclined on the planking to all sides of him.

"Oh, oh!" a fat gentleman sighed.

"Add more steam, add more!" shouted a youth.

A fellow with a pince-nez energetically flogged himself on his wasted hips. Uncle Ipat in the meantime stretched out on one of the upper rows of planks. He handed Lyonka a besom and ordered him to thrash his back. Lyonka began to thrash, but mildly, without applying much force.

"What's the matter with you, no strength in your arms?" Uncle Ipat said peevishly. "That's better. Ah! That's the way," and shivered with pleasure.

The old man lingered long under the steam, and suddenly said:

"I still say that things were better under the tsar."

At these words the youth standing near them pricked up his ears. Others followed suit.

"Of course things were better," repeated Uncle Ipat.

"The fellow with the beard is speaking the truth," purred the fat gentleman.

"Who said that he's right?" shouted the man with the pince-nez. He began to climb up on the planking:

"Citizens, we fought for Russia's freedom."

"Who fought? Did you fight?"

Somebody took a swipe at the orator. A hand grabbed at Uncle Ipat's beard.

"Give him a drubbing!"

"Let turn his beard into a floor mop!"

The old man shrieked, slipped and collapsed on the floor. People began to mill around in the steam house, wash-basins tumbled about, a cacophony of voices rose into the air. The emaciated fellow again climbed to his plank over the stove.

"Citizens, we struggled for the freedom of Russia..."

The manager of the baths came running at the sound of the turmoil. He halted at the door and shouted in a distraught voice:

"Gentlemen!" then he paused. "Citizens, that is!" and finally, imploringly, "Comrades!"

The turmoil didn't subside. Somebody grabbed a wash-basin and thoroughly doused the owner. The latter spat out water, cursed, and stomped out.

In a short time an armed patrol appeared at the bath-house. A burly fellow in a sailor's pea-jacket, apparently the man in command, tried to make his voice heard over the hubbub. Once again no one paid any attention. At that point the sailor drew out his mauser and fired a shot.

Everyone turned around. All fell silent.

"Get up, old man," said the sailor, extending Uncle Ipat his hand.

The old man stood up. He looked with trepidation at the sailor and his mauser.

"What's going on?" the sailor asked.

The fellow with the pince-nez raced up and began to hastily explain, as if he feared that he would once again be cut off:

"Comrade soldier, that person," he pointed at Uncle Ipat, "was carrying out propaganda against us."

The sailor glanced at the fellow with the pince-nez then turned to Ipat and asked:

"Is that true?"

The old man fidgeted nervously, blinked his eyes, pulled at his beard, let go then, tugged once again.

"Is that true?"

Uncle Ipat remained silent.

"He, permit me to say," the emaciated man persisted, "did just that. He said that things were better under the tsar."

"Get your things together and come with me, old man," pronounced the sailor and pointed to the door.

"What's the story with you?" asked the sailor when they moved onto the street. "What don't you like about Soviet power?"

"Oh, it's alright. It suits me," answered the old man. "The only thing is, how can we get along without a tsar? It doesn't seem to be a serious effort."

"Not serious?" grinned the sailor. "Isn't that something!"

Near the Sukharev market somebody called out to the sailor.

"Wait here," he said to Uncle Ipat and Lyonka.

However, no sooner had the sailor left than the old man grabbed the boy's hand and darted hastily into a gate-way. He then climbed over a fence, Lyonka barely managing to keep up with him.

From that day on, after they had taken flight to avoid the sailor, the old man lived in a state of constant anxiety. He waited, fearing that the next moment would bring with it his arrest. Finally, after five days there came a knock on the door. Lyonka hastened to open the door but Uncle Ipat shouted at him:

"Where are you going? Stop! Stay where you are!"

Once again they heard the knocking, but then they listened to footsteps moving into the distance. The old man breathed a sigh of relief.

But suddenly the sound of footsteps once again carried to their ears and they could make out voices beyond the door. Marya was talking:

"How can it be that he's not home? Of course he's there. Go ahead in."

Uncle Ipat blanched and quickly hid behind the curtain, dragging Lyonka along with him.

The door opened and two people entered the room. The boy squinted through a hole in the curtain and caught sight of the pair. One was a tall man holding a briefcase, the other ... the same sailor with the mauser hugging his hip, the one they'd encountered at the baths. The newcomers surveyed the room, the sailor casting his glance over the ceiling. Lyonka followed his gaze. There, to the right on the ceiling was a wet spot. He looked down at his feet. The rotted boards had opened up wide chinks through which moisture passed freely.

"Let's see, it's Ipat Ignatyevich Dremov, right?" said the man with the briefcase.

"He's the one," replied Marya.

"And you're his natural sister?"

"Sister."

"And the child is whose, if you don't mind?"

"His name is Lyonka. He is an orphan, the son of our sister Varvara."

"I see," uttered the tall man. "And we've come to you from the Soviet of Workers' and Soldiers' Deputies."

"With important business at hand," added the sailor.

Lyonka glanced at his uncle. Ipat stood with bated breath.

Suddenly Lyonka knocked against a bucket which clattered as it fell. Uncle Ipat shuddered and the sailor reached for his mauser.

"Who's there?"

Uncle Ipat held his silence, all the while making the sign of the cross. Aunt Marya walked up and shoved aside the curtain.

"What are you doing hiding there?" she exclaimed. "And fix your beard. You have guests who came to see you."

Uncle Ipat glanced at the guests, saw the sailor and edged backwards.

"Ho-ho!" the sailor hooted. "The monarchist. Our old friend!"

Uncle Ipat backed up another step, knocked against a bench and tumbled onto the floor.

The sailor broke into gales of laughter. The fellow with the briefcase rushed over to Ipat.

"What's the matter with you. We're from the Soviet." He held out a sheet of paper to the old man. "This is your warrant. You're going to be moved to a more comfortable apartment in the home of General Insarov."

Uncle Ipat stood up, looked first at the document, then at the sailor and finally at Aunt Marya. He couldn't make heads or tails of the situation.

"Offer your thanks," Aunt Marya nudged the old man in the side. "You're disgraceful! Have you lost your bearings from joy?"

The new room was located on the second floor. It was large and well-lit, with two windows looking over Sadovaya Street. When Uncle Ipat stretched out on the soft wide bed during the first evening there, he looked furtively in all directions, then said:

"You see, this is how they lived during the tsar's time. Those were the days!"

"Simmer down, you old fool," Aunt Marya said angrily.

Uncle Ipat fell silent.

One day later Ipat Dremov was invited to the local Soviet and offered work—he was put in charge of supplies in a children's home. He returned home pleased, stroking his silvery beard. "That means they've taken notice of me," he judged. "I'll set Lyonka up there too." On the way he ran into the sailor again.

"Ho-ho," the sailor hooted. "Monarchist!"

Uncle Ipat frowned.

"That's enough of that kind of talk," he scolded the sailor. With no further word he passed by. "Pah," the old man spat in vexation. "What an unpleasant epithet that fellow's thought up. 'Monarchist'!" he repeated to himself. Then he grinned, came to peace with himself, and strolled home.

THE MILL

The peasants of the village Telegino received a mill built out of bricks in inheritance from the landlord Kryakov.

The mill was old and dilapidated, without a roof or sail-arms. How could it be saved and restored? The peasants thought over the worth of such a project and backed away.

"It's not worth thinking about. Let's tear it down and divide up the bricks equally. A fair share to everybody."

No sooner said than done: the mill was pulled apart.

"What times these are," sighed the rich peasant Afanasi Blinov. "No good will come of this new power if it just destroys things."

"You're no prophet. Don't croak at the new system," Saveli Makhotin, recently a soldier, replied to Blinov. "Impatient yokel, you're like pus in a wound. You need to be drained out so that the organism can regain its health. Just give a date, we'll build a new and better mill."

"You go ahead and build it," snarled Blinov, "you just find the material!"

The times were in fact hard. Bricks were worth their weight in gold. Iron was next to non-existent. Locating such material was next to impossible.

A village Soviet was soon organised in Telegino. Makhotin was elected the first chairman.

After two months had passed he began to propagate the idea of a new mill.

"We need it, no doubt," agreed the peasants. "We can't get along without one. We acted without thinking. What we did was rash, out of anger at Kryakov."

The chairman was encouraged by these words and immediately took to the task at hand. It was necessary to gather together the bricks which had been distributed, find some nails and iron for the roof and—to the job! The peasants hemmed and hawed, procrastinated and finally backed off.

"We don't have any more bricks, we used them on stoves. We built fireplaces. And Ivan Sinebryukha, well, he took his share and sold the whole lot!"

"Where are we to find iron?"

"Do you think we have a nail factory hidden somewhere?"

Makhotin couldn't make any progress with his plan.

"You didn't believe me," sneered Blinov. "Hey, soldier, you don't know the peasant soul at all. When he gets his paws on something he doesn't give it back."

Spring passed and summer set in. The rye grew and ears formed on the stalks. It stood high and elegant in the fields, gathering nourishment from the land. It was no longer the landlord's rye—it now belonged to the peasants.

Ears of barley stuck out like hedgehogs, their long beards reaching towards the clouds. Peasants' barley, for the landlord was gone.

Oats darted into the air, then bowed heavily in the breeze. They were no longer landlord's oats—they now belonged to the peasants.

It was a pleasure to feast one's eyes on these fields.

The opinion then began to take hold among the villagers:

"You know, Makhotin was right after all."

"What'll we do without a mill?"

"We'll be the barnyard joke."

"Even the dogs will howl at us."

"It's not for the rich and blue-blood, after all, we should do it for ourselves."

"Chairman, how about calling together a peasant gathering."

The gathering was called. Noisy, crowded, everyone tried to drown out the voices of their competitors.

"Citizens," Makhotin called their attention. "Quiet! Citizens! Quiet! If you want to speak, come over here."

The peasant Dormidont Savelyev took his turn.

"There's not much to say, let's simply build the mill and that's that."

"Let's build it. Let's build it," the peasants echoed.

"A new one."

"An efficient one."

"Strong enough to last for our children and grandchildren."

Makhotin grinned and said provocatively:

"How can we build it, there aren't any bricks, nor any iron? And what about nails? What do you think we are, a nail factory?"

"Yes, there are bricks," the congregation shouted. "We saved the ones from Kryakov. We won't spare them. If we run short, we'll hunt some up, from the neighbours, from the peasants in Voloshino. They need a mill too and they have bricks left over from their landlord's stable."

"Alright," Makhotin conceded, "so there are bricks. But what about iron?"

"We'll find that too," interrupted the peasants. "We'll go to the people from Lisya Nora. They've got iron from the roof of their landlord's kennel."

"And what about nails?"

"We'll get them. We'll have a collection, two from each home. If that's not enough we'll go to the Adamovo peasants. They've got a pile from the fence of their landlord's."

"Well, now," Makhotin asked Blinov after the gathering had ended, "what do you have to say about the peasant soul now?"

"I don't understand it," Blinov waved his arms, "very surprising."

The mill was built in an amicable spirit, with songs and jokes accompanying the work. The peasants from Voloshino, from Adamovo and from Lisya Nora lent a hand. The mill was built solidly and on a good foundation. Their children and grandchildren would live to enjoy it.

It stands even today. If you drive along the road from the provincial centre to Telegino, you'll see it to the left of the road, on a hillock. Only the old sail-arms are gone. Steam power has replaced the work of the wind.

CROQUET

The landlord Vodoleyev, the teacher Pinalov, the land surveyor Dyatlov and priest Grekhovodov loved to play croquet doubles together.

Croquet is a refined and sedate game. All you do is strike your mallet against the ball, driving it forwards and backwards over the playing area.

Whenever Pakhom Arepin walked past the estate of the country squire he would inevitably stop to watch the gentlemen entertaining themselves.

"Gentlemen's game, and so peaceful," was the judgement. "Not like our own type of fun, bloodying each other with our fists."

When Vodoleyev's property was redistributed Arepin chose to take the croquet set for himself.

"What a ne'er-do-well, no horse sense at all," his neighbours laughed. "His **armyak**'s in rags, he's owned the same **lapti** for two years. He could have taken a pair of Vodoleyev's shoes or his **caftan,** but no, he wants to amuse himself with the frolics of the rich!"

Arepin and his son Grisha began to play a game of croquet and the local peasants began to crowd around the wattle fence, watching and laughing.

"Arepin's playing the role of Vodoleyev."

"And Grisha's imitating Dyatlov, yes, Dyatlov for sure."

"They're taking after Pinalov and that priest Grekhovodov."

Arepin, however, pretended not to hear the peasants' conversation. He concentrated on the effort to hit the balls right as he drove them back and forth across the field.

The jokes and laughs gradually began to subside as curiosity slowly got the better of the peasants. The first to step forward was Prokhor Nemytov.

"Well, after all, Pakhom, let me have a try at it."

Arepin let Nemytov into the game. After Nemytov followed Korytov, and after him Sechkin. After Sechkin came Grechkin, and after him still others...

The peasants took a liking to the game of croquet. At first free moment they would make their way to the home of Pakhom Arepin.

The holiday to celebrate the harvest was approaching, and it was the occasion of much celebration.

The peasants got drunk and would sing songs until their voices were hoarse, and then the fights would begin: first one against another, then one street against another, and finally whole villages would join the mêlée. This year the usual preparations were made for the holiday. The country doctor Sorokin was most worried about the upcoming event: "I hate to think of all the bashed skulls, all the new casts and splints, and all the wasted iodine."

The holiday came, but no casualties drifted in.

"What's going on?" the astonished Sorokin wondered. He took a stroll into the village. All was quiet and peaceful. He turned into the side street where Pakhom Arepin's cottage was located and saw a crowd gathered there. It looked like the country-fair, there were so many people! Sorokin pushed his way through the throng to the centre and saw a clearing there. In the square little wickets had been set into the ground. The peasants held wooden mallets in their hands and balls were scattered about the area.

"Why, it's a croquet set," the country doctor said in amazement. "How strange, the first time I've ever seen such a thing. A gentlemen's game and so peaceful, and the peasants..."

The croquet game was only the beginning. Soon other activities were established in the village.

A reading-room was opened, subscriptions to newspapers entered and a chess club formed. After that a new school and a village club were opened. Radio appeared in the village and electricity lit up the homes.

It didn't all come at once of course, not in a single day. It all took time.

THE TEACHER

A new person arrived to teach in the village of Malye Kochki. He was a Baltic sailor and a member of the crew of the cruiser *Aurora*. He had no experience in teaching and only intended to remain until someone with training could be found to fill the gap left by the sudden flight of the former teacher.

When he arrived the first day the children fell silent, waiting for him to begin drills on the alphabet.

But the sailor suddenly began telling them about the *Aurora*. Then he talked about the storming and seizure of the Winter Palace. His next subject was the Bolshevik Party, Soviet power and Lenin.

The children were interested. They fixed their gazes upon the sailor and sat quietly as they listened.

After a few days had passed the sailor began to test their understanding of all that he had said.

"What is the *Aurora*?"

"The *Aurora* is a revolutionary ship of the Baltic fleet which participated in the attack on the Winter Palace by firing with its artillery."

"Excellent work! Just right! Now tell me what the Bolshevik Party is?"

"It stands for all the best," the children hastened to answer. "The Bolshevik Party stands for the redistribution of land to the peasants and the factories to the workers. It stands for peace among all peoples."

"True," the sailor nodded his head. "But what is Soviet power?"

"That's when the country is governed not by the tsar, not by the bourgeois, but by the labouring people."

"Right. Now who can tell me about Lenin?"

"Me, me, me," a chorus of voices rose.

"You speak, Eremei Toropygin."

Toropygin jumped up.

"Lenin is the leader of all labouring peoples. Lenin spent time in prison and was sent in exile. Lenin gave his whole life to the struggle for the working class."

The sailor was pleased; just look how informed the children had become!

The sailor began now to explain how to write the letters "a" and "b" and how to add one and one and two and two. He didn't proceed any further, for at this point he was called away.

Soon a real teacher arrived in the village. A woman and a Bolshevik, her name was Zoya.

"Well, what have you been studying here?"

"We've learned 'a' and 'b'."

"How to add one and one and two and two."

"And what else?"

The children hesitated.

"We didn't have time for more, the sailor was called away."

"All in all, it's not very much to show. I guess you're not very diligent students?"

The children felt insulted at these words. Eremei Toropygin stood up.

"On the other hand we learned about Lenin."

"He's right, he's right!" shouted the children.

"And about Soviet power."

"And about the Bolshevik Party."

"And about the storming and seizure of the Winter Palace."

Zoya smiled.

"Who told you all this?"

"The Baltic sailor from the ship *Aurora*."

Zoya thought to herself: "A smart fellow that Baltic sailor, he began with the essentials." She regretted missing the opportunity to meet him. The children also regretted that the sailor had left. But after all a seaman isn't a teacher, he has his own matters to take care of.

AN IMPERIAL PERSONAGE

When Soviet power was established the imperial stables of the court were liquidated and the tsar's horses sent to various points in Russia.

A horse by the name of Marquis ended up in the village of Zakharovka. All the peasants not owing horses were called together to draw lots for the horse. The winner was Kuzma Polosukhin.

The peasant was stunned by the unexpected turn of fate and couldn't believe his new-found happiness. The steed was tall and stately. Its mane and tail were smartly trimmed, its legs elegant and its neck finely formed. This was no ordinary horse but an imperial steed.

Polosukhin led the steed home by the bridle, he was followed by a crowd of peasants.

"What a horse!"

"The tsar himself probably rode it!"

"The tsarina, tsarina!" laughed the peasants.

"Wait a minute, how can you plough with that horse? He's never been hitched to a plough before in his life."

Polosukhin led the horse to the little shed at the back of his house and tried to harness it to a cart. The horse kicked and reared up in resistance, stamping the ground with its hooves.

"You devil," cursed Polosukhin. "Hold it, hold still! Whoa! Whoa, I say!"

It was of no help.

The peasants were mirthful.

"You should be a little tender, more gentle to it," instructed one.

"You should talk in French," guffawed a second. "It doesn't seem to know Russian very well."

"You should address him more formally, by his titles."

Kuzma lost his temper and drove Marquis into the barn. The peasants went their separate ways.

For a whole week Kuzma slaved away trying to accustom the horse to the bit and harness it to the cart. In vain, his efforts were rewarded only by several hits from its sharp hooves.

"Well then, you can go to the devil," Kuzma finally lost his temper. "I'll sell you to the first Gypsy that comes along."

So he did.

But then a letter arrived at the rural Soviet which announced that Marquis had been mistakenly given to Zakharovka, that it was an extremely rare breed and that it was necessary to turn him over immediately to the stud-farm in Orel.

The peasants fell upon Kuzma:

"How dare you sell him?!"

"Such a rare horse, and the Lord knows where he is now!"

"Get moving and find the Marquis!"

Kuzma just barely managed to fend off their anger. He rushed off to search for the Gypsy. He travelled from village to village, from market to market and finally located him.

"Give me back the horse," he said.

"What do you mean?"

Polosukhin explained the situation.

The Gypsy grinned.

"You're late. I already sold the horse."

"To whom?"

"To a rich peasant named Nikifor Uvarov in the adjacent district."

Polosukhin raced to the nearby district and found Nikifor Uvarov.

"Give me back the horse."

"What are you talking about?"

Once again Kuzma explained his predicament.

"Well," said the rich peasant, "I gave it away."

"To whom?"

"To my son-in-law, for his farmstead."

Polosukhin next rushed to the farmstead and found the son-in-law.

"Give me the steed," he ordered.

"What are you talking about?"

For a third time Kuzma explained.

"You're late. I already made an exchange."

"Oh Lord!" Kuzma winced.

"But he's not far away, in the village of Zakhrebetnoye, at Pereplyuev's, the person who owns the local store."

Polosukhin trudged to the village of Zakhrebetnoye and appeared before Pereplyuev, the shop-keeper.

"Give me back my horse."

"What in the world?"

Polosukhin repeated the story.

"Alright," agreed the shop-keeper, "only now the price has gone up. To be exact, it has tripled."

"Have you lost your mind?" shouted Polosukhin. "The horse is needed by the government. It's to be sent to the Orel stud-farm for breeding purposes," repeated Kuzma.

"If you don't agree, that's your business. I also can make use of the horse."

Polosukhin returned to Zakharovka and told his fellow villagers about Pereplyuev.

The peasants once again raised a storm of protest and shouted vituperatively at Kuzma for selling the horse. Then they decided in the following manner:

"To the devil with him, that Pereplyuev. Of course, merchant money-bags can't understand the needs of the society as a whole. Soviet power doesn't base its actions on shop-keepers but on the interests of the common peasant."

The peasants gathered the money together to buy back Marquis and sent him off to his destination.

"What's a horse? The heart of the matter lies elsewhere," the peasants reasoned. "Just think how much pressing business faces the Soviet authorities, and yet they remembered the Marquis. There's a good head on the shoulders of the new power. It has a good nose for practical affairs."

THE SKY

Soviet power came to the village of Old Farmsteads. The children observed how the grown-ups redistributed the land, stock and inventory of the nobility, and began to dream.

"We should think of something to divide up as well."

Since, however, there was nothing left to redistribute; everything had been taken care of, Kolka Ryabov suddenly proposed:

"Why don't we divide up the sky?"

"What an idea, how in the world could we do that!" laughed his friends.

"Here's how: to each an even share!"

"That's understood. But if we divide it, what do we do next? How do we use our shares?"

"What do you mean? Do whatever you like: build a cottage, plough it, pasture the horses on it."

The children were surprised and entertained by the idea.

There were four of them: Kolka Ryabov, Eryomka Dudarov, Grishatka Kobylin and Marfutka Dygai.

"As you wish. If you want to divide it up, let's do so."

They drew out lines across the length and the breadth of the sky. Then they drew lots to see who would receive which parcel.

The children gathered in a pasture outside the village and sprawled out on the grass, their backs to the ground and eyes to the sky. It was a good feeling to be the one running the show. Do anything that crosses your mind, as you will!

Eryomka Dudarov decided to sow his section with corn. His fields turned into amber fields of rye. Grishatka Kobylin led his horses out to pasture in the evening. He lit a camp-fire at the very edge of the sky. Marfutka Dygai beautified her sector with clusters of camomiles and cornflowers.

Kolka Ryabov was occupied with the same business. His eyes widened and his mouth opened slightly as the years rushed by him. He was astounded by the roll of a drum. The blare of a bugle drifted invitingly into range. And a banner, a red banner, unfurled across the sky. Kolka caught sight of himself astride a fierce steed and carrying a lance.

And from that point where the sky merges with the fields, from the clouds which concealed the sunset, crawled a horde of terrible monsters.

"Strike them, beat them! Destroy!" the heroic Kolka rushed at the enemy. "Hurray!" he waved his arms wildly.

Eryomka Dudarov tapped his friend on the shoulder: "What's got into you?"

The embarrassed Kolka didn't reply. The clatter of hooves still resounded in his ears, and his hands continued to firmly grip the lance.

The children thoroughly enjoyed their new form of entertainment. At night they wandered into the streets, their necks craned upwards, counting the stars. How many had they each received? They counted and recounted, but each time lost track. They laughed as they argued.

"From the beginning! Once again!"

The work began all over.

During the first thunderstorm of the spring season the children raced barefoot through the meadows to the bridge over the stream.

"Look how the sky's aflame!"

"Listen to the thunder growl!"

Lightning. Thunder. Clouds. The river seethed and frothed along the banks. The wind whistled like a bandit in the forest. The rain pattered busily against the logs.

"I'll bet it's good for the harvest."

"Our sky will give us a bumper crop!"

"And you didn't want to divide it up!"

The children lived together in harmony. But then at the beginning of the summer they gathered together once again on the meadow. Once again they sprawled out and began to occupy themselves with their parcels. The sun raced through the sky, the wind whispered in the grass. Somewhere in the distance the cry of a quail could be heard.

Suddenly Grishatka Kobylin noticed an injustice: he had received a parcel of the sky on the north side, where the rays of the sun didn't fall.

Grishatka frowned and stood up:

"I've been swindled!"

The children jumped to their feet. What was the matter?

"You took all the sun, but I've been left in the lurch!" Grishatka exclaimed, pointing his finger at the sky.

The children looked and agreed.

"But didn't we draw lots?" said Eryomka Dudarov.

"And it was only fair," tossed in Marfutka Dygai.

"I want a parcel with some sunlight, some sunlight," persisted Grishatka. "I want to plant watermelons."

The children began to shout at each other, hardly noticing how their conversation had turned into an argument. They grew bitter, separated and went home.

Once home they began to rethink the situation.

"It turned out badly for us," decided Eryomka Dudarov.

"How silly that we fought," said Marfutka Dygai, with tears swelling in her eyes.

Kolka reasoned to himself: "After all Grishatka is right, everyone wants a bit of the sun."

Kolka then gathered the children together once again:

"Why don't we make the sky communal."

The children stared at Kolka, then shouted in unison:

"That's right, that's right! Let's make it communal!"

"There's only one sun," declared Kolka. "Let it shine on all."

A PLEASANT SURPRISE

Artemi Teplov, a worker in Tula, sent a letter to his native village. It was a concise letter, in all eight words: "Expect guests. Be ready for a pleasant surprise."

The peasants scratched their heads and shrugged their shoulders in bewilderment.

"Something's unclear here. Who is coming and for what purpose? Most important, what will this pleasant surprise be?"

Ten days passed when suddenly a workers' delegation arrived from Tula. But this wasn't the whole story, for they didn't come with empty hands. They carried with them sickles and scythes, pitchforks, iron axles for the carts, hinges, nails and other metal odds and ends.

The peasants gasped in surprise:

"So this is the pleasant surprise!"

In fact there was an extreme shortage of sickles, scythes and other iron tools in the countryside at that time. The peasantry simply had to get by as best it could.

The peasants' eyes glittered.

"Will you sell them?"

"Not on your life," replied the workers.

"How about an exchange?"

"No."

The peasants didn't understand what the point was.

"We brought them to you as a gift," the workers explained. "From us, the working class."

The peasants were astonished.

"Free?"

"That's right, straight from our hearts. Please accept this token from the workers."

This was straight from a fairy tale! Such a precious gift!

The peasants bustled about making preparations, then dragged the workers to their tables in the cottages.

The workers had a bite to eat:

"Thanks very much. So long. It's time for us to leave, we have to be back at the factory."

The guests bowed and took their leave.

"Isn't this something!" The villagers couldn't quite get a grip on the situation. "Out of the goodness of their hearts! No other motives! A miracle, to put it mildly!"

Soon after this Artemi Teplov himself arrived in the village.

"Well, how are the scythes and the pitchforks? Was it a pleasant surprise?"

"And how!" shouted the peasants in reply. "The scythes are excellent, and so are the sickles and pitchforks. As for the pleasant surprise, it's more the fact that the working class turns out to be our friend, more like a blood-brother."

THE SMALL GIFT

The peasants from the village of Beryoza resolved to send a small gift to Vladimir Ilyich Lenin as soon as the first harvest was in.

They gathered together a sackful of grain, carried it to the mill to be milled and sent a letter off:

"Dear Comrade Lenin!

"First, we extend our thanks for the land, the pastures and the forests. Our grain yield is higher now. There's enough to go around now and we decided not to forget you either.

"We don't grow wheat, so we're sending you rye meal. Don't hesitate, it's good flour. We milled it three times so that it would please you..."

Then they paused before adding:

"Please give our respects to the entire Bolshevik Party. From all the peasants of the village of Beryoza, in the hand of Epifan Dyra."

The peasants thought of sending the gift through the mail, but then decided against it. Instead they persuaded one hearty peasant, Prokop Gmyrya to deliver it. They placed him in a cart, brought him to the station, and made sure that he and the sack got onto the train.

"Directly to him!" they shouted in parting. "Right into his hands, do you understand?"

"It couldn't be clearer," he said.

Gmyrya returned after an interval of a week.

"Well, did you see him?"

"And did you give it to him?"

"I saw him and gave it to him."

"Good work."

"Isn't that something!"

"Lenin himself!"

"So what did Lenin say? Did he like it? Did he give his thanks?"

"What do you think? He said: 'Give my heartfelt thanks to our comrades, the peasants.' He said it twice, both for the grain and for the respects offered to the Bolshevik Party."

"Isn't it interesting that he addressed us so politely."

"And with sympathy."

"So what else did Lenin say?"

"He said that we should hold firmly to Soviet power, that we should try to think of the needs of all and not forget the workers. 'You,' he said, 'and the working class are building together a new life.'"

"Well said," agreed the peasants.

"We don't, in the end result, differ all that much from the workers."

In a word, the peasants were pleased.

About one month had passed when the peasants from Beryoza suddenly received a letter from the city of Nizhni Novgorod, from the workers of a ship-repair yard.

The peasants read through the letter in astonishment. It thanked them for the sack of flour and explained that it had been divided among the sick and the children of the area. The flour was excellent, they wrote, the bread was rich. Towards the end they added:

"It is clear that among you there is a wise and understanding person. Our grain situation is truly bad, which means that we couldn't even attempt to establish a value for your gift. Thank you for remembering about us, about the workers."

The peasants wondered out aloud:

"What sack?"

"What flour?"

"Could it be that very same flour?"

The peasants soon grasped the essence of the situation. The letter from the workers was warm and gracious. Nevertheless the peasants were offended and gathered together at the hut of Prokop Gmyrya.

"As it turns out our present didn't please Comrade Lenin."

"He turned his nose up."

"The expressions of gratitude were just for appearances."

Gmyrya thought fast and hard.

"You people," he uttered, "for appearances you say. Lenin sacrificed his own pleasure, he doesn't think only of himself. It wasn't an accident that he mentioned the working class at that time."

The peasants looked at Gmyrya.

"As a matter of fact, that's true."

"He stated it well."

"Just look: there wasn't a word about Lenin in the letter. As if it were a present from us. Lenin, he is a modest one, isn't he!"

"This is what I think, men," declared Gmyrya. "We shouldn't be frugal about sending grain to Nizhni Novgorod. Not just one sack. Afer all, what help is such a small amount to them? Our harvest was good, should we send out more?"

"Well said, let's send some more!" the peasants responded with enthusiasm. "We should give our support to the working class. We are building a new life together. Lenin was perfectly right!"

On the following day the peasants sent off two cartloads of grain in the direction of the station. Once again Gmyrya was delegated.

The office worker weighed the load and took down the delivery address.

"To the workers?" he repeated.

"They're the ones."

"A present?"

"Right on the nose."

"Well, from whom. What should I say?"

Gmyrya squinted his eyes and looked cunningly at the clerk.

"Write, but make it clear and nice..."

The clerk dipped his pen in the ink-well, shook off the excess and prepared to write.

"From Vladimir Ilyich Lenin," added Gmyrya.

WITNESSES

Fomka woke up, tossed about on his bunk for a moment, then rose and went into the street to relieve himself.

It was late night and very dark. Fog drifted across the street. Fomka stepped behind the corner of the factory barracks and suddenly heard footsteps.

The boy froze still and listened. The steps became louder and louder and soon were very close to him. Fomka was by now completely on the alert. He watched three men emerge out of the darkness and fog. Two were dragging a box and a third was holding a spade.

Fomka peered intently—it was the former owner of the factory, Elizar Elizarovich Moikin. With him were his two sons.

"A box and a spade. Where could they be going?" wondered Fomka. He fell into step behind them.

The Moikins went to the factory pump-house and placed the box down on the ground. Next they began to dig a hole in great haste, glancing furtively in all directions and listening for the slightest sound.

"They're burying a treasure," thought Fomka.

He waited until the Moikins had finished their task, then circled about the pump-house, marked off the spot and returned home.

Fomka lay restlessly on his bunk, unable to fall asleep again. At the crack of dawn he raced to find his friend Kapka Zatvorov.

"Kapka, Kapka," Fomka tugged at his friend. "Get up, Kapka."

Kapka opened his eyes.

"What's with you?"

"A treasure, a treasure!"

"What kind of treasure do you mean?"

"A real, authentic one!"

Fomka told Kapka about the late evening events. His friend jumped out of bed and got ready to leave.

The children grabbed spades and raced to the pump-house.

"There must be piles of money there," said Fomka.

"What do you mean money? Money's just paper. This treasure will be gold and diamonds," Kapka corrected his friend.

The children let their fancy run free, imagining what they would do with their fantastic wealth.

"We'll buy cookies," said Fomka.

"What do you mean cookies!" answered Kapka. "We'll buy real éclairs, crème-brouillé, the best they can offer."

Fomka glanced at him. That Kapka, he could always think of something better to say! Although all these treats were completely foreign to him, he pretended he knew how delicious they were.

The boys' imaginations ran free. They decided to buy their mothers luxurious shawls, their sisters calico for dresses and ribbons and their fathers new boots. Then they began to count off their friends and neighbours. Ten pounds of groats for the Malinins, for they had many mouths to feed. Felt boots for Uncle Kharlamov. A new crutch for the lame Zarubin—he had dreamed of one for a long time. And for Vavilin the metal-craftsman, a cap.

"He's a Bolshevik, he wouldn't accept it," declared Kapka.

As soon as the boys arrived at the pump-house they set to work feverishly.

"Faster, faster!" Kapka ordered.

In their haste the boys jostled one another, impeding their work. Finally, however, their spades struck against the box.

"Tick-tock, tick-tock," the children heard.

"A clock, it must be a wall clock," declared Fomka.

"A wall-clock!" grinned Kapka. "It's either an alarm-clock or a real Paul Bourée!"

The boys were so absorbed in their business that they didn't notice someone approaching from behind. They turned around and suddenly caught sight of Vavilin, the metal-craftsman.

"Well, what have you here?"

The boys hesitated in confusion.

"A treasure," Fomka finally answered. "There's gold here. There's Paul Bourée with an hour chime. Can you hear it ticking?"

"A clock!"

Vavilin hurriedly bent over the pit and listened.

"Hey, now, move away!" he shouted at the boys.

They moved backwards.

Vavilin stretched his hand towards the box, fussed about for a moment and silenced the clock. He stood up, wiped off the sweat which had formed on his brow and grinned.

"A treasure, that it certainly is! This treasure is called dynamite!"

The boys were dumbfounded.

"But there's a clock in the box!"

"A clock, but not the kind you imagined. It's a special mechanism for explosives. Now tell me the whole story as you know it."

The boys told him what they knew.

"Yes indeed," said Vavilin, "that's your Paul Bourée for you."

"Darn, there go our shawls and ribbons," sighed Fomka.

"Shawls and ribbons, and so what!" objected Kapka. "The pump-house is much more valuable."

Vavilin broke out in laughter:

"You're a sharp one, Kapka!"

That very day Moikin and his two sons were arrested. They were brought to court and punished severely according to revolutionary law.

Fomka and Kapka also went to court and related their story once again. They were listed in the court protocol as witnesses. However both the judge and all those who observed the trial were aware that the name wasn't exactly correct. They weren't simply witnesses, they were the protagonists in this matter.

FATHERS AND SONS

A group of children began to imagine what would they each like to contribute to the people's power.

"I would like to plant grain," said Kolka Zaborov.

"I want to be a worker in a factory," was the expressed wish of Dimka Petrov.

"I want to serve in the Red Army," Goshka Izvekov blurted out, "and protect the Soviet power from its enemies."

"And I," declared Lyuba Kozulina, "want to study and study and study. Then I'll teach children how to read and write."

The children were on the right track. Each of these types of work are both honourable and needed by the country.

Years passed and the children grew up.

Kolka is no longer Kolka—he's called Nikolai Mitrofanovich. He's a tiller of the soil and helps supply the country with its grain needs.

Dimka is no longer Dimka—Dmitri Andreyevich he's called. He's now a skilled worker standing at the smelting furnace and providing the country with metal for its needs.

Goshka is no longer Goshka, but Grigori Ivanovich. He stands guard on the borders of the Soviet Union, protecting the peace of the country.

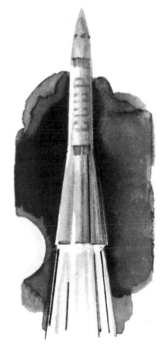

Lyuba teaches children in the school system. Her name is now Lyubov Antonovna.

Everything turned out as they dreamed. And why? Because power is now in the hands of the Soviets and all paths are open to the common people.

At one point all four met once again in their native village. The only difference now was that they all had children.

The former Kolka had a boy named Semyon.

The former Dimka had a boy named Seryozha.

The former Goshka had a boy named Andrei.

The former Lyuba had a girl named Zina.

Semyon, Seryozha, Andrei and Zina all became acquainted and then, in the course of a day, began also to dream of what they could do for the people's power.

"I want to be just like my father and help provide the country with grain," announced Semyon. "I want to be an agronomist."

"I want to smelt the strongest steel," Seryozha answered his new friends. "I'm going to work in a factory, like my father."

"I want to become a fearless pilot," Andrei revealed his cherished secret.

"I want to study, study and study," Zina told her new acquaintances. "I'll become a famous professor."

The years passed and Semyon, Seryozha, Andrei and Zina reached adulthood.

Semyon is no longer Semyon, but Semyon Nikolaevich. Just as he wished, he is now an agronomist. He directs a state farm in the Tselinny region in distant Siberia.

Seryozha is no longer Seryozha, but Sergei Dmitrievich. He invented new means of smelting and new alloys of steel. Now he is designing rockets and helping the effort to send man into space.

Andrei is no longer Andrei, but Andrei Grigoryevich. He is a very distinguished man, a pilot and a fearless general. He fought bravely against the nazis and now wears the star of a Hero of the Soviet Union on his chest.

As for Zina, Zinaida Kuzminichna that is, she is now a professor and a well-known historian, engaged in writing scholarly books. If you read these books you will learn what our past was like and what a great power we have become.

These children have also seen their dreams come true. Their contributions to our country have been large indeed.

When you grow up you should follow their example. Remember about these fathers and sons.

1. In February 1917 a bourgeois-democratic revolution occurred in Russia. The power of the tsar was overthrown. In April Lenin returned to Petrograd from emigration in Switzerland. "Long live the socialist revolution!" he proclaimed (Engraving by P. Staronosov).

2

3

4

2. Painting by Pavel Sokolov-Skalya, "Storming of the Winter Palace" (October 1917). 3. The revolutionary cruiser **Aurora**. A salvo from this ship was the signal to begin the storming of the Winter Palace. 4. Smolny Institute. Bolshevik Headquarters during the October Revolution. 5. Guarding Smolny during the October days.

6

6. Painting by Vladimir Serov, "Speech by Lenin to the Second All-Russia Congress of Soviets".
7. The Great October Revolution has taken place. The first decree of the young Soviet government was "The Decree on Peace" proposed by Vladimir Lenin at the Second All-Russia Congress of Soviets. "Peace to all peoples!"—with these words the first workers' and peasants' state in the world was born. To all countries drawn into the World War Soviet Russia proposed the conclusion of an immediate peace without annexations or indemnities.

№ 208.
Пятница,
27 октября 1917 г.

ИЗВѢСТІЯ

ЦѢНА:
въ Петроградѣ **15** коп.
на ст. жел. д. **18** коп.

Центральнаго Исполнительнаго Комитета
и ПЕТРОГРАДСКАГО СОВѢТА
РАБОЧИХЪ и СОЛДАТСКИХЪ ДЕПУТАТОВЪ.

Адресъ конторы: Лиговка, Сайкинъ пер., д. № 6. Телефонъ № 218-41.
Адресъ редакціи: Смольный Институтъ, 2-й этажъ комната № 14. Телефонъ № 38-89.

Декретъ о мирѣ,

принятый единогласно на засѣданіи Все-российскаго Съѣзда Совѣтовъ Рабочихъ, Солдатскихъ и Крестьянскихъ Депутатовъ 26 октября 1917 г.

Рабочее и крестьянское правительство, созданное революціей 24—25 октября и опирающееся на Совѣты Рабочихъ, Солдатскихъ и Крестьянскихъ Депутатовъ предлагаетъ всѣхъ воюющимъ народамъ и ихъ правительствамъ начать немедленно переговоры о справедливомъ демократическомъ мирѣ.

Справедливымъ или демократическимъ миромъ котораго жаждетъ подавляющее большинство истощенныхъ, измученныхъ и истерзанныхъ войной рабочихъ и трудящихся классовъ всѣхъ воюющихъ странъ миромъ, котораго самымъ опредѣленнымъ и настойчивымъ образомъ требовали русскіе рабочіе и крестьяне послѣ сверженія царской монархіи — такимъ миромъ правительство считаетъ немедленный миръ безъ аннексій (т. е. безъ захвата чужихъ земель, безъ насильственнаго присоединенія чужихъ народностей) и безъ контрибуцій.

Такой миръ предлагаетъ Правительство Россіи заключить всѣмъ воюющимъ народамъ немедленно, выражая готовность сдѣлать безъ малѣйшей оттяжки тотчасъ-же всѣ рѣшительные шаги впредь до окончательнаго утвержденія всѣхъ условій такого мира полномочными собраніями народныхъ представителей всѣхъ странъ и всѣхъ націй.

Подъ аннексіей или захватомъ чужихъ земель Правительство понимаетъ сообразно правовому сознанію демократіи вообще, и трудящихся классовъ въ особенности, всякое присоединеніе къ большому или сильному государству малой или слабой народности безъ точно, ясно и добровольно выраженнаго согласія и желанія этой народности, независимо отъ того, когда это насильственное присоединеніе совершено, независимо также отъ того насколько развитой или от-

сталой является насильственно при-соединяемая или насильственно удерживаемая въ границахъ даннаго государства нація. Независимо, наконецъ отъ того, въ Европѣ или въ далекихъ заокеанскихъ странахъ эта нація живетъ.

Если какая бы то ни была нація удерживается въ границахъ даннаго государства насиліемъ, если ей, вопреки выраженному съ ея стороны желанію все равно, выражено ли это желаніе въ печати, въ народныхъ собраніяхъ, въ рѣшеніяхъ партій или возмущеніяхъ и возстаніяхъ противъ національнаго гнета — не представляется права свободнымъ голосованіемъ, при полномъ выводѣ войска присоединяющей или вообще болѣе сильной націи рѣшить безъ малѣйшаго принужденія вопросъ о формахъ государственнаго существованія этой націи, то присоединеніе ея является аннексіей т. е. захватомъ и насиліемъ.

Продолжать эту войну изъ-за того, какъ раздѣлить между сильными и богатыми націями захваченныя ими слабыя народности, Правительство считаетъ величайшимъ преступленіемъ противъ человѣчества и торжественно заявляетъ свою рѣшимость немедленно подписать условія мира, прекращающаго эту войну на указанныхъ равно справедливыхъ для всѣхъ безъ изъятія народностей условіяхъ.

Вмѣстѣ съ тѣмъ Правительство заявляетъ, что оно отнюдь не считаетъ вышеуказанныхъ условій мира ультимативными, т. е. соглашается разсмотрѣть и всякія другія условія мира, настаивая лишь на возможно болѣе быстромъ предложеніи ихъ какой бы то ни было воюющей страной и на полнѣйшей ясности, на безусловномъ исключеніи всякой двусмысленности и вся-

кой тайны при предложеніи условій мира.

Тайную дипломатію Правительство отмѣняетъ со своей стороны выражая твердое намѣреніе вести всѣ переговоры совершенно открыто передъ всѣмъ народомъ, приступая немедленно къ полному опубликованію тайныхъ договоровъ, подтвержденныхъ или заключенныхъ правительствомъ помѣщиковъ и капиталистовъ съ февраля по 25 октября 1917 года. Все содержаніе этихъ тайныхъ договоровъ, по-скольку оно направлено, какъ это въ большинствѣ случаевъ было къ доставленію выгодъ и привилегій русскимъ помѣщикамъ и капиталистамъ, къ удержанію или увеличенію аннексій великороссовъ, Правительство объявляетъ безусловно и немедленно отмѣнен-нымъ.

Обращаясь съ предложеніемъ къ правительствамъ и народамъ всѣхъ странъ начать немедленно открытые переговоры о заключеніи мира Правительство выражаетъ съ своей стороны готовность вести эти переговоры, какъ посредствомъ письменныхъ сношеній, по телеграфу, такъ и путемъ переговоровъ между представителями разныхъ странъ или на конференціи таковыхъ представителей. Для облегченія такихъ переговоровъ Правительство назначаетъ своего полномочнаго представителя въ нейтральной странѣ.

Правительство предлагаетъ всѣмъ правительствамъ и народамъ всѣхъ воюющихъ странъ немедленно заключить перемиріе, причемъ со своей стороны, считаетъ желательнымъ чтобы это перемиріе было заключено не меньше, какъ на три мѣсяца, т. е. на такой срокъ, въ теченіе котораго вполнѣ возможно, какъ завершеніе переговоровъ о мирѣ съ участіемъ пред-

ставителей всѣхъ безъ изъятія народностей, или націй, втянутыхъ въ войну или вынужденныхъ къ участію въ ней, такъ равно и созывъ полномочныхъ собраній народныхъ представителей всѣхъ странъ для окончательнаго утвержденія условій мира.

Обращаясь съ этимъ предложеніемъ мира къ правительствамъ и народамъ всѣхъ воюющихъ странъ, временное рабочее и крестьянское правительство Россіи обращается также въ особенности также къ сознательнымъ рабочимъ трехъ самыхъ передовыхъ націй человѣчества и самыхъ крупныхъ участвующихъ въ настоящей войнѣ государствъ: Англіи, Франціи и Германіи. Рабочіе этихъ странъ оказали наибольшія услуги дѣлу прогресса и соціализма и великіе образцы чартистскаго движенія въ Англіи, рядъ революцій, имѣвшихъ всемірно-историческое значеніе, совершенныхъ французскимъ пролетаріатомъ, наконецъ, въ героической борьбѣ противъ исключительнаго закона въ Германіи и образцовой для рабочихъ всего міра длительной, упорной дисциплинированной работѣ созданія массовыхъ пролетарскихъ организацій Германіи. Всѣ эти образцы пролетарскаго героизма и историческаго творчества служатъ намъ порукой за то, что рабочіе названныхъ странъ поймутъ лежащія на нихъ теперь задачи освобожденія человѣчества отъ ужасовъ войны и ея послѣдствій, — ибо эти рабочіе всесторонней рѣшительной и беззавѣтно энергичной дѣятельностью своей помогутъ намъ успѣшно довести до конца дѣло мира и вмѣстѣ съ тѣмъ. дѣло освобожденія трудящихся и эксплуатируемыхъ массъ населенія отъ всякаго рабства и всякой эксплуатаціи.

8. Together with "The Decree on Peace" on the very same day the Soviet government published a second decree of major significance—"The Decree on Land". In conformity with this decree gentry ownership of the land was abolished and all land was to be turned over without compensation to the cultivator—the peasant. The land, mineral resources, the forests and waterways were declared to be the property of the people. 9. Painting by Victor Ivanov, "The Decrees of the Soviet power being read to the people". 10. Soon, in 1918 the first Soviet constitution was adopted. The constitution proclaimed the building of socialism in the USSR and the complete elimination of exploitation of man by man. "He who does not work, neither shall he eat" — was written into the first constitution.

КОНСТИТУЦИЯ

РОССИЙСКОЙ СОЦИАЛИСТИЧЕСКОЙ ФЕДЕРАТИВНОЙ СОВЕТСКОЙ РЕСПУБЛИКИ

1918

11

12

13

14

11. The beginning of new, collective work. Repairing agricultural implements. May, 1920. 12. The peasants called electric light bulbs "the Ilyich light" in honour of Lenin, the originator of the plan for the electrification of Russia. 13. The Soviet President, Mikhail Kalinin, of peasant origin (third from the right) at a grain-collecting station on the Volga at the town of Khvolynsk, observing grain-weighing. 14. The first radio in a peasant club.

VLADIMIR ILYICH LENIN

THE ELDER

Some representatives of a peasant community in Kostroma province arrived one day at Smolny in Petrograd in search of Comrade Lenin.

The peasants from Kostroma province looked around, casting glances to all sides, in search of Vladimir Ilyich Lenin.

As it turned out Lenin happened to be walking at that very moment in their direction. The peasants said to him:

"Dear friend, who's the elder here?"

"Who's that?" Lenin asked in reply.

"The elder," the peasants repeated. "The one who rules Russia now."

"Oh, the elder," grinned Lenin. Vladimir Ilyich cast a glance about. "There's the elder," he said pointing behind their backs. He grinned mischievously and continued on his way.

The peasants turned and looked: behind them stood a group of workers in the corridor. Beside them some soldiers were engaged in a heated argument. A sailor from the ship *Aurora* was puffing peacefully on his cigarette. Slightly to the rear peasants were milling about, also dressed in sheepskin coats, caps with ear-flaps and **lapti**. These peasants were also carrying knapsacks, a sure sign that they too were representatives from some distant place.

The peasants from Kostroma looked first on the workers, then on the soldiers, then on the sailor and finally on their fellow peasants.

"The elder can't be in this group," they said in disbelief. "The fellow with the beard must have been mistaken."

"What's your business, old men," the peasants suddenly heard a voice. A youth had strolled over from

ELDER — the elected or appointed head of the peasant village community

the group of workers. "It's your first time here, apparently?"

"Our first time. We're looking for Lenin, kind fellow."

"For Lenin?"

"That's right, for Volodimir Ilyich."

The youth cast a questioning glance at the peasants: "But you were just talking with Lenin."

The peasants' mouths opened wide in amazement.

"Who? The fellow with the beard?"

"He's the one," the youth answered.

The peasants related the substance of their conversation with Vladimir Ilyich, at which the worker broke into laughter.

"I see, you were looking for the elder, the one who rules Russia now? Well," the youth paused in thought, "Comrade Lenin was telling you the truth. Now, if you want to see Lenin, go up to the third floor."

The peasants grabbed their knapsacks.

"Well, I'll declare," uttered one, "it's all beyond me."

"Strange," agreed another.

They looked at a third one of their group, the eldest. But he maintained his silence. The old fellow was deep in thought. Wrinkles ran up his brow like waves.

"What are we to make of this, Afanasy Danilovich?" the peasants assailed him.

"What? It's just as they said it, that's all there is to understand," said the old man, his face suddenly breaking into a smile.

The Kostroma peasants went up to the third floor and approached Lenin's office.

"Who are you looking for?" asked the secretary at the entrance.

"Comrade Lenin."

"Who shall I say is calling?"

The old man looked at his group, grunted to add weight to his voice, and wiped his whiskers with his palm:

"Tell him that the elder has arrived. The one who rules Russia now."

THE VOICE IN DISAGREEMENT

Peasants from the village of Zavidovka handed over their quota of grain to the state, but then came to the conclusion that too much in fact had been taken from them. The times were difficult, hunger was rampant and food precious. Bread was worth its weight in gold. Thus, the peasants wrote a letter to the local government. No answer was forthcoming, however.

"We must turn to Lenin, to Lenin himself," Ivan Khomutov insisted noisily.

Khomutov convinced his fellow peasants. They chose Khomutov, Petrov and Sizov to represent as delegates before Comrade Lenin.

They promptly set off for Moscow.

"Whatever Lenin decides is good enough for us," Khomutov thought along the way. "I agree with him on all points."

Lenin received the peasants to hear out their problem.

"You're aware," he said, "that we're living through very difficult times."

Ivan Khomutov became very cautious. "Comrade Lenin wouldn't say such things without good reason."

"Difficult, but not hopeless," continued Vladimir Ilyich. "Without a doubt the country will surmount all its troubles and you peasants, our comrades, will aid us, I'm sure."

"So that's how it stands," Ivan Khomutov realised. "Comrade Lenin is about to deny our request."

But suddenly: "As far as you're concerned," said Vladimir Ilyich, "you're entirely right in this matter. Any grain taken over and above the proper amount is subject to be returned."

Lenin drew up the necessary papers for the local Soviet and handed them to the delegates.

The peasants bowed deeply.

Ivan Khomutov was triumphant.

"Well, did you see? Did you hear? Right on the nose! I'm completely in agreement with Lenin."

During these years workers and peasants, upon arriving at the Kremlin for matters of a business nature, often received coupons to eat at the dining hall of the

Council of People's Commissars. The delegates from Zavidovka also received such coupons.

The peasants were content: they had met with Lenin and now they faced a hearty meal.

"This ought to be interesting!" Ivan Khomutov smoothed his moustache. "This won't be our fare of thin cabbage soup or gruel. We'll have something to tell the people in the village!"

The peasants entered the dining hall and received the first course. They took a look—it was cabbage soup. Watery, sour. A piece of unappetising herring floated in each bowl in place of the usual meat.

"This is news!" exclaimed the astonished peasants.

The second course was brought on next. Sure enough, it was a thin gruel without any kind of enrichment and boiled in water rather than milk.

The peasants considered of pulling some of their pork fat from their bags but thought twice of it.

The peasants finished eating and left the dining hall.

"It must have been a different dining hall," said Ivan Khomutov. "It certainly wasn't the one for the Council of People's Commissars."

As they stepped away from the entrance they noticed Vladimir Ilyich proceeding along the corridor. He walked briskly, his coat unbuttoned. As he approached he said:

"Well, did you have a bite to eat?"

"Yes."

"That's fine. I'm told that the porridge is delicious today."

"I'll say delicious!" thought Ivan Khomutov. "Perhaps they'll serve Lenin from a different pot."

Vladimir Ilyich walked into the dining hall. The peasants returned to the door and watched Lenin through a slit. They wanted to see what would be served to Comrade Lenin. They watched, only to see the very same cabbage soup, and after it, the very same porridge dished out to Vladimir Ilyich.

"Isn't that something," said Ivan Khomutov, unable to restrain his surprise.

The peasants then returned to Zavidovka.

"Well, tell us, did Lenin receive you?"

"He did."

"Did he honour your request?"

"He honoured it."

"Did he give you the papers?"

"That he did."

The peasants showed the documents to the others, who reacted with pleasure:

"Harness up the wagons and let's be off to the district centre. Our thanks to Comrade Lenin. He decided correctly, and justly."

But at that moment:

"No brothers," Khomutov shook his head, "there was no justice in the decision."

The peasants stared at Khomutov.

"No justice," repeated the latter. "I'm not in agreement with Lenin."

"What in the world?! What is this?" asked the bewildered peasants. "Perhaps Ivan left his mind along the road! He's the one who complained loudest, and now he's against the decision."

A chorus of voices rose up in protest.

"Quiet, now. Quiet." Ivan interrupted. "Do you eat pork fat?"

The peasants exchanged glances.

"We do..."

"We can assume that there's corn in the bins?"

"Well, yes, we can."

"We're not dying from hunger for the time being, am I right?"

"That's right," the peasants answered.

"Well, there you are!"

Khomutov related the events which had transpired in the dining hall for the Council of People's Commissars. The embarrassed peasants fell silent.

"No, Lenin shouldn't have given us the documents. I don't agree with what he did. I don't agree," repeated Khomutov. "It wasn't a just decision."

ONE, TWO, THREE

It was a rare day that Vladimir Ilyich succeeded in freeing himself from important business that required his immediate attention.

Nevertheless, on occasion he would find the time to take a ride in an automobile to the woods somewhere outside of the city.

During one such stroll, emerging from the forests into a field, Lenin caught sight of a little girl.

The little girl was wearing an oversized hand-me-down coat; her braid spilled out from under a kerchief. She stood under a birch, crying miserably and holding a basket under her arm. In her basket was one lonely mushroom, an orange cap boletus.

"Why are you crying?" asked Vladimir Ilyich.

The girl didn't answer. Instead she began to cry even harder.

"Well, for such a big girl," Vladimir Ilyich shook his head, "aren't you ashamed of yourself?"

This didn't help either. Lenin could see that she was a stubborn little girl. He rummaged in his pocket, then leaned towards the basket.

"One, two, three—may a nut appear at the bottom of your basket." He glanced into the basket.

Her curiosity overcoming her, the girl fell silent and took a look. Sure enough, there was a nut there!

"That's really something!" the girl exclaimed in surprise. She wiped the tears from her eyes and looked in astonishment at Lenin.

"What's your name?" asked Vladimir Ilyich.

"Varya."

"Tell me, Varya, what happened to you?"

"I got lost," she whimpered.

"Where's your home?"

"I came from Mironovka."

"Don't feel sad. We'll find your Mironovka."

Lenin took Varya by the hand and led her along the overgrown path to the automobile.

As they walked along he asked her:

"And where are all your mushrooms?"

She had had poor luck in finding mushrooms in the woods and her basket was empty.

"It's not good to return home with empty hands," said Vladimir Ilyich. "We'll have to straighten this matter out."

He stepped off the path, stooped and suddenly:

"One, two, three—may a white mushroom appear!"

The little girl cast a glance. There it was, a mushroom! A mushroom with a thick stem and fleshy bonnet, standing like a soldier under an oak tree. Varya bent over and caught sight of a second, and then a third mushroom. The area was full of them and soon her basket was overflowing. The little girl looked in surprise at Lenin.

They proceeded a short distance further in the woods. Lenin then stopped, squinted his eyes mischievously and said:

"One, two, three—may an automobile appear!"

Varya looked beyond a bush and a fir tree. Miracle of miracles—an automobile was standing there in the glade.

"Well, have a seat," said Vladimir Ilyich, opening the door for Varya.

The girl climbed in hastily.

The machine moved first along a road through the forest, then through fields and up and down hills. Soon they caught sight of Mironovka.

Varya wasn't happy to see Mironovka, however. She was sad that her adventure was drawing to a close.

Lenin drove her to the outskirts of the village, waved good-bye and drove into the distance.

Varya raced home to tell her story of how she had lost her bearings in the forest, how a strange man had appeared before her and how a series of miracles had happened: first the nut, then the mushrooms, and finally the automobile.

"He can do anything you wish," whispered Varya. "He's that kind of man."

For a long time the residents of Mironovka tried to guess who it was that had led Varya out of the woods.

THE LET-DOWN

It was Matvei Toropygin's first trip to Moscow. He was an agile and resourceful youth, and moved quickly from the Okhotny Row to Tverskaya and Neglinnaya streets, finally deciding that it was time to pay a visit to the Kremlin.

The Kremlin at that time included a barber-shop, though to be sure, a small one. It caught the eye of Toropygin, who decided on the spot that it was time for a shave. A souvenir, of sorts, of the Kremlin!

He entered and took a seat. The barber was busy, so a wait was in order.

Five minutes passed when the door once again creaked open, Matvei lifted his gaze—at the threshold stood Comrade Lenin.

Matvei Toropygin jumped out of his seat and froze as straight as a column, his hands to the hips in the fashion of a soldier.

"Good day. What are you standing for? Have a seat," said Vladimir Ilyich.

Toropygin couldn't muster up the courage to sit.

"Sit down, comrade," Vladimir Ilyich smiled.

Matvei finally slipped into his chair, hanging, to be sure, on the very edge. Lenin took a place next to the youth and fixed his gaze upon him:

"Are you from the countryside?"

"Yes," Matvei answered, blushing.

"Be so kind as to tell where precisely."

"Vyazma."

"Where in Vyazma?"

"Anisovka ... that's the name of our village."

"I see," said Vladimir Ilyich, "how are things with you people in Anisovka? You're not offended by the new system? How are the winter crops this year? Do you have a school in your village? Do the newspapers reach you? I'd like to hear your answers, in detail if you could."

Matvei pondered how to begin, what exactly to answer. "Not offended," he uttered about Soviet power. "The crops will be good," he declared concerning the winter plantings. "There aren't any schools yet, but one's sure to open next year."

At this point their conversation was interrupted—a seat had been freed for the next customer in line.

"Go ahead," Vladimir Ilyich addressed Matvei. "Take a seat, please."

Matvei lost his bearings.

"Well I ... you see ... yes I'll wait."

"No, no," answered Lenin. "It's your turn."

"I'm in no hurry, Vladimir Ilyich."

"Let's not argue about this!"

Matvei glanced at the barber, but he was apparently accustomed to this type of event, for he stood with a trace of a smile on his face. Matvei turned his gaze to Lenin:

Vladimir Ilyich pulled a magazine out of his pocket, opened it and even turned away from Matvei, to avoid embarrassing him any further.

"Step up," said the barber.

With little choice left Matvei, the poor fellow, took the seat. He now regretted coming at all and sat as if upon pins and needles. His only thought was to conclude the business at hand as rapidly as possible.

The barber finished shaving him and Matvei grabbed for his hat.

"Well, now, I guess it's my turn," Vladimir Ilyich said lightly. "You look younger now, old man. What a handsome fellow! Pass on my greetings to the people of Vyazma."

Toropygin returned to his native village Anisovka.

"You don't say!" the peasants exclaimed in surprise. "You really saw Lenin!"

"What's he like? What did he have to say?"

"Greetings to us? Isn't that something!"

"So where did you meet Comrade Lenin?"

Toropygin told them.

"Tell us more of the detail."

Suddenly the peasants scowled.

"You didn't give up your place? Why, you insolent young pup!"

Matvei hemmed and hawed. You see, it just happened that way! I didn't like the idea myself!

What more could he say? The peasants had already heard quite enough.

"You've put us to shame, smeared our name. You've let down Anisovka. Even more, you've shamed all tillers of the land."

At this very time, as it turned out, elections were being held for the rural Soviet. Matvei Toropygin's name had been mentioned and everyone had stood solidly behind him. But now....

No sooner had the peasant gathering been called:

"We don't want him," the peasants suddenly shouted. "We don't want him. He wouldn't give up his place to Lenin. We're not for him!"

Thus, Matvei was not elected to the Soviet.

That was how Comrade Lenin had let Matvei down.

NEW FELT BOOTS

Katya's responsibilities were minor in nature—she was called a "runner". She worked as a messenger in a Soviet institution.

One day Katya's superior summoned her to his office and handed her an important parcel to be delivered immediately to the Kremlin and to be handed personally to Comrade Lenin.

Katya set off in a hurry. On the way her attention fell upon her felt boots. They were old, ancient in fact, with gaping holes. It was well past the time to throw them out, for Katya had worn them thin running from one office to another with her deliveries.

Katya was embarrassed to appear before Vladimir Ilyich in these boots, but what could she do? In those days footware was a deficit item.

The girl arrived at the Kremlin and was permitted to enter Vladimir Ilyich's office. She handed the parcel to Comrade Lenin, making every effort to conceal her boots from his gaze.

Katya expected to hand him the package and leave quickly. However Vladimir Ilyich detained the girl with questions about how long she had worked, where she had attended school, how many years she had completed and if she had parents.

Katya answered Vladimir Ilyich's questions, heard him wish her luck and offer his farewells, then left.

After two days had passed Katya was again summoned to her superintendant's office. She crossed the threshold to his room and froze in her tracks: the superintendant was holding up a pair of new felt boots with galoshes.

"Well, now, take them, they're yours," he said to the disoriented girl.

Overwhelmed, Katya didn't dare to take a step forward.

"Take them," laughed the superintendent.

Katya took the felt boots, ran downstairs and tried them on. They fit her perfectly.

She walked along the frozen Moscow streets in her new boots, the snow crunching beneath her feet.

"Isn't he a wonderful superintendent," she thought to herself. "He takes such good care of us."

AN AMAZING DAY

Vladimir Ilyich was off to spend a day hunting.

Lenin arrived at the village of Modenovo in the district of Vereya. He stopped the automobile, took his gun and, with a guide, set off for the woods.

"Lenin has come!"

The news flashed through the village and soon spread to fellow peasants in the neighbouring settlements.

Vladimir Ilyich and his guide, their guns under their arms, passed through the wintry forest. It was a fine day, not too cold. The sun lingered high in the sky. The night before there had been a light snowfall, so they knew that any tracks they caught sight of would be recent. For a hunter it was the best of circumstances.

"As if made to order for you," said the guide. "The weather, Vladimir Ilyich, is just right. Over there, about a half-verst away, is the best location. At the bend we turn left and ..." the guide waved his hand to indicate where the best hunting would be found.

They came to the bend, but suddenly heard footsteps behind them, as if someone was following their tracks. Vladimir Ilyich and his partner turned around and caught sight of two youths. Both were covered with sweat from their effort to catch up. Breathing heavily, they came to a halt.

"Comrade Vladimir Ilyich, excuse us. We're looking for you."

"What's on your minds, comrades?"

"We're from the village," the youths explained.

"We're carrying a written request for you, Vladimir Ilyich, from the villagers," and the youths handed him a sheet of paper.

Vladimir Ilyich took the paper and smiling, opened it up. He read: "To the leader of the world revolution, Comrade Lenin, from the citizens of the village of Modenovo." Below were the words: "We invite you to meet us for a conversation."

Vladimir Ilyich looked at the youths and then at his guide.

"What a people," the latter grumbled, "they're like burrs. No conscience at all." He turned to the youths: "Comrade Lenin needs a few hours of relaxation."

The messengers hung their heads. They wanted to excuse themselves and leave.

"Hold on," Vladimir Ilyich stopped them. "Wait a minute. After all, I haven't given an answer and, if I'm not mistaken, the note was addressed to me."

"To you, that's right," the youths said with renewed fervour.

"Alright now," said Vladimir Ilyich, "return to your village and tell them that I accept and thank them for the invitation. Let them know that I won't be long."

"Thank you!" shouted the youths and raced back to Modenovo. Vladimir Ilyich turned in the same direction.

"Oh my," sighed the guide. "What a day it is to lose! The rabbits will have a chuckle over this!"

"Chuckle?" Lenin said gaily. "Well, what of it. Let the rabbits live today. It's a remarkable feature of our people, their burning interest in everything. It just wouldn't be right to refuse them."

The young men rushed into the village.

"Well, what happened?"

"He's coming, he's coming. He's following behind us!"

"You don't say. That certainly does fit his character."

The peasants gathered in the cottage belonging to Praskovya Afanasyevna Kochetova. The room was soon overflowing. Others began to arrive from surrounding villages, anxious to hear Lenin speak. There simply wasn't enough room for everyone, so some had to be content with the passageway and others to crowd about the entrance.

Lenin arrived. He talked about the military situation in the country, about how **Wrangel** had been driven into the sea. He talked about the difficulties they were having with grain supplies but assured them that the crisis would be met. He said that the transportation system was in ruins, but that the necessary manpower would be found to repair it as soon as the enemy was driven out of the country. Then he talked of his great and marvellous plan—the electrification of all of Russia.

The peasants listened raptly, as if in a dream world. Each word went directly to their hearts.

Vladimir Ilyich concluded his report, after which ensued a discussion. Question followed question in rapid succession. Soon the conversation became so animated, and the peasants so wrapped up in their own exchanges, that it seemed as if Lenin were not even present.

Outside it was growing dark. It was winter and the days were short. The conversation, however, continued in full swing.

Nadezhda Konstantinovna was waiting in Moscow for Vladimir Ilyich.

"Well, at last he has had the opportunity to relax," she said happily. "He's got some fresh air in the fields, in woods and the weather turned out to be perfect."

Vladimir Ilyich returned home. He walked in with an animated and pleased look on his face.

"Wasn't it a beautiful day today, Volodya!"

"Marvellous!" answered Vladimir Ilyich.

OLD FARMSTEADS

The fire raged out of control all day. By evening all that remained of the village Old Farmsteads were stoves and chimneys. The cottages had burned down, the barns had all gone up in smoke. Even the bathhouses in the gardens had disappeared. Everything was lost: wooden chests and icons, tables and floorboards, carts and sleighs. Worst of all, the year's harvest perished.

WRANGEL — a general of the tsarist army; one of the leaders of the counter-revolutionary forces in the Civil War in Russia

Such a catastrophe was a rarity, but it had indeed happened here. All that remained were the victims. They gathered at the ruins of their homes. The wail of women cut through the air.

Who could lend a hand at such a time?

The situation with lumber was poor, for forests were scarce in the area. Nails were nowhere to be found, and iron—impossible! How could they get by with no grain? Two hundred hungry mouths! Autumn was knocking at the door.

They had to turn to Lenin, for he was their only hope for relief.

Somebody suggested this alternative, but then cut himself short.

"So where can Lenin obtain lumber?"

"Who ever heard of grain leaving Moscow for the countryside?"

"Be that as it may, neighbours," someone found the words, "we'll tell him our story and let the chips fall as they will."

The peasants made their way to Lenin and related their misfortune to him. He listened in agitation.

"Tell me, how are the children?"

"They're living for the time being in neighbouring villages."

"And what about the rest of you?"

"We'll live in dug-outs, because there's no lumber available, Vladimir Ilyich."

"We can help you with that end of it. It'll be more complicated to rebuild everything on such short notice. How can you manage it?"

"All we need is lumber. God will help with the rest."

"God has nothing to do with it. He won't be of any help." Lenin paused thoughtfully. "Tell me, are there any military units quartered in your district?"

"There's a machine-gun unit in training."

"Now that's even better, things are looking brighter. We can find some grain for you as well. You'll all receive the minimal ration. Seeds are the first priority."

"We are very grateful," the peasants began to bow. "Heartfelt thanks from the entire village."

"It's early yet," Vladimir Ilyich interrupted them. He picked up his telephone receiver.

"I have some peasants here who are in deep trouble," and Lenin continued on the subject of the need for lumber.

He hung up the receiver, then dialled another number.

"I have some peasants here in need of help," and gave some instructions concerning the cadets.

Vladimir Ilyich then made a third call to arrange for the procurement of grain.

"Well, there you are," he said. "I hope everything turns out all right for you."

The peasants again made professions of gratitude.

"That's entirely unnecessary," Lenin cut them short. "It's my responsibility, my obligation, so to speak, to you and to worker-peasant power. Once again, I wish you good fortune, comrades."

The lumber and grain soon arrived at Old Farmsteads. Not long after a company of cadets appeared in the village. In no time the busy hum of saws and axes rose over the area. Everyone set to work with a heart.

In the interval of one month a new village was built from the ashes. Smart and dainty new houses stood elegantly in rows parallel to the street.

The peasants gathered around their cottages.

"The name Old Farmsteads no longer fits. We have to think up a new name for the new village."

"That's right," agreed the peasants.

Suggestions were tossed out:

"New Farmsteads."

"Radiant Farmsteads."

"Modern Farmsteads."

"It won't do, it simply won't," voices clamoured. "They're not bad, but they're not quite right. Something more appropriate."

And suddenly:

"Let's name it after Lenin," someone shouted.

"That's it!" the peasants cried triumphantly.

Old Farmsteads no longer exists. In its place now stands a village named in honour of Lenin.

LEFT BEHIND

Lyonka was swimming in the Pakhra when Lenin appeared on the bank of the river. He had been given strict orders by his doctor to come to Gorki for an urgently needed rest.

Lenin fixed his gaze on Lyonka—the boy was already a superb swimmer. He performed somersaults and graceful dives into the water. He did the crawl and the backstroke, swam with and against the current and crossed from one bank to the other and back again without the slightest rest.

Lyonka also noticed Lenin but he didn't recognise him for who he was. Lyonka had only recently arrived in Gorki and took Lenin for just another man off the street.

When the boy crawled out of the water Lenin asked him:

"Well, how was the water?"

"Wet," Lyonka conceded. He wasn't a talkative child.

"Wet it is," laughed Lenin. The youth caught his fancy.

Vladimir Ilyich sat down on the gentle slope, looked first at the water then at Lyonka, repeated the process and finally turned to the boy to speak:

"Let's see who's fastest."

"If you wish," said Lyonka with a shade of self-importance.

Lyonka was a strong swimmer but Lenin was also very agile in the water. He was, after all, from the Volga region. It was a rare day that someone managed to overtake Lenin in the water.

Vladimir Ilyich and Lyonka swam hard, but the latter soon outdistanced Lenin, who returned home stung.

"That's not a good sign. He beat me. I'm growing old. My strength just isn't what it used to be."

Lyonka had in fact spoiled Lenin's mood that day. He, however, was very pleased. He returned to Gorki to inform everyone that he had outswum a grown man in the Pakhra.

"Well who was he?" his friends inquired.

"Not very tall, medium height I'd say."

"With a beard?"

"That's right."

"And a moustache?"

"With a moustache."

"Did he have a high forehead?"

"Yes, he did."

"That grown man," shouted the children, "is Lenin himself!"

Lyonka's mouth dropped wide open in surprise. He felt uncomfortable now about the day's events: he had both beaten Lenin and talked somewhat curtly to him. He resolved to make amends for his negligence.

The next day the boy again raced to the Pakhra and lingered there until evening. Lenin, however, didn't appear. For more than a week Lyonka returned every day to the river. It was only on the tenth day he once again caught sight of Lenin.

"Well, how is the water?" asked Vladimir Ilyich.

"Warm," shouted Lyonka, "quite warm. You wouldn't believe how warm it is, Vladimir Ilyich."

"I guess that means it is certainly warm," laughed Vladimir Ilyich.

Lyonka in fact wanted to entice Lenin to jump into the river.

"The water's lovely. It's like lying on a featherbed!"

Lenin and Lyonka agreed to race once again. They tossed a stick into the water and off they went! Lyonka had waited impatiently for this moment.

Lyonka swam along, but in reality held himself back. He was subtle, however, and made every effort to conceal the fact. To strengthen his case he made a great show of breathing very heavily.

Despite this Lenin soon noticed. He turned to Lyonka:

"What tricks are you up to?"

"What are you saying, Vladimir Ilyich," Lyonka protested. He was lying, lying to Lenin, and without even blushing. Lenin could see that Lyonka was lying.

He decided to call him to accounts.

Vladimir Ilyich slightly slowed down his own pace. He looked back—Lyonka had followed suit. Lenin slowed down even more and Lyonka still didn't gain on him. The closer they came to the stick, the slower they proceeded. Now they had stopped entirely.

Lenin stopped and turned to Lyonka:

"I've caught you now!"

Lyonka realised that he'd been discovered and lowered his gaze in shame.

"That won't do, Lyonya, it just won't do." They were already on the shore at this point. "We'll just have to start over again."

Once again they tossed the stick and once again dove into the water. It was clear to Lyonka that deceit wouldn't work, so he swam as hard as he could. He exerted himself but couldn't keep up with Lenin. He quickened his pace in hopes of overcoming Vladimir Ilyich, but to no avail. His arms pumped even harder but to no visible gain, it was no use. He was no longer pretending as he huffed and puffed, but he was simply not capable of catching up with Lenin.

Lyonka lost the race and returned home confused and with an air of defeat.

Vladimir Ilyich, on the other hand, returned home beaming with pleasure.

"Well, that shows that our side hasn't tossed in the towel. There's still some strength there..."

As he walked along the path he thought to himself:

"That's great. It means I can wrap up my period of rest. There's still some powder left in the old powder keg."

Lyonka, poor soul, dragged home disconsolate. Things had worked out just as he had wanted, he had after all intended to yield first place to Lenin. Still ... he hadn't quite expected the outcome as it developed.

STEPA-A-A-N MARKELYCH!

"Vladimir Ilyich!"

Lenin didn't reply.

"Vladi-i-i-mir Ilyich!"

Silence was the only answer. Only the wind murmured through the branches of the fir trees.

The old peasant, Stepan Markelych, accompanying Lenin on a hunting expedition, began to grow anxious.

He glanced nervously about, and listened for the slightest sound.

He and Lenin had separated an hour ago, agreeing to meet here in the clearing under an old elm tree. Markelych waited another twenty minutes, but there was still no sign of Lenin.

"What can have happened?" Stepan Markelych wondered and began to rack his brain for an answer. Markelych knew that Lenin was a very punctual person. He must have got lost. Perhaps, though, something had happened to Vladimir Ilyich. He had best go to look for him.

The old man left, and after a few moments Lenin appeared at the elm tree. He glanced about, Markelych wasn't at the pre-arranged place.

"What can have happened?" wondered Lenin. Vladimir Ilyich knew that Markelych was a punctual person, which indicated that something must have gone wrong. He began to take alarm, paced back and forth for a while near the elm, and set out to search for the old man.

Lenin walked along in the woods:

"Stepan Markelych!"

He stopped to listen for a reply.

"Stepa-a-an Markelych!"

At this time Markelych was also wandering in the woods, but in a different area.

"Vladimir Ilyich!" resounded the voice of the old man. "Vladi-i-mir Ilyich!"

Markelych's quest met with no luck, so he decided to return to the original spot under the elm.

Vladimir Ilyich, encountering the same frustration, came to an identical conclusion.

Just as the old peasant came abreast of the elm, he caught sight of Lenin emerging into the clearing.

At the sight of Vladimir Ilyich the old man's face visibly relaxed.

Lenin, of course, also breathed more easily to learn that Markelych was alive and intact. He was also slightly embarrassed at his nervousness. His guide could have been taking care of his own business, after all. Lenin decided to conceal the fact that he had been searching for Markelych. The old man, too, felt uncomfortable about his earlier uneasiness. He pretended he hadn't budged from his spot near the elm tree.

"I'm sorry, Stepan Markelych," said Vladimir Ilyich. "Please don't be angry. Just imagine, I was so enchanted with these woods!"

"Think nothing of it, Vladimir Ilyich," answered the old man. "Who keeps track of time here anyway! I myself got involved in watching a woodpecker. Its noise just drew my attention."

"That's good to know," said Vladimir Ilyich.

Lenin was pleased that he had managed to conceal his anxiety from Markelych. The latter, in turn, was happy for the very same reason.

However as they were proceeding through the clearing, the old man could not refrain from confessing:

"You know I went looking for you, Vladimir Ilyich."

"What are you saying?" Lenin said in astonishment. "Looking for me!"

"I couldn't help but think that you'd run into some misfortune."

"You are a nervous old fellow, aren't you!" Vladimir Ilyich declared.

"Nervous," Stepan Markelych confessed.

Lenin broke into a grin.

The old man looked at him. "What in the world? I don't think that what I said was so funny. What is Lenin laughing about?"

WATERMELONS

All summer Mishatka and Rodka, two boys who were also neighbours, were kept busy with their crop of watermelon.

Their first task was to keep the birds from the garden. The summer was hot and dry and the boys had to run constantly to the river for buckets of water to pour over the parched soil. Finally, they spent entire days at a stretch hiding in burdocks adjacent to their gardens to prevent other children from stealing their watermelons. The melons ripened under the sun, unaware that Mishatka and Rodka had secret plans for them. The youths were growing them to present as a gift to Comrade Lenin.

The watermelons grew to an enormous size; each weighed perhaps eight kilograms. The children were pleased and began to arrange for their delivery to Moscow.

Mishatka was a little uncertain about the exact location of that city.

"It's in that direction," explained Rodka, "behind that field, that meadow and the forest. About twenty versts in all."

In reality, the distance from their homes to Moscow was just a little short of a thousand versts.

The boys secretly gathered together some provisions for the trip. They both stored up some rusks. Rodka withdrew a strip of pork fat from the pantry and Mishatka took a few eggs from the brood-hen.

They prepared for the journey, but suddenly—something would have to happen!

Mishatka's mother noticed that the eggs were missing and Rodka's soon realised that her supply of pork fat in the pantry had mysteriously dwindled.

It didn't take them long to find the guilty ones.

At first, of course, the children denied everything. They assured their mothers that they were pointing the finger in the wrong direction, that they hadn't gone near the chicken-coop and that Rodka hadn't touched the pork fat. Then their fathers returned home and matters took a turn for the worse. The boys finally were forced to make a clean slate of it all.

But to their surprise:

"Well, it's true," said their parents, "our Kuban watermelons would after all be a nice present for Comrade Lenin."

Everyone in the Cossack village was receptive to the idea. The residents decided to arrange for the delivery of the watermelons to Vladimir Ilyich. One person was appointed to bring them to Moscow. He appeared in Moscow before Comrade Lenin with the watermelons nurtured by Mishatka and Rodka.

Vladimir Ilyich looked intently at the beauties from the steppe region, poked them with his finger, stepped back and squinted his eyes—in a word, he was delighted.

"Marvellous, marvellous," said Lenin. "They're simply gorgeous."

Vladimir Ilyich requested that his heartfelt gratitude and personal greetings be communicated to the boys.

The children were extremely proud to hear the news. In turn the whole village was pleased.

Only one problem bothered the boys: whose watermelon had tasted the best?

Mishatka was assured that his, of course, was the sweetest.

Rodka, however, didn't hesitate to differ, and loudly: "No, mine! Without any doubt, mine was sweeter!"

The boys wanted to send Comrade Lenin a letter to receive his answer on this subject.

They couldn't quite muster up the courage, however.

It was best that way. What could Lenin have told the two boys? He didn't even try the watermelons. Instead Vladimir Ilyich, thinking of the joy of other children, sent them, after he had admired them thoroughly, to an orphanage in the Khamovniki workers' district.

THE TROUBLE-MAKER

Lenin once received the following letter:

"Dear Vladimir Ilyich, please accept our greetings. By October you will receive a gift from us."

"Here we are, another gift," Vladimir Ilyich reacted with displeasure.

The peasants didn't specify the nature of the gift, having decided to keep it a secret.

"It's always more interesting when you don't know ahead of time what kind of gift you'll receive," the peasants judged.

In fact it was a rather common gift. They had decided to send Vladimir Ilyich meat and pork fat for the October holiday.

They were quite content with their decision. But, as is bound to happen in any situation, a trouble-maker had to speak out. In this case it was a former Red Guard who had served with Budenny by the name of Seliverst Dubtsov.

"Well, headless wonders," he grumbled to the peasants, "do you really call this a gift?"

"What's with you?" objected the peasants. "Vladimir Ilyich is human too. Do you think he doesn't eat our kind of food? The pork fat is bound to please him."

"Pork fat," laughed Dubtsov, "you have no imagination."

"You're nothing but a trouble-maker," his fellow villagers cursed.

For a whole week Dubtsov pestered the peasants, repeating relentlessly:

"You have no imagination, none whatsoever. Your brains are located where you sit down!"

The peasants lost their tempers and finally asked of Dubtsov:

"Indeed, tell us of your fantasy."

Dubtsov in fact made a suggestion which was met by such gales of laughter that the roof of the cottage was almost lifted from the walls.

He proposed that the peasants take up their picks and shovels and without delay lay down a road from their village to the nearest station (a distance of almost 9 versts!).

"A road!" hooted the peasants.

"And what would that mean to Lenin?"

"It would be a gift to ourselves!"

"A trouble-maker for you, and a man who fought with Budenny no less!"

But then, after a few days had passed and the villagers had had their fill of laughing, someone rather meekly suggested:

"You know, brothers, he may be right. Perhaps Lenin would approve of such a project."

"Perhaps he would," the peasants hesitated.

"There's no perhaps about it," emphasised Dubtsov. Dubtsov had convinced the peasants.

They gathered together the women, drove the old men from their perches on the stoves, and set to work. The road was finished just in time for October. Even a bridge was built across the Kamenka River.

The peasants composed a letter to Vladimir Ilyich, extending holiday greetings and, at the end, communicating the news about the road. They added that, if he liked, he could look upon the project as their gift to him. If he didn't like it, they asked that he not be offended. The guilty one was the trouble-maker Seliverst Dubtsov, a former soldier under Budenny.

They received a reply in short notice.

"It's just right, perfect in fact." Vladimir Ilyich wrote that it was a marvellous gift, that he couldn't have thought of a better one. The letter ended with the statement that the nine-verst road was yet another step for the country in the direction of communism.

The peasants read the letter.

"Isn't this something!"

"What an answer!"

"Just see how Lenin responded!"

"It was worthy of Vladimir Ilyich," the peasants decided. "Perhaps for May we'll have another gift ready..."

A DESSIATINA OF LAND FOR LENIN

"Lenin, don't forget about Lenin, Volodimir Ilyich," shouted Ivan Perepletov during the redistribution of the land formerly belonging to the gentry estate.

In fact how could they forget? Just the evening before the decision had been made to put aside a parcel of land for Lenin out of that which was to be redistributed.

"It has to be that way."

"Everything happened because of him, after all."

"Let him have some land to use as well."

They took a long time choosing the right parcel, for they wanted it to be choice land. They argued over which side of the village would be best and took care that it would be neither too moist nor too dry and that the soil would be clay with an admixture of black earth. They measured out the **dessiatina**, then wrote a letter to Moscow. They asked Lenin to come and take possession of his land.

In no time they received an answer.

Lenin thanked the peasants for their kindness, but asked them to forgive him if he was too busy at present to work the soil. He had pressing business in the Council of People's Commissars. The letter ended

DESSIATINA—a Russian unit of land area equal to 2.7 acre

with Lenin's recommendation that the peasants dispose of the land according to their own discretion.

"It's true, he has no time for the land at this point," said the peasants.

"We shouldn't try to tear him away from the business of the state."

"All the same, it's a pity—he'd make a good neighbour."

The peasants accepted his decision. They had one matter to take care of: Lenin had asked them to "dispose of the land according to their own discretion". He hadn't given any precise instructions what to do.

The peasants tried hard to come to a decision. They thought and thought.

Finally they decided not to give the **dessiatina** to anyone else nor to divide it up amongst themselves. Instead they resolved to maintain it for common usage, to sow, plough and harvest it jointly. In turn the harvest would be stored in a barn for the use of the whole community.

That is exactly what happened.

It was wise idea. Now the peasants had a communal supply of grain for use in case of need. When the situation arose, they would have something on which to fall back.

When the crop failed the Pakhomov family the peasants didn't go hungry nor did they fall into debt. Instead they received help from Lenin's **dessiatina**.

Their needs were many. For example, when they decided to buy a thresher they didn't have to squeeze out contributions from every cottage. Instead they sold the communal grain.

Then they decided at a gathering:

"Why don't we send the workers a gift?"

"We'll send one, it's a must."

They filled some sacks and sent them off with an accompanying letter: "It's not just common bread, it comes from Lenin's **dessiatina**!"

Ten years passed and collective farms began to be established in the villages. The peasants now had more land and stock. Lenin's **dessiatina** now became part of the collective farm. It wasn't forgotten or neglected, for the people's memory is eternal.

Whoever passes by this spot, whether on horse or by foot, comes to a stop, and recalls Lenin. The memory of Lenin is kept alive on this collective farm.

A SECRET REQUEST

Many gifts were sent from the workers and peasants to Lenin. They sent bread, groats, sugar (the food situation was difficult at the time) and other edibles. Gifts of a different nature arrived as well. Leather-workers sent Vladimir Ilyich a sheepskin coat. Lace-makers from Vologda sent him a bed-spread embroidered in folk style. Textile workers from Petrograd gave him a soft rug.

Upon receiving such gifts Lenin would frown.

"What's the matter, Vladimir Ilyich," his comrades at work would defend the gifts. "They're straight from the hearts of the people, expressions of their gratitude."

"Well, that I understand," agreed Lenin, "nevertheless, don't you see, it's awkward, not quite right. It's a vestige of the past, a continuance of the old ways: a gift to the lord, a gift to the priest for forgivance, a gift... It's time to call an end to it. An end," sternly repeated Vladimir Ilyich.

Once Lenin received a letter from the distant city of Klintsi in Gomel region. The workers were writing from the Stodol cloth factory.

Vladimir Ilyich read the letter congratulating him on the approaching fifth anniversary of the October Revolution, wishing him good health and then, further promising that: "... we will send you before the holiday ... a modest gift made by our own hands." The gift would be a length of cloth.

The letter was signed not by one, two, or even three people. There were 400 signatures.

Vladimir Ilyich began to lose his temper, but soon checked himself. There was no point in insulting the workers just before the holidays. Lenin took up his pen and paper and wrote a reply to the workers:

"Dear Comrades:

"My warmest thanks for the greetings and for the present. I must tell you in confidence that no presents should be sent to me. I ask that you pass this secret request around among as many workers as possible...

"Yours,

"V. Ulyanov (Lenin)"

The workers of Klintsi received Lenin's letter and read it through. It pleased them thoroughly, for it was a nice letter, a warm one, and with an expression of thanks.

However, the workers also fell to thinking. They understood clearly that Lenin didn't approve of gifts. As far as the request was concerned, the workers also understood the gist of the matter, though it be secret. They interpreted Vladimir Ilyich's request as a strict order and communicated it to all the other workers in Klintsi. In fact the whole region soon learned of it.

At one point Stepan Sherstobitov, a worker at the Stodol factory, returned to his native village near Minsk and related Lenin's request to his neighbours.

The peasants, of course, were disappointed. They were at the time preparing to send Vladimir Ilyich a gift of some fragrant honey for the New Year holiday. However, a request is a request, and the peasants felt obliged to comply.

It so happened that a soldier from the Red Army, Ivan Dodonov, was spending his leave in this very village and at that very time. He returned to his unit, carrying with him the request sent out by Vladimir Ilyich. When soldiers of the unit had served their time in the Red Army, they returned to their villages and cities, telling all they met about the secret request made by Comrade Lenin.

Word was passed from mouth to mouth. It went out to near and distant places. It even reached us today.

And now I pass the word on to you. You in turn should tell all you know. Only don't forget—the request is highly confidential.

What about the gifts? Did the workers and peasants really stop sending Comrade Lenin presents? No, in fact they didn't.

How do you explain that?

It's hard to explain. Russia is a huge country. Maybe word didn't reach everyone. Or perhaps there's another explanation...

THE MONUMENT

The peasants of a small Siberian settlement decided to erect a monument to Lenin while he was still living.

They sent delegates to Moscow with the mission of receiving permission from Vladimir Ilyich.

The delegates arrived and were received by Lenin:

"Good day. How was your trip?"

"Pleasant," answered the peasants.

"How are the crops this year?"

"The Lord blessed us."

"Are there any shortages of goods in your area?"

"They're being delivered, Vladimir Ilyich. We have enough calico, we have nails, and there is no shortage of soap."

"Well, that's good to hear," smiled Vladimir Ilyich. "I guess that exhausts my questions. Now what can I do for you?"

The delegates explained their proposal to him.

"A monument?!" exclaimed Lenin.

"A monument," answered the peasants. "We've already obtained the stone for the foundation," they related, not without a touch of pride. "And the location, Vladimir Ilyich, is superb, on an elevation. There are tall birches and a stream in the vicinity. The view is beautiful. You won't be insulted at the sight of it, Vladimir Ilyich."

"That I would," answered Lenin. The smile disappeared from his face. "Not only insulted, but very insulted."

The peasants lost their composure. They hadn't expected events to take this direction.

"The location, I agree, is excellent," continued Lenin. "But as far as the monument is concerned, I'm definitely against it. Categorically, you might say," Lenin waved his arms. "Tell that to your comrades in Siberia. I make myself clear, I hope. Thanks for coming. I wish you all the luck..." and Lenin bid them farewell.

The delegates returned to their settlement and related their conversation with Lenin.

As might be expected, an animated discussion ensued.

"As it turns out, Lenin doesn't approve."

"Perhaps the location doesn't suit him?"

"You explained everything to him? You told him that we'd already obtained the stone?"

"Of course, of course," answered the delegates. "The location pleases him. We made ourselves as clear as day. That just wasn't the problem, brothers. You see, Lenin's a very modest man."

The peasants wanted to proceed with their plans to erect a monument despite Vladimir Ilyich's objections. But then they wavered. After all, Lenin did say that he was strongly against it.

"Perhaps he understands better..."

The peasants began to think what to do with the stone and how to utilise the location. It would be such a waste to leave it idle.

After lengthy arguments and counter-arguments they suddenly came to an agreement: to build a school, of a sort that would be the envy of the whole area, near the ancient birch trees.

Once decided, they soon carried out the project.

It stands there to this day, on the elevated spot, in complete harmony with the Siberian sky. The birch trees give forth new leaves each spring and the brook murmurs its way through the ravine.

The air is replete with the sound of children's laughter.

The years pass by, one after another. Events fade and disappear into the past.

The school, however, remains.

There is an eternal monument to Lenin in a little Siberian settlement.

WHERE WAS COMRADE LENIN BORN?

One Sunday at the market some peasants got involved in a dispute over the location of Comrade Lenin's birthplace.

"It's far away, beyond the Urals," said one.

"You're wrong," a second interrupted him. "He

was born in this area. He's a local, from our own district."

"A local!" a third couldn't hold back. "I know for sure. Vladimir Ilyich is a Siberian, he's from region of the Lena River, and that's that."

"He's not a Siberian," a fourth cut in. "Vladimir Ilyich was born in Petrograd, the city that used to be called Saint-Petersburg."

"Moscow," a fifth asserted.

"Tula," added a sixth.

"Smolensk."

"He's from Kursk region, from the city of Glukhov."

"Tambov, I say."

"Ryazan."

"Tver!"

Where was Lenin born? The peasants' argument didn't subside.

"From Orel, I'm sure."

"Penza."

"At the Elnya station."

"In a village."

"No, you're all wet. He was born in a city."

Newcomers joined the argument. The peasants asked anyone they thought would give an answer.

"Dear fellow," they asked, "where was Comrade Lenin born?"

The person addressed paused to think.

"I'm not sure precisely. I only know that Lenin was born in the mountains. That's where he got his keen eyesight. He has eagle eyes."

The peasants turned to a second:

"Dear fellow, where was Comrade Lenin born?"

This one also thought for a moment:

"Lenin was born in the steppe region," he answered with conviction. "There can be no argument about it. That's why he is such an expansive person. Large-scale, that's what Leninist means."

Now the peasants turned to a third. This fellow took his time before answering, as did the others:

"Here's your answer," he said. "Vladimir Ilyich is from the forest region. I'm sure of it—the forest region. How else could he have such a strong constitution. Where else could his strength of conviction come from?"

The peasants were completely lost.

Where, after all, was Lenin born?

The question was a difficult one to answer.

It's hard to say how the argument would have ended. Fortunately one wise fellow suggested:

"Let's go to the district Soviet, to the chairman himself."

They followed his advice, and went directly to the chairman of the Soviet to explain their dilemma. The chairman heard them out, smiled as he looked at the peasants, and answered:

"Comrade Lenin was born in Simbirsk, on the Volga, that wide, free river."

He paused, looked anew at the peasants, and added:

"So that there will be no opportunity for an argument among you, let's just say, comrades, that Lenin was born here, at home, in Russia."

2

1. Vladimir Ilyich Lenin. 2. Painting by Vladimir Serov, "Peasant delegates conversing with Lenin". 3. In 1920 the peasants of Kashino, near Volokolamsk built their own electric power station. V. I. Lenin and N. K. Krupskaya were present for the inaugural ceremonies. 4. From the horse—to the tractor!

3

4

5

5. V. I. Lenin at his work desk in his office in the Kremlin, October 1918. 6. In this building, located in the Kremlin, were housed the Council of People's Commissars and the All-Russia Central Executive Committee of the Soviet of Workers' Deputies. 7. Lenin's study in the Moscow Kremlin. 8. A gift to Lenin on his fiftieth birthday from the workers of Omsk—a train bearing foodstuffs for the people of Moscow, April 22, 1920.

6

7

8

9. V. I. Lenin, N. K. Krupskaya and Lenin's sister Maria Ulyanova in a motor vehicle after the parade of the Red Army on May 1, 1918. 10. Delegates to the Third All-Russia Komsomol Congress receive their bread rations. 11. The Leninist plan for the cooperation of agriculture is put into effect—peasants registering for the collective farm. 12. V. I. Lenin, N. K. Krupskaya and Lenin's sister Anna Elizarova with nephew Viktor and Vera, the daughter of a worker. (Gorki, near Moscow, 1922.)

9

10

11

12

13

13. V. I. Lenin out for a stroll. (Gorki, early
August, 1922.)

THE GREAT PATRIOTIC WAR

MOSCOW

STALINGRAD

BERLIN

THE EXPLOIT OF 28 HEROES

November 1941. World War II was raging. The nazis were tearing towards Moscow. The enemy mounted a major tank assault against the division commanded by General Panfilov.

The Dubosekovo Halt. 118 kilometres from Moscow. A field. Hills. Copses. In the vicinity the Lama River wound its course. Here in an open field on a hill the heroes from Panfilov's division blocked the nazis' path.

In all they were 28. They were headed by a political instructor named Klochkov. The soldiers were dug into the ground. They clung to the edges of the trenches.

The tanks plowed forward, their engines humming. The soldiers counted them.

"Jesus, there are twenty of them!"

Klochkov grinned:

"Twenty tanks. That means less than one per person."

The soldiers smiled. Their political instructor was a real brave.

"Less than one," said Emtsov, a private.

"Of course, less," affirmed Petrenko.

The heroes moved into battle. A field. Hills. Copses. In the vicinity the Lama River wound its course.

"Hurray!" the shout rose from the trenches.

The first tank had been put out of action.

Once again a cheer went up. A second tank hesitated, its engine chugging, its armour clanking ... and came to a halt. And again a cheer. And again. Fourteen out of twenty tanks were dispatched by the heroes. The remaining six turned and retreated.

Sergeant Petrenko chuckled:

"It looks like we've strangled the bandits!"

"That's right. They put their tails between their legs and ran."

The soldiers rested, then once again saw an avalanche moving upon them. This time the nazis had thirty tanks.

Klochkov looked at his soldiers. They were all silent, frozen in place. The clank of steel was the only audible sound. The tanks came closer and closer.

"Friends," said Klochkov, "Russia is immense, but there's nowhere to retreat. Moscow is at our backs."

"We understand, Comrade," the soldiers answered. "Moscow!"

The soldiers again moved into action. Their ranks became thinner and thinner. Emtsov and Petrenko fell. Bondarenko perished. Trofimov died. Narsutbai Esebulatov was killed. Shopokov fell next. Soldiers and grenades became scarcer and scarcer.

Klochkov himself was wounded. Still he rose up to face a tank, threw a grenade and blew the tank up. The joy of victory swept across his face, but at that very moment a bullet cut him down. Political instructor Klochkov fell.

General Panfilov's heroes struggled fiercely. There were no limits to their courage. They didn't budge before the nazis. Russia owes them a debt of gratitude for this.

The Dubosekovo Halt. A field. Hills. Copses. In the vicinity the Lama River winds its course. The Dubosekovo Halt is a sacred spot in the heart of every Russian.

"TRY OURS!"

It appeared, unheralded, from the clear blue sky. It appeared, as if in a fairy tale...

A fierce battle was taking place to the north-west of Moscow on the road to Leningrad. The nazis were pushing towards the little city of Klin. Soviet companies were falling back. The troops made their way up a hillock. To the left was a low-lying region, through which a river, covered by a layer of ice, flowed. Here

the nazis were gathering together their forces. They were packed tightly in the area. They numbered in the hundreds—perhaps even a thousand. This was the rallying point for a new attack.

The soldiers looked down at the nazis. Someone said:

"Oh, for a few cannisters to throw into that mass."

"That's right, cannisters would do it," a second affirmed.

"They'd be just the thing," a third agreed.

The soldiers let their fantasies run free.

"How about a cannon right here," uttered one of them.

A second added:

"And a few shells for it."

"And some fellows with backbone to handle the gun," a third concluded.

The soldiers dreamed away. And suddenly, from the other side of the ravine, on a slope just as steep as that on which they were standing, appeared a piece of artillery.

The soldiers rubbed their eyes—they thought they were still dreaming. But no! It was all real. Horses. A gun. Two soldiers. An officer near the cannon.

The gunners looked down into the low-lying area; they also caught sight of the nazis and came to a halt.

The soldiers looked at the artillery-men in astonishment. They had appeared, unheralded, from the clear blue sky ... as if in a fairy tale.

The gunners stood for a moment on the steep incline, then turned and rapidly descended. The nazis now saw the artillery, but they couldn't at first tell whether or not they were hostile. While they were wondering the artillery came within range. The gunners pointed the gun and stuffed a cannister shell down its barrel.

"Well now, try ours!" shouted the officer. "Fire!"

The cannister flew out of the cannon, and behind it a second.

"Try ours! Try ours!" shouted the officer. "Fire! Fire!"

A third explosion, then a fourth. A fifth kicked up a cloud of snow.

"Try ours!"

"Try ours!"

The low-lying area was soon covered with the bodies of nazis. Those who were still alive rushed up the steep slope directly towards the companies of soldiers. They were met with blasts of machine-gun fire. For a while it was feverish going.

When the soldiers once again looked below, the team of horses had already disappeared. It was gone from view. Like a bird, like a song, it had come and gone as if it had entered back into the pages of the fairy tale.

The soldiers lingered long on the slope.

Who were these heroes? Who were the daring artillery-men? The soldiers had no way of knowing.

"Try ours!" was the only memory that remained of the courageous artillery-men.

A TANK BATTALION

A fierce battle was waging near the station and settlement of Kryukovo. The nazis were pressing very hard against the defence. Manpower was short. The soldiers were on the verge of falling back.

The commanders called up their superiors to ask for immediate reinforcements. There was no help on hand, however, all reserves had long ago been sent into battle.

The situation was worsening by the moment at Kryukovo. Once again the commanders called in to headquarters.

"Alright," their superiors told them, "be expecting a tank battalion."

True enough, a tank officer appeared at the command point for the battle. The officer was young and handsome, dressed in a leather-jacket and helmet. His eyes were blue, the colour of the azure in the May skies.

The tank officer approached the regimental commander, saluted sharply and introduced himself:

"Comrade Commander, our separate tank battalion reporting at your service. At your disposal Senior Lieutenant Logvinenko."

The regimental commander was speechless with joy. He embraced the officer:

"My thanks, brother, my heartfelt thanks." Then he set right down to business: "How many tanks do you have in your battalion?"

"One tank," answered Logvinenko. His azure-blue eyes peered at the commander.

"How many did you say?" the commander couldn't believe his ears.

"One tank," the officer repeated. "Only one is left... It's a T-37."

The nazis had taken heavy casualties around Moscow. But our troops had suffered as well... All the joy drained from the face of the regimental commander, as if he'd been suddenly struck by a blast of cold wind. The T-37 model was the most obsolete of Russian tanks. The most obsolete and the smallest. One machine-gun—that was the extent of its firepower. Its armour was as thin as your little finger.

"I stand ready to receive battle orders," said the officer.

"Go to the devil—that's your battle order," was on the tip of the regimental commander's tongue, but he overcame his first impulse and restrained himself.

Instead he ordered: "Put yourself at the disposal of the first battalion. It's the one coming under the heaviest attack from the nazis."

The tank officer no sooner joined up with the battalion than he threw himself into the battle along with the infantry. He manoeuvred cleverly, supporting the infantry first in one place, then rapidly altering his position. Soon he would be seen at another spot. The soldiers saw the armoured tank and their spirits were boosted. The rumour rapidly spread—a tank battalion had arrived.

Now the heroes held their ground, not budging an inch to the nazis.

They repulsed a second attack, and after that four more. By this point the tank officer was rendering aid not only to the first battalion but to the whole regiment.

The battle ended. The tank officer emerged—young, agitated, handsome. His eyes were blue, the colour of azure in the May skies.

The regimental commander approached the officer and embraced him warmly.

"My warmest thanks, brother, from the bottom of my heart. Now I understand that a tank battalion really did arrive."

ZOYA

Like a dove-coloured ribbon the road winds to the west. Automobiles race down this road. Some 85 kilometres from Moscow. If you look to the left you'll see a marble pedestal, and on the pedestal the frozen form of a girl. Her hands are tied. She has a proud, open demeanour.

This is the monument to Zoya.

Zoya Kosmodemyanskaya was a Moscow schoolgirl. When the enemy began to approach the city she enlisted in a partisan detachment. The girl crossed the front lines and joined the avengers of the people. Many residents of the Moscow area rose up at that time against the nazis.

The detachment was very fond of Zoya. She endured bravely all the hardships and adversities of this dangerous life. She was given the pseudonym "Tanya".

At one point a large detachment of nazis stopped at the village of Petrishchevo. During the night Zoya made her way into the village, cut all telephone communication and set afire the homes in which the nazis were quartered. Two days later she returned to Petrishchevo, but this time the nazis seized the young partisan.

The commander of the division himself, a lieutenant-colonel named Rüderer, interrogated Zoya.

"What's your name?"

"No comment."

"Is it you that set fire to the homes?"

"That's right."

"Your goal?"

"To destroy you."

They began to torture Zoya, demanding that she yield information about her comrades, where she had come from and who had sent her on the mission.

"No", "No comment", "I won't say"—answered Zoya.

The beating would begin again.

At night Zoya was subjected to new tortures. She was sent, almost unclad, into the streets several times to walk in the snow barefoot.

Once again:

"Say who you are."

"Who sent you?"

"Where'd you come from?"

No answer was forthcoming from Zoya.

In the morning Zoya was led out to be executed. She was brought to the square in the centre of the village and the local peasants were driven to watch the spectacle.

The girl was marched up to the scaffold and stood on a box. A hangman's loop was tossed around her neck.

It was the last moment, the last breath of a young life. How did she use this breath? What does a soldier do in the face of death?

The officer in charge prepared to give the signal. He raised his arm, but paused there. One of the nazis got hold of a camera at that moment. The officer assumed a dignified air, after all one has to present oneself properly in a picture! During this interval:

"Comrades! Have no fear," rang out the voice of Zoya. "Be brave, struggle, smash the nazis, crush them!"

A nazi standing nearby rushed to Zoya with the intention of striking her, but she pushed him away with her foot.

"I don't fear death, comrades," said Zoya. "I'm proud to die for my people." Turning slightly, she addressed her tormentors: "There are 200 million of us. You can't hang us all. No matter what you do victory will be ours."

The officer in charge gave a jerk and his arm fell...

The road to Minsk. Some 85 kilometres from Moscow. A monument to a heroine. People come to pay their respects to Zoya. The blue sky. The wide expanses. Flowers...

TULA COOKIES

Tula cookies are oh so delicious! A crust forms the outer layers and the filling in the centre is sweet...

Having encountered heroic resistance from the Soviet troops in the west, the nazis intensified their attempt to break through to Moscow from the south. Nazi tanks began to rumble up the road leading to Tula.

The city prepared to meet the enemy.

Workers' battalions were organised to join the Soviet Army in the defence of Tula.

One of the city enterprises mastered the task of producing anti-tank mines. The workers of a former confectionery factory lent a hand on the production line. Among these helpers was a young apprentice pastry-cook named Vanya Kolosov. He was an imaginative youth, resourceful and gay. One time he showed up at the shop where the mines were being produced. Under his arm he carried a bundle. He unwrapped the bundle and pulled out handfuls of labels which were used on the boxes in which the Tula cookies had been packaged. Vanya took some of the labels and began to attach them to the finished mines. Soon the workers looked, and on each mine they saw the words "Tula cookies".

The workers broke into laughter:

"Here are some sweets for the nazis."

"A nice little present for the Fritzes."

The mines were shipped out to the front lines of the city defence network. The sappers, busy at setting up minefields on the approaches to Tula, began to unpack the mines only to see before their eyes "Tula cookies"! They laughed heartily also.

"What a surprise for the nazis."

"A present for the Fritzes."

The soldiers wrote a letter to the workers: "Thanks for your efforts and for the mines. We look forward to another party with 'Tula cookies'."

On the 29th of October, 1941, the enemy reached the approaches to Tula and began to storm the city. They didn't succeed, however. Soviet troops and workers' battalions successfully held them off. Many tanks were blown up by the mines. All in all, the nazis lost a hundred of them during the battle for Tula.

The Soviet soldiers took a liking to the expression "Tula cookies". Everything that was produced in Tula and sent to the front—shells, bullets, mortars and mines—came to be known as "Tula cookies".

The nazis continued to storm Tula for a long time, but all in vain. They never did seize the city.

Apparently Tula cookies are very good!

"I'LL WRITE YOU FROM MOSCOW"

The nazis couldn't break through to Moscow from the south, so they tried from the north. Their efforts failed, however.

"Take the city by storm, take it at all costs!" the nazi generals ordered.

It was the eve of a new attack. Lieutenant Albert Neimhan went down into his dug-out, got out some paper and began to write a letter to his uncle, a retired general living in Berlin.

"Dear uncle!" Neimhan began his letter. "Ten minutes ago I returned from the headquarters of our grenadier division. The company commander has received orders for the final assault upon Moscow..." Neimhan added hastily: "Moscow is ours! Russia is ours! Europe is ours! I'm in a rush, headquarters is calling me. In the morning I'll write you from Moscow."

The nazis opened the attack on Moscow from the very nearest point on the Western front. The enemy division broke through the front near the town of Naro-Fominsk and pushed forward.

"Hurray, hurray!" the nazi generals shouted triumphantly. "The road to Moscow is open."

A dispatch was rushed out to Berlin.

"The road to Moscow is open!"

The nazi tanks and motorcycle units rushed in the direction of Moscow. They covered five, ten, fifteen kilometres to the village of Akulovo. Here, near Akulovo, the enemy encountered a covering detachment. A deadly battle broke out. The nazis couldn't push any further.

They now tried to cut through to the south of Naro-Fominsk. They covered five, ten, fifteen kilometres to the village of Petrovskoye. Here at Petrovskoye the enemy met another covering detachment. Another deadly battle flared up and the nazis were again halted in their tracks.

The nazis turned to the north. They rushed to the Golitsyno station. They covered five, ten, fifteen kilometres, then ran into yet another covering detachment in the villages of Burtsevo and Yushkovo. For a third time a deadly struggle ensued and for a third time the nazis were halted. The attack bogged down at this point.

The Soviet troops had beaten off the new assault on Moscow. The nazi tanks turned and rumbled off to their starting point. They left, but nevertheless the nazis still underestimated the strength of the Soviet troops. The nazi generals consoled themselves:

"Nothing to worry about, nothing at all. We'll rest up, put our shoulders to the wheel and take care of them!"

The generals made preparations for a new assault on Moscow. At the same time fresh Soviet reinforcements were gathering to the north, south, and here to the west of Moscow. The new divisions came from Siberia and the Urals and new tanks and artillery were sent in with them. The Soviet Army prepared to strike a crushing blow against the enemy.

The troops were ready, waiting only for the signal to attack.

And the signal came.

On the 6th of December, 1941, the troops defending Moscow launched a massive attack. The Soviet Army began to annihilate the enemy, driving him to the west.

And what about the letter of Neimhan's? Did the officer have a chance to write it?

He never did get time, for Lieutenant Neimhan perished in the battle. He was left lying in the snow next to his letter on the outskirts of Moscow.

THE HOME

The Soviet troops were on the offensive. The tank brigade under Major-General Katukov was dashing ahead in pursuit of the enemy.

Suddenly they came to a halt. The bridge ahead of the tanks had been destroyed. This happened on the road to Volokolamsk in the village of Novo-Petrovskoye.

The operators of the tanks cut their engines. Before their eyes the nazis pulled away from them. Someone fired at the German column but it was simply an idle waste of shells.

"Auf Wiedersehen!" cried the nazis.

"Let's ford the river, Comrade General," someone suggested to the major-general.

General Katukov looked down at the steep banks and rushing water of the Maglusha River. His tanks couldn't make it up those steep slopes.

The general lapsed into thought.

Suddenly a woman with a child appeared in front of the tanks.

"The going is easier over there, near our home, Comrade General," she addressed General Katukov. "It's only a stream there and the slopes are gentler."

The tanks set into motion behind the woman. The house came into view. It was set in a hollow located above the stream. It was true, this spot was better. Still... The tank drivers and General Katukov looked about. The tanks couldn't cross here without a bridge either.

"We have to have a bridge," said the drivers. "We need logs."

"There are logs," the woman answered.

The drivers looked around but couldn't see any logs.

"There they are, take a look," said the woman, pointing to her home.

"But that's a home!" objected the drivers.

The woman looked at her home, then at the men:

"So what's a home—wooden boards. In comparison to what the people have lost it isn't much to cry about. Isn't that right, Petya?" she said, turning to the child. Returning her gaze to the soldiers she said: "Take it apart."

The soldiers couldn't muster the nerve to touch the home. A heavy frost had already set in, winter was around the corner. How could they get by without a home at this time of year?

The woman read their minds.

"Say, we'll get by in a dug-out, don't worry," and again turned to the boy: "Right, Petya?"

"Right, mom," Petya answered.

Nevertheless the soldiers hesitated and fidgeted.

The woman then grabbed an axe, walked to a corner of her home and struck the first blow along the log sidings.

"Well, what can we say ... thanks," said General Katukov.

The drivers dismantled the home, improvised a bridge and crossed the river in pursuit of the nazis.

As the tanks crossed the new bridge the woman and her child waved their hands in farewell.

"What are your names?" cried out the drivers. "Who should we say a good word for?"

"Alexandra Grigoryevna Kuznetsova, and Pyotr Ivanovich Kuznetsov; my son."

"Our deepest regards to you, Alexandra Grigoryevna. You'll grow up to be a brave man, Pyotr Ivanovich."

The tanks raced forward and caught up with the enemy column. They crushed the nazis, then pushed further to the west.

The thunder of war passed into the distance. The dance of death and tragedy came to a halt. Every year the war fades further into the background of our memories. But the memory of heroic deeds remains fresh.

The memory of the valorous deed at the Maglusha River hasn't been forgotten either. Take a drive to the little village of Novo-Petrovskoye. Today a house stands in the very same spot in the very same hollow. The inscription over the door reads: "To Alexandra Grigoryevna and Pyotr Ivanovich Kuznetsov for their heroic act performed during the time of World War II." The tank drivers returned to build this home.

The Maglusha River winds its course. Over the river stands a home with a veranda and a porch. The windows look out upon a bright world.

WHAT KIND OF TROOPS ARE FIGHTING?

The Soviet Army was on the offensive. It hit the nazis from the east, the north and the south. They drove the enemy from the outskirts of Moscow. They rolled forward irrepressibly.

At one point during the offensive the commander of the Western Front, General Zhukov, arrived with his staff officers at the front lines. He watched with great interest his troops in action.

"Those fellows are great!" he said over and over again.

He watched and watched, and then turned suddenly to the officers standing nearby and said:

"What kind of troops are fighting?"

At that very moment the infantry surged forward with a loud "Hurray!".

"Infantry, Comrade Commander," the officers answered their commander. "Infantry—the matron of the fields."

"Right you are, so right, infantry," agreed Zhukov.

He stood and stood, then once again asked:

"So what kind of troops are slugging it out?"

The officers exchanged glances. Really, hadn't they given an answer?!

Precisely at that moment the artillery stepped up its action. The gunners were firing excellently; their aim was true. There was no mercy for the nazis from these quarters. And now a salvo of the **katyusha** rockets flew out. Metal and flame spewed out. The nazis hit the dirt.

Zhukov turned to his officers. He waited for their answer.

"Artillery, Comrade Commander," shouted the officers. "Artillery—the god of war."

"True, true, the artillery," agreed Zhukov.

He continued his survey of the battle.

"Such fellows, such warriors!" and for a third time he turned to his officers with the same question:

"So what kind of troops are fighting?"

The officers shrugged their shoulders. How was one to make sense of the commander? Had they really been mistaken in their answer? The officers saw that the general was waiting for an answer.

The Soviet tanks thundered out at that moment. An avalanche of iron moved forward.

"Tanks, Comrade Commander. Tanks!" the officers cried out.

"Right, tanks," agreed Zhukov. "What eagles the tank drivers are!"

The general observed closely the crushing onslaught. He stood and stood, then spoke again.

"So what kind of troops are fighting?"

The perplexed officers stood silently still. No one moved forward with an answer.

At that very moment Soviet airplanes began their attack. Bombs exploded in dull thuds and dirt flew into the air.

"Well, what about it?" Zhukov expected an answer.

"Aviators," someone said timidly. "Aviators, Comrade Commander. Our winged hawks."

"Right you are," agreed Zhukov. "Glory to the Soviet hawks." He bowed to his officers, then said quietly: "So what kind of troops are fighting?"

The officers were completely flustered. They didn't know what more to say.

Zhukov waited for a moment, then pointed to the attacking forces.

"Invincible," he said smiling.

The troops moved forward triumphantly. They clearly had the upper hand over the nazis.

The Soviet Army liberated 11 thousand settlements in the battle around Moscow. They destroyed 38 nazi divisions. In all of Europe there had been no force capable of defeating Hitler's troops. But now there was—the Soviet Army. The great battle for Moscow ended in crushing defeat for the nazis.

Zhukov stood watching his troops advance. He feasted his eyes.

"So what kind of troops are fighting?" the commander asked once again of his officers.

"Invincible," his officers answered in one voice.

1

1. Early in the morning on the 22nd of June, 1941, nazi Germany treacherously and without a declaration of war, sent its troops against the Soviet Union in violation of the Non-Aggression Pact. Thus began the Great Patriotic War waged by the Soviet people against the nazi aggressors.

2

3

2. "Mother Russia calls", one of the first military posters, by I. Toidze. 3. The nazi officers look through their binoculars at Moscow. At this time there is taking place a military parade of Soviet troops on Red Square. The date is November 7, 1941.

4

5

6

7

4. Artillery battery stationed around Moscow, here in firing position. 5. General Zhukov, Commander of the Western Front. 6. The legendary Katukov, Major-General of a tank formation, reports to Konstantin Rokossovsky. 7. "Katyushas" being launched. A woman's name Katyusha was given by the soldiers to the first Russian mortar rocket. 10. Mortar shell. 8. Soviet medium-size bomber IL-4 in flight. 9. Moscow. Troops leaving for the front.

8

10

9

12

13

11

11. Soviet automatic weapon. 12. Political Instructor Klochkov, who led the 28 Panfilov's heroes in their courageous stand, with his daughter. 13. Soviet troops during the liberation of Volokolamsk. 14. Heroine of the Soviet People, Zoya Kosmodemyanskaya. 15. The execution of Zoya Kosmodemyanskaya. This photograph was recovered from the body of a dead nazi officer. 16. Soviet troops moving into Klin, 1941.

14

15

17

18

19

20

17. Destroyed German equipment along the roads leading to Moscow. 18. Homecoming.
19. Trophy—a captured artillery piece. 20. Retreat. Defeated nazis on the approaches to
Moscow.

21

22

21, 22. They wanted to enter Moscow, and in fact they did—captured nazis being led through the streets of the capital.

MAMAYEV KURGAN

In the summer of 1942 the nazis mounted another offensive. Having suffered defeat near Moscow, they mounted their main thrust this time to the south in an attempt to seize the regions rich in grain and oil. The enemy advanced far, emerging at the banks of the Volga to begin the assault on Stalingrad.

Lieutenant Chernyshov was a handsome devil. His brows were arched like a crescent, his curls as black as tar.

September, 1942. Stalingrad. Seven nazi divisions stormed the city. Thousand of guns opened fire. Five hundred nazi tanks advanced in a wave.

The battle for Mamayev Kurgan was especially bloody. Mamayev Kurgan was the highest point in the city. From its top wide expanses were visible. One could see the Volga, the steppes and the left bank of the Volga.

The summit of the hill had already traded hands several times. The nazis attacked our troops and drove them off, then we recaptured the position. Our troops held the summit for a while, only to lose it once more to the enemy. Lieutenant Chernyshov led his troops to the attack five times. From a vantage point he could be picked out, his brows arched like a crescent, his curls black as tar.

Chernyshov began the sixth attack while the first was still fresh in his mind. The troops had raced then to the summit, running in sprints. They would lie down to wait out a fierce volley from the enemy, then stand up and again race forward.

"Forward! Forward!" shouted Lieutenant Chernyshov, though exhausted to the point of delirium and hoarse in the throat.

MAMAYEV KURGAN — Mamayev burial mound

Once again the soldiers hit the dirt. The lieutenant waited and then once again:

"Forward!"

The soldiers lay still, making no motions to stand up.

"Forward!" shouted Chernyshov. He grabbed his automatic and nudged first one, then another with the muzzle.

"Forward!"

The soldiers lay still.

Anger rose in the throat of the officer. His face contorted from shouting. His brows crossed like sabres.

"Forward!" shouted Lieutenant Chernyshov.

The soldiers lay still.

Sergeant Kutsenko suddenly appeared next to the lieutenant.

"They're dead, can't you see, comrade?" Kutsenko quietly said to him.

Lieutenant Chernyshov shuddered and looked around at the burial mound and at the soldiers. He realised—the soldiers were in fact dead. He and Kutsenko were the only two survivors. They retreated from the hill to their own troops.

There at the bottom of the hill Chernyshov was appointed to command a new group. Once again he moved to the attack. Once again the assault bogged down in blood. They didn't reach the summit the third time, or the fourth, or the fifth.

Night set in, a night which saw no respite from battle. As long as they could stand on their legs the soldiers fought. Chernyshov staggered about on his feet like a drunk man.

When dawn broke it cast light on a sight horrible to the eyes. The slopes of the hill were covered with the corpses of soldiers. It was as if the soldiers, exhausted from a march, had lain down for an hour's rest. Play the reveille for them and they'll come to!

The soldiers would wake no more. Their sleep was eternal.

"To the attack!" once again the command sounded.

Once again Chernyshov led the soldiers to the summit. "Oh, if only we were fresh!" Suddenly he heard a thunderous peal of "Hurray!". "What in the world?" He decided that he had imagined the noise. Turning around, he saw fresh companies rushing to the hill. The troops were in formation: as if molded in a cast they were identical, one to another. From the left bank of the Volga men from the 13th Rifle Division under General Rodimtsev had come to help.

"Hurray! Hurray!"

The troops flew to the summit. They attacked in waves, like the surf against the shores. The summit was in our hands.

Lieutenant Chernyshov stood on the summit of the hill. Beside him was Sergeant Kutsenko. They looked on the Volga and into the distance on the left bank of the river.

"Just the same we took it," uttered Lieutenant Chernyshov and suddenly began to laugh joyfully like a child. He took off his cap and wiped his grimy brow.

Kutsenko's eyes fell upon Chernyshov. He wanted to say something but the words didn't come. He looked: where were the lieutenant's black curls? Chernyshov's head was bathed in silver like the moon. Only his brows were the same, arched like a crescent.

DANKO

Danko is a legendary hero in one of Maxim Gorky's tales. To save some people in a dark forest Danko tore out his heart from his body. The heart lit up in a radiant flame which revealed the road out of the forest to the people.

Stalingrad was an unusual city. It extended in a long strip for sixty kilometres from north to south along the right bank of the Volga.

At the end of September extremely heavy fighting broke out in the northern section of the city. This was the factory region where the "Red October", the "Barricades", and the famous "Stalingrad" tractor plant were situated. The residents of Stalingrad were proud of their factories, which were the glory of the workers. Here, in the factory region, the nazis were trying to break through. From morning until evening a fierce battle raged. Day was turned into night by the tremendous smoke, dust and fire. In turn endless fires turned the night into day.

Mikhail Panikakha, a sailor and member of the **Komsomol,** was not one to stand out in a crowd. He was of average height and average built. An ordinary sailor. He wore a sailor's cap and a striped shirt. True, his bell-bottoms were stuffed into his boots.

Mikhail Panikakha was a marine. He was fighting here alongside his battalion in the factory region.

The nazis threw their tanks against the marine infantry. An unequal battle developed.

The tanks had armour, cannon and machine-guns. The marines had only grenades, and a limited supply at that.

Mikhail Panikakha was in the trench, struggling with his comrades against the armour, cannon and machine-guns. But the moment came when his supply of grenades was exhausted. He was left with only two bottles filled with explosive fluid. Yet the tanks kept coming and coming. No end to the battle was in sight.

One of the tanks headed directly towards Mikhail Panikakha. There was no way to escape his fate. Steel moved on a collision course with human flesh.

The sailor clung to the trench, waiting for the tank to come still closer. He gripped the bottle in his hand. He aimed carefully, for he didn't want to miss. Now the tank was near enough. The sailor stood up in the trench, raised the bottle over his head, ready to toss it under the steel mass, when a bullet suddenly struck and shattered the glass. The fluid burst into flames and poured over Panikakha. In an interval of seconds the sailor was a living torch.

People about him froze in horror. The sky froze in position. The sun in the sky stopped its course...

"No, you're not going to take it," the sailor cried out.

He grabbed the second bottle filled with gas. The living torch jumped out of the trench and raced to the nazi tank. The bottle lifted into the air and struck against the engine-lid. The nazi tank roared, then sputtered and choked. A flaming fountain spewed up into the sky.

The battle has long since died down, the soldiers returned to their homes. The memories have faded. But the deeds of these fearless people are immortal. The memory of Mikhail Panikakha's feat lives on: it is ageless.

Danko of Stalingrad—so his comrades called him. So his name entered history.

THE DEFENCE OF STALINGRAD

The troops were defending Stalingrad, fending off the attacks of the nazis.

The army defending the central and factory section of the town was commanded by Lieutenant-General Vassili Ivanovich Chuikov.

Chuikov was an audacious and decisive general.

Moving into the factory region the nazis tore towards the command point of the army headquarters. They were only three hundred metres away and moving closer.

The staff officers and adjutants became very agitated.

"Comrade Commander, the enemy is at our doorstep," it was reported to Chuikov.

"That's just fine," said Chuikov, "he's just what we need."

The soldiers took heart at the fighting spirit of the general. They hurtled themselves at the enemy and destroyed him.

Adjacent to the command point was an oil-storage area. An open basin filled with mazut was situated on the premises. Nazi airplanes bombed the area and set the mazut on fire. The flames spread in the direction of the command point. For two whole days the conflagration raged. For a week the command point was surrounded by an inferno of heat and smoke.

Once again the adjutants were distressed:

"It's dangerous here, Comrade Commander, the fire's at our doorstep!"

"That's just wonderful," said Chuikov. He looked at the smoke and flames. "Just wonderful, it's excellent camouflage."

Next a battle took place near Chuikov's headquarters. It occurred so near, in fact, that when food was carried over to the headquarters fragments of mines and shells often turned up in the pots and dishes.

Glinka, the cook for headquarters, ran up to Chuikov:

"Comrade General, have you ever seen such a thing! Fragments in the plates, mines in the **kasha,** shells in the soup!"

The commander grinned:

"That's just magnificent, Glinka. It's battlefield spice. Front-line vitamins to build up the anger inside!"

"Some vitamins!" grumbled Glinka. He liked the answer, however, and passed it along to the other soldiers.

The soldiers were pleased. Their general was audacious.

Chuikov was in command of the army charged with the defence of Stalingrad. He considered, however, that the best type of defence is to attack. Chuikov attacked the enemy relentlessly, not giving him a moment's peace.

A new division arrived and was placed under the disposition of Chuikov. The commander of the division appeared before the Commander-in-Chief to receive his instructions. He tried to imagine where and what kind of defensive position he would be ordered to take up. In his mind he ran through the military code and manual—what, scientifically speaking, would be the best type of defence.

Chuikov leaned over his maps. He looked carefully, repeating over and over: "Let's see now, where would it be best for you to take up the defence? There's a gap here. And here they need men. And here—they'd be grateful!" He finally took a pencil, drew a circle and from the circle made an arrow:

"Here now," he said, "together with the men on your right flank you'll begin the attack. Your objective—to wipe out this concentration of the enemy and to end up here, at this point."

The division commander glanced at the general:

"That looks to me like a full-scale offensive, Comrade Commander, not a defence."

"No, it's a defence," said Chuikov, "a Stalingrad defence."

Chuikov was an aggressive general, always on the offensive. He participated in many of the battles of World War II. In 1945 troops under his command were among the first to enter Berlin.

TITAYEV

November. A blizzard. The snow fell heavily...

The life of a signalman wasn't an enviable one. Snow, bad weather, mud, sudden attacks from the sky, shells tearing up the ground, bullets strewing death—nevertheless the signalman was ready for action. If a line was damaged by a bomb, or torn by a shell, or sabotaged by a nazi scout, the signalman had to find it and re-establish communications.

In November the battle at Mamayev Kurgan broke out once again. At the very height of the battle the communications lines with the divisional command point were cut. At that very time the command point was engaged in giving target coordinates to the artillery. The communications were cut and the artillery fell silent.

Titayev, a signalman, was dispatched to repair the damage.

He crawled along the line, looking for the break. Low clouds hung over Titayev and a furious ground wind was blowing. To the left were the enemy trenches. Mortars flew over and submachine guns chattered away. The battle was in full swing.

Titayev crawled along, staring intently at the wire and searching for the break. Bullets whistled over the soldier. The ground wind fought to drive him off his path.

"Hey, you won't drive me away," shouted the soldier to the blizzard.

"Hey, you won't catch me," he defied the bullets.

He crawled along. There, on the hill, the battle raged. There had to be artillery support. Titayev realised it and moved quickly. Some thirty metres ahead he could see a crater from an explosion: he'd found the damage. Ten metres to go. Five. He crawled towards the crater. Now he was at the very edge. There lay the line, severed by the shell fragments. Titayev grabbed one end, then quickly pulled up the second...

The telephone receiver was silent for a long time at the command point, then suddenly it was working. The commander breathed a sigh of relief.

"First-rate men," he praised the signalmen.

"It was Titayev," someone replied. "He's a first class soldier."

Titayev was well-known and liked in the division. At the company command post they waited for him to return. For some reason he didn't show up.

Two soldiers were sent to look for the signalman. They crawled along, following the same path. Low clouds hung over them. The ground wind blew in their faces. The submachine guns chattered away. The battle raged. The Soviet artillery was now firing, drowning out the other sounds of battle. It was music to the ears of the soldiers.

The soldiers crawled along, peering ahead. They caught sight of the crater, and recognised Titayev at its edge. He was lying on the ground.

"Titayev!"

"Titayev!"

Titayev remained silent.

The soldiers crawled closer. They looked—he was immobile, dead.

The soldiers had become accustomed to many sights during the war. But this...

As it turned out, at the very moment when Titayev, having discovered the break in the line, tried to reconnect the severed ends, a fatal bullet had hit the soldier. He didn't have the strength left to repair the damage.

But parting with life, his consciousness rapidly ebbing, the soldier managed in the last second to put both ends of the line between his teeth. He clenched it like a vise with his teeth. Communications were re-established.

"Fire! Fire!" the command raced along the wires. And the answer came back:

"Firing commenced. How's the connection?"

"The connection is excellent."

And again:

"Fire! Fire!"

The troops crushed the enemy. But there, at the edge of a crater lay a soldier. No, he wasn't lying, he was standing at his post.

The soldier stood at his post.

THE FORTRESS

The nazis couldn't take Stalingrad. The rumour was circulated that the city was an inaccessible fortress. It was said that impassable ditches, walls and embankments surrounded the town. Each step taken, it was bruited, was met by powerful defensive networks and fortifications, by traps and various engineering ruses.

The nazis wrote that the city blocks were not blocks at all, but rather fortified zones. Houses were not houses, they said, but forts and bastions.

"Stalingrad—it's a fortress, a fortress," insisted the nazis.

In this vein the German soldiers and officers wrote home. In Germany they read the letters:

"Stalingrad—it's a fortress, a fortress," the word circulated.

Their generals fired out reports. Each line said one and the same thing:

"Stalingrad—it's a fortress. An impenetrable fortress. It's full of fortified regions and insurmountable bastions."

The nazi newspapers printed articles repeating one and the same point:

"Our soldiers are storming the fortress."

"Stalingrad—it's the strongest fortress in Russia."

"Fortress, fortress," screamed the newspapers.

Even the leaflets circulated at the front wrote about it.

But Stalingrad wasn't a fortress and never had been. It had no special fortifications. It was a city like any other city. Houses, factories...

Soviet soldiers obtained one of the nazi leaflets. They had a good laugh: "The nazis aren't writing this because they're having an easy time of it." Then they showed the leaflet to Kuzma Akimovich Gurov, member of the Military Council, Divisional Commissar of the 62nd Army. They wanted to show the commissar what fantasies the nazis were concocting.

The commissar read through the leaflet and astonished the soldiers by saying:

"Everything written here is true. The nazis are right. Of course it's a fortress."

The soldiers were confused. Maybe it was so after all. The authorities usually had a clearer picture than they did. Nevertheless they looked at the commissar with doubt in their eyes.

"A fortress," Gurov repeated. "Your hearts and your courage, that's the invincible fortress, that's where the impassable boundaries and fortified zones are. That's where you'll find the walls and bastions."

The soldiers smiled. What the commissar said was understandable and even a pleasure to hear.

Kuzma Akimovich Gurov was telling the truth. The valour of the Russian soldier, that was the wall against which the nazism collided and broke his neck at Stalingrad.

TAKE ANY...

The troops were engaged in the defence of Stalingrad. In the meantime...

General Headquarters had been developing for a long time a gigantic and daring plan to destroy the nazi troops at the walls of Stalingrad. Generals Zhukov, Vassilevsky, Voronov and other military authorities had spent many sleepless nights working out the details of the future battle. This was how the plan looked: driving from the north and south they would surround the nazis in the region of Stalingrad and trap them in a huge circle and annihilate them.

November 19, 1942, this huge offensive by Soviet troops was initiated.

The Soviet units struck rapidly. The lead detachment of the 26th Tank Corps moving from the north with a daring assault seized the bridge over the Don River and after it the city of Kalach.

Correspondents from the army newspapers arrived at the Don in the region of the fighting. They began to ask for details of the assault and for the names of people who had distinguished themselves.

The first question:

"Who took the bridge?"

"An advance tank detachment," was the answer to the correspondents' query.

"Who was in command?"

"Lieutenant-Colonel Filippov."

At this point the correspondents learned the story of how the bridge was taken. Lieutenant-Colonel Filippov and his tanks had made a swift assault on the bridge. The nazis had been caught by surprise and even thought at first that the tanks were their own. When they caught on it was already too late. Soviet tanks were now on the bridge and had control of both banks.

The correspondents jotted down notes for a dispatch on the tank raid and moved on further, to the city of Kalach.

Members of the tank column met them there. The correspondents turned to the drivers and asked:

"Who took Kalach?"

"An advance tank detachment."

The correspondents scribbled down some information.

"If we're right, your commander's name is Lieutenant-Colonel..."

"Exactly, Lieutenant-Colonel. Lieutenant-Colonel Filippenko," the soldiers specified.

"What's that, Filippenko you say? But we thought Filippov!" the journalists objected.

"To the tanks!" the command rang out.

The drivers dove into the heavily-armoured hatches of their tanks.

The correspondents were left alone with their note pads. They looked at the surname they had written down for the commander of the advance detachment and tried to guess which was correct: Filippov or Filippenko.

They decided to check again. Soon they ran into another soldier.

"What's the last name of the commander of the advance tank detachment?" the correspondents asked.

"Lieutenant-Colonel Filippov," the soldier replied.

"That means it is Filippov after all," the correspondents decided.

Nevertheless they decided to double-check.

"What's your commander's last name?" they asked of a bypassing lieutenant of the tank detachment.

"Lieutenant-Colonel Filippenko," was his answer.

"He's the commander of the advance tank detachment?"

"Precisely, that's him."

The journalists were in a complete muddle. They had no idea what was going on. "Filippov or Filippenko? What name should they send out for their articles?"

They returned to their newspapers. There they sat, trying to guess which of the surnames to use.

But guessing was of no use.

It turned out that among the attacking tank drivers there were both a Lieutenant-Colonel Filippenko and a Lieutenant-Colonel Filippov. Both were in command of advance tank detachments and both received the Hero of the Soviet Union award. The first received it for seizing the bridge on the Don, the second for taking the city of Kalach.

There were many heroes at Stalingrad, and many had similar names. There were Ivanov, Ivanenko, Ivanyan, Ivanidze, Ivashchenko. There were radio operators named Litvina, Litvinenko, Litvinova; tankists named Grigoryan, Grigorenko, Grishchenko, and infantry men named Petrov, Petrashvili, Petrosyan, Petronavičius. There were many heroes and many surnames.

Would you like to write about heroes?

Pick any name...you won't go wrong.

ROUT

Soviet troops surrounded the nazis pressing in on them in an enormous circle. The final and concluding stage of the battle of Stalingrad had begun.

"Hold that line! The Führer commands you!" shouted the commander of the surrounded German army, Colonel-General Friedrich von Paulus. "The Führer will remember you. Hold that line! The Führer is with you, he won't abandon you."

The soldiers believed Paulus, they believed in the Führer. They fought on to death as rivers of German blood flowed.

The Germans fought stubbornly, but matters got worse and worse. The circle got tighter and tighter and Soviet units pressed against the nazis. An inferno blazed on all sides.

Paulus didn't weaken:

"Men, don't move from your positions! Die like soldiers. The Führer won't abandon us."

The soldiers still believed. In fact, however, the order had already gone out to cease the attempt to rescue the surrounded troops.

The soldiers didn't know this. They fought on like lions, like beasts. Their belief in the Führer was sacred.

On the 9th of January, 1943, the Soviet command sent the encircled troops terms for capitulation, that is, for laying down their arms. Their safety and food and shelter were guaranteed. As soon as the war ended they would be sent home.

The soldiers, exhausted from the ferocious battles, breathed a sigh of relief. Here was an escape from their fate. They rejoiced at the prospect of an end to the battle. Only they soon learned that Hitler had issued a stern order forbidding his soldiers to surrender. The nazi generals declined the Soviet offer.

Once again the soldiers threw themselves in battle and once again rivers of blood flowed.

The Soviet encirclement grew tighter and tighter. Our troops drove the nazis into and confined them in Stalingrad, the very city they had destroyed. The nazi soldiers crawled into the cellars and basements of ruined buildings, into trenches and caves... into any chink they could find.

The Commander-in-Chief of the surrounded German army, Friedrich von Paulus himself, huddled in the cellar under the former central department store of Stalingrad.

Paulus was no longer simply a general. He had been elevated in rank to the position of General and Field Marshal as a reward for his fidelity to the Führer and to nazism.

"Take courage! Hold the line!" Paulus shouted from the cellar.

Here in the cellar were the headquarters for the encircled army, or, more accurately, for what remained of it. Only a few soldiers dragged themselves into the city and continued to fight. The rest gave up the struggle as a lost cause.

"Hold on!" Paulus shouted from the cellar.

It's hard to tell how long he would have kept this up. At this point, however, Soviet tanks broke through into the centre of town. The tank drivers approached the cellar in which Paulus was hidden and descended the stairs.

"Be so kind as to put your hands up, Field Marshal Paulus."

The Field Marshal surrendered.

On the 2nd of February, 1943, the nazi troops encircled within Stalingrad lay down their arms once and for all. The remnants of the huge 330 thousand men army of Hitler's surrendered into the hands of the Soviets. The Soviet troops had destroyed or completely annihilated 22 nazi divisions; 91 thousand nazi soldiers were taken prisoner, among them 2,500 officers. In addition to Field Marshal von Paulus Soviet troops captured some 23 of Hitler's generals.

The nazi army which had fought at Stalingrad now ceased to exist. Victory was total at Stalingrad, total and great. Its glory will not fade over the centuries.

1

2

3

4

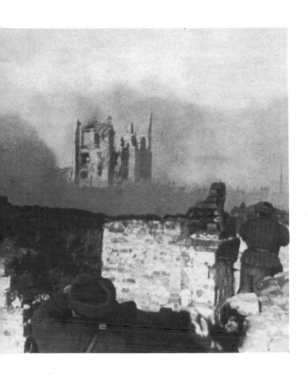

5

1. In the Stalingrad trenches. 2. General Vassili Chuikov headed the army which carried out a heroic defence of the central and northern sections of Stalingrad. In 1945 the army under Chuikov was one of the first to enter Berlin. 3. Street-fighting in Stalingrad. 4. Fighting in a workshop in the "Red October" Factory. 5. "The workshop is ours!"

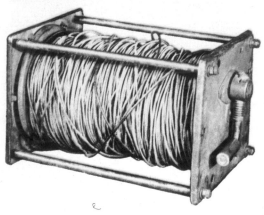

Смерть немецким захватчикам!

Прочитай и передай товарищу!

СТАЛИНГРАДЕЦ!
БУДЬ СТОЙКИМ, КАК
МАТВЕЙ ПУТИЛОВ

Он был рядовым связистом и часто находился там, где вражескими снарядами и минами каренились провода, где разрывающиеся бомбы непрерывно выводили из строя связь- нерв Сталинградской обороны. Сегодня на линии вражеской миной ему раздробило руку. Теряя сознание, он поднёс концы проводов в рот и крепко зажал провод зубами. Восстановив связь, он умер с проволокой в зубах!
ОТОМСТИМ ЗА МАТВЕЯ!

6. M. M. Putilov, Komsomol and signalman. Wounded in action, he clenched the severed lines between his teeth. Thus restoring communications, he died with the lines held between his teeth. 7. Leaflet describing Putilov's exploit. 8. Coil belonging to signalman Putilov. 9. Lieutenant-Colonel Filippov, Commander of the 14th Motorised Brigade under the 26th Tank Corps—a hero of the Stalingrad Battle. 10. "Katyushas" near Stalingrad. 11. Soviet fighter planes. 12, 13. The entire population lend a hand in the struggle. Men departing for the front were replaced at work by their wives and children.

10

11

12

13

14

15

16

14. Victory at Stalingrad. Nazi soldiers surrendering. 15. Enemy equipment put out of operation. 16. Commander of the surrounded nazi army, General Field Marshal Paulus on the day of capture.

17

17. Stalingrad has emerged victorious!

ON TO BERLIN!

The Stalingrad battle was the turning point in the course of World War II. From this point on a major offensive was launched by the Soviet armies on all fronts. The enemy retreated, but fought back bitterly.

There were still many conflicts and battles to come. There were the famous battle for Kursk, the struggle to win back the Dnieper and the city of Kiev, the encirclement of the nazis near Korsun-Shevchenkovski. The breaking of the nazi blockade of Leningrad, the liberation of Sevastopol and Odessa and the huge operation called "Bagration", which completed the rout of the nazis and their elimination from Byelorussia.

Soviet troops drove the aggressors from the borders of the Soviet Union, then began the liberation of the enslaved nations of Europe. They freed Poland, Rumania, Bulgaria and Hungary. They fought to liberate Czechoslovakia and Yugoslavia.

In the spring of 1945 the Soviet armies approached Berlin, the capital of nazi Germany. On the 16th of April the last major struggle of World War II commenced—the battle for Berlin.

The 16th of April. Late night. Three o'clock Berlin time. Suddenly a torrent of fire descended on the nazi defences. The First Byelorussian Front under the command of Marshal Zhukov began its assault on Berlin.

All life on the opposite side huddled and clung to the ground in an attempt to hide. The nazi artillery remained silent. How could they reply: it was too dangerous to lift one's head or even wave the hand!

Among these soldiers a certain Ruschke also lay down and concealed himself. He tried to figure out the situation.

What was going on? Night. Three o'clock Berlin time. And suddenly an artillery barrage! Would there be a break-through? But a break-through during the night? How can you attack in the darkness? How could tanks operate? After all they see virtually nothing during daylight hours. How could the field artillery sight its targets? How could the soldiers launch an attack?

How indeed?

Ruschke struggled to understand, but couldn't make heads or tails of it. Maybe the Russians were just trying to intimidate them. Perhaps they had got their timing confused.

The other soldiers were just as puzzled. The generals were in a state of confusion.

Meanwhile the artillery hammered away.

The Russians had undertaken something mysterious.

The hurricane lasted 30 minutes, laying waste everything in its path. Then, just as suddenly as it had begun, it came to an end. The firing came to a halt. All was still. Silence enshrouded the positions.

The surviving nazi soldiers crawled out of their shelters. The generals followed suit. Ruschke crawled out with his compatriots and looked around.

And suddenly...

Nobody understood what was happening at first. Dozens of strange beams of light suddenly burst blindingly into the eyes of the nazis.

They squinted and closed their eyes in reaction. What in the world? When they re-opened their eyes everything was as light as day. Beams of light splattered, burned and seared the eyes. Fearsome shadows raced about before them.

The nazis only now came to their senses; they were in fact searchlights. They stretched over a distance of several kilometres along the front lines. Blazing up simultaneously, they turned night into day.

The light, striking the nazis directly, served to blind them. On the other hand, it helped our troops by lighting up the road for the tanks and by illuminating the darkness for the artillery, infantry and other combat troops.

The nazis were in a state of turmoil. Never had they witnessed such a thing!

A phenomenal and victorious barrage rolled over them.

Meanwhile the air was already filled with the roar of Soviet airplanes. They began to make strikes. Strikes with unprecedented force! Unprecedented boldness!

"THE FÜHRER'S GUARD"

The troops of the First Byelorussian Front under the command of Marshal Zhukov were tearing into the nazi lines.

At the same time the troops of the First Ukrainian Front under the command of Marshal Konev were breaking through the nazi defences.

But if Zhukov's forces were attacking at night, flooding the nazis with beams from searchlights, here under Marshal Konev the situation was different, in fact, quite the opposite.

Here the front line ran parallel with the Neisse River. The river had to be crossed in order to penetrate Hitler's defence line. It had to be forced, but it wasn't a crossing that could be accomplished easily. Bridges had to be built, fordings planned. It was no simple matter. Crossings couldn't be begun in broad daylight. Thus, Marshal Konev was in need of the cover of darkness, not the illumination of searchlights.

"Now we'll bring on the darkness," pilots reported to the marshal.

Soviet airplanes had taken to the sky and carpeted the Neisse with a curtain of smoke. Smoke rolled over the Neisse and settled on both banks.

The weather was peaceful, without a trace of wind. The smoke hung in the air over the Neisse without budging and concealed the Soviet units.

These clouds of smoke helped. In the spot where the main break-through was made, 133 crossings were accomplished.

The Soviet troops thrust forward at the three defence lines of the nazis.

The first line didn't hold. It collapsed.
The second line didn't hold. It fell.
Soviet units then took the third line.

Having breached the nazi defences, Marshal Konev's troops together with those of Marshal Zhukov launched an overpowering march on Berlin. The tanks plowed forward.

"100 kilometres to Berlin," the Soviet tank drivers read the road sign in the morning.

"75 left to go," they said in the noon.

Then 60, 55, 50 flashed by...

The tank divisions raced ahead, but nazi troops remained to the rear of the Soviet forces near the city of Spremberg. They pressed on the right flank of Konev's troops and presented a serious threat. Among the opponent's forces was a tank division named "The Führer's Guard". This division caused no little trouble for the Russians.

It was necessary to surround and eliminate these forces. Soviet troops therefore hurtled once again into battle. They fought, muttering:

"Well, how's 'The Führer's Guard' doing?"

Our troops were successful in surrounding the enemy, squeezing him in a ring of steel. Then the area was hammered into dust by artillery fire.

General Lebedenko was responsible for the task of destroying the cluster of nazi troops.

"Well, how's 'The Führer's Guard' now?" Marshal Konev inquired after the conflict.

"Destroyed, Comrade Marshal!" Lebedenko reported.

"Well, that means," said Konev, "since the Führer's Guard is eliminated, it's time now to go after the Führer himself."

"OH!"

Dürinshof is one of several small towns located in the vicinity of Berlin. They weren't expecting the Russians here for they weren't expecting the headlong speed accomplished by our break-through.

But suddenly, like lightning out of a clear-blue sky, Soviet tanks appeared in the city. After a short engagement the nazis who were dug in here were destroyed, and tanks rumbled along the streets.

The drivers opened the hatches and looked about. One of these drivers was Lieutenant Andrei Melnik. As the tanks rolled past stores and homes, he read the signs over the shops: "Bread", "Pharmacy", "Ideal Milk". And here was another which read "Telephone Station".

Something flashed into the mind of the lieutenant as he read.

"Stop!" he cried to the mechanic.

The tank's brakes were applied and it swerved out of the way to allow the others in the formation to pass.

Lieutenant Melnik emerged from the tank and ran into the station. It was clear that he'd thought up something mischievous, for his eyes already twinkled.

As he raced into the building which housed the station, Melnik caught sight of two telephone operators who cried out in unison in astonishment at the sight of a Soviet officer:

"Oh!"

They both then collapsed in a dead faint.

"Don't be afraid," shouted the lieutenant. "Don't be afraid."

He approached one and then the other to help bring them back to consciousness. They opened their eyes and looked askance upon the Soviet officer.

Melnik smiled and began to talk in German. Indeed he had a good command of the language:

"Connect me up, *Mädchen,* with Berlin."

He no sooner said this than:

"Oh," once again.

And once again into a dead faint.

Once again, Lieutenant Melnik tried to bring the girls to, but without success. The terrified operators were beyond reach.

Melnik thought and thought, then decided to ring up Berlin himself. His first attempt brought success. He heard a voice from the receiver:

"Berlin speaking."

"Take down a telephone message, please."

"Ready," answered the Berlin operator.

Melnik dictated:

"To the officer in charge in Berlin, General Weidling. Did you get it?"

"Got it," the operator answered.

"Expect us in Berlin. Soon'll be there. Be ready with accommodation. Did you get it?"

"Got it."

"A warrior's greetings," the lieutenant continued to dictate. "This telegram was sent by Lieutenant Melnik, commander of a platoon of Soviet tanks."

No sooner had the officer uttered these words than he heard through the line:

"Oh!"

Silence followed.

"Hello, hello!"

There was no response from the receiver.

It was clear to the lieutenant that *Mädchen* in Berlin had also fainted.

He pushed back his tankist helmet and grinned. Grinning, he raced to the exit and returned to his own men.

"What was going on in there?" they crowded around with the question.

"Well, you see," smiled Melnik, "I just called up an acquaintance of mine."

WHERE
THE ACTION IS

Private Mikhail Pankratov had just recently been conscripted into the army. His parents bade him farewell:

"Don't cast mud on our name as soldiers," his father said to him.

"Don't let your courage desert you in battle," his mother called out to him.

The words of his parents were superfluous. The soldier was proud of his destiny. He was anxious to lock horns with the nazis.

The troop train rushed to the west. It puffed its way up slopes and clattered past junctions. The soldier sprawled out on his bunk, dreaming about feats of war. In his imagination he dashed after the enemy, then fought madly, firing rounds from his automatic. He carried out a daring reconnaissance mission and brought back a "tongue". He led an attack and was the first to penetrate the fortress-city of the enemy. Again he was the first to raise the banner of his troops over the city.

The soldier dreamed of heroic deeds. He glanced at his chest—it was decorated with a festoon of medals.

The soldier wanted to hasten fate.

"Faster, faster," he begged the train.

The kilometres raced by in quick succession. Fields, woods, cities and villages rushed by the window.

Wouldn't it be great to be sent to Berlin, where the action was taking place—that was the soldier's cherished hope. Fate smiled on him: the train went in that direction and joined up with the troops moving on Berlin.

Pankratov was delirious with joy at his luck. He dashed off a letter to his parents. He couldn't say exactly where he was going, such direct information was forbidden during wartime. He could only hint, but it wasn't hard to grasp the message; he was headed where the action was. "Await word from Berlin," he ended the letter.

He posted the letter and again he dreamed about military exploits. Here he was, marching into Berlin!

The great day for Pankratov finally came. The troops moved out for the offensive.

But just a moment?! The troops left, but Pankratov's company was held back.

Pankratov and his fellow soldiers rushed to their sergeant:

"What's going on, Kuzma Vassilyevich?"

"Quiet down," said the sergeant. He lowered his voice and brought his finger to his lips: "We going to have a special assignment."

"TONGUE"—the slang for a prisoner captured in order to extract information

And right he was. After an interval of a day they were seated in trucks. The motors roared out and the trucks rolled down the road.

The soldiers sat in the wagons of the trucks, quite content with their lot. They had, after all, been honoured with a special mission.

The wheels raced over the kilometres, then the trucks roared into a huge field. It was an abandoned and empty field, ripped up by craters and torn by huge gashes.

"Hop out," the command came.

The soldiers jumped out of the trucks and, at the order of the commander, fell into formation.

"Comrades," the commander's hand swept towards the field.

"What in the world is this?" the soldiers wondered. "Maybe there's a secret unit on the field? Perhaps there's an underground factory or headquarters?"

"Comrades warriors," repeated the commander, "we've received distinguished orders—to plough and seed the field."

They gasped.

"That's distinguished! That's a mission!"

But a command was a command. The soldiers took to the work. However the drone of voices didn't die down.

Pankratov muttered along with the rest:

"So this is where the action is! What'll I write home now? What can I tell my parents?"

At that very moment the sergeant was within earshot of Pankratov. He glanced at the young soldier and, unable to restrain himself, said sharply:

"Young, and a fool at that. Not that," pointing to the west, where the battle for Berlin was about to come to an end, "but here," now pointing at the field, "is where the action is. People weren't born to kill and wage war. Life and peace are what's sacred to man."

Pankratov fell silent, and the other soldiers followed suit. The spades dug into the moist spring earth. The fragrance of the soil, ripe with the newness of the season, greeted the nostrils of the toiling soldiers.

DEATH STALKS
THE STREETS

On the 25th of April the troops of the First Byelo-russian and the First Ukrainian fronts completed the total encirclement of Berlin. The battle moved to the centre of the city.

Berlin is a huge city. At that time it numbered over 600 thousand homes. Death stalked every street.

The nazis erected barricades and other obstructions in the streets. Mine fields blocked the approaches to these barricades. Machine-guns ranged in upon every square metre of land. Every home in Berlin was turned into a veritable fortress, every street, a battlefield.

On one of the Berlin streets the barricades were especially redoubtable. The nazis had erected them out of steel, iron and flagstones. Infantry first tried to storm the wall, but they made no progress. The soldiers simply died in vain. Soviet tanks next approached the wall and opened fire with their heavy cannon in an attempt to rip a breach in the barricades. But the shells from the tank cannon weren't powerful enough. The barricade held up like reinforced steel. It blocked the road to the infantry and tanks. All movement halted here.

The infantrymen and tank drivers stood looking at the iron, the steel and the flagstones:

"If only we had some demolition experts, some sappers."

And suddenly, as if in response to their statement, the soldiers caught sight of a sapper moving upon the barricade. He crawled along, dragging behind him explosives, a Bickford fuse and line. He stopped and paused a bit, crouched down, then leaped from house to house. Once again he began to slither along the ground.

The soldiers' eyes were glued upon him. They knew exactly what would come next. He raised himself up on one of the stones and lay down. Then he carefully placed the charge under the stone and began to set up the Bickford fuse.

The soldiers closely followed the sapper's movements. Soon he would light the fuse and the spark would race down the line towards the explosives. The sapper, jumping quickly from the stone, would crawl hastily away from the barricade. The spark would reach its destination, the wall shake from the detonation, and a breach would appear in the barricade. The soldiers would then pour through the breach.

So it began. The sapper pulled a match from his pocket, struck a flame then held it up to the fuse. Then suddenly the sapper threw his arms out, fell on the stone and lay still. "They killed him!" someone said.

But no. The soldier began to move.

"Brothers, he's not dead, only wounded."

The sapper moved slightly and lifted his head. He glanced at the stone, then at the fuse, evidently making a calculation of some sort. His hand reached for the matches. Once again he held the box in his hands, struggling to light the match. He struck it against the box, but he was so weak that the sulphur didn't ignite. Again he sprawled out on the flagstone.

The soldiers watched the flagstone turn red. The sapper was losing both strength and blood. But he hadn't yet given up. For a third time he took the box of matches in his hand, and for a third time struck the sulphur. Hurray! It caught! He held the flame towards the fuse and finally made contact. Smoke, winding along the fuse like a snake, raced towards the explosives.

"Jump! Jump!" the soldiers screamed at the sapper.

The latter lay without motion on the stone.

"Jump! Jump!"

Only now the soldiers realised—the sapper had no strength left to jump.

The hero lay without motion on the stone.

The powerful charge exploded in a flash. Flagstones and huge fragments flew into the air and a gaping hole was opened in the wall. The soldiers poured through it.

Eternal glory to the brave. Eternal praise for the courageous.

DANKE SCHÖN

A temporary kitchen was set up on one of the Berlin streets when the smoke and dust of battle were just beginning to settle. The soldiers rushed to receive their ration: **kasha** was just what they needed after a battle. They wolfed their food down ravenously.

Sergeant Yurchenko, head cook in the field kitchen, pottered about among the pots and pans.

He was pleased to hear the soldiers praising the **kasha**.

"Who would like seconds? Who wants more?"

"I wouldn't refuse," spoke up Private 1st Class Zyuzin.

Yurchenko filled up Zyuzin's tureen again, then returned to his work. Suddenly it seemed to him that he was being watched from behind. He spun around, and so it was. A pint-size little boy stood in the gateway of a nearby home looking with hungry eyes at Zyuzin and the kitchen.

Sergeant Yurchenko signalled to the boy:

"Hey there, come on over here."

The urchin approached the kitchen.

"You there, you're not any too shy, are you?!" Private Zyuzin added.

Yurchenko took a tureen and filled it with **kasha.** He held it out to the little boy. *"Danke schön,"* the boy said. He grabbed the tureen and disappeared through the gate-way.

Someone shouted after him:

"Don't eat the tureen too! Make sure you return it."

"Hmm... looks like he's been hungry for a long time," said Private Zyuzin.

Ten minutes passed, then the boy returned, holding out the tureen and with it a plate. He handed back the former but cast his eyes meaningfully upon the plate.

"What's it now, seconds?"

"Bitte, von Schwester," he said.

"He's entering a plea for his sister," somebody sitting nearby explained.

"In that case, bring some to her," replied Yurchenko.

"*Danke schön,*" the boy uttered. Once again he disappeared through the gate-way.

Another ten minutes had passed when the child showed his face a third time, again carrying a plate. He went up to the kitchen holding the plate before him:

"*Bitte, von Mutter.*"

The soldiers broke into laughter:

"You're quite a nimble fellow, aren't you!" The boy received some **kasha** for his mother as well.

This fellow was only the first. Soon a group of children congregated about the kitchen. They stood at a distance, gazing at the tureens, the kitchen and the **kasha.**

Looking at the hungry children, the soldiers lost their appetites. The **kasha** no longer seemed so tasty, it wouldn't go down.

They exchanged glances. Zyuzin looked at Yurchenko and Yurchenko at Zyuzin.

"Well then come on over," Yurchenko then shouted at the children.

The urchins rushed to the kitchen.

"One at a time, one at a time," Zyuzin tried to maintain order by having them form a line. They received their shares of **kasha:**

"*Danke schön!*"

"*Danke schön!*"

"*Danke schön!*"

"*Danke schön!*"

From the way they gulped down the food it was clear that they'd been hungry for quite some time.

Suddenly an airplane winged overhead. The soldiers looked up... it wasn't ours, it was German.

"Get into your homes! Home with you!" Private Zyuzin drove the children away from the kitchen.

They didn't budge. The **kasha** was at their fingertips and it was a pity to part with it.

"March!" shouted Zyuzin.

The plane went into a dive, a bomb raced to the ground.

The children scattered in all directions. Only Zyuzin lingered on. After the bomb hit there was no kitchen, no Zyuzin. Only **kasha,** as if alive, spilling over the stones, over the hushed street.

THE BANNER OF VICTORY

Soviet troops broke into the centre of Berlin and began to storm the Reichstag.

"Sergeant Egorov!"

"Present."

"Private Kantariya!"

"Here."

The commander was summoning the soldiers to entrust them with an honourable task. They were handed the battle flag and instructed to place it on the Reichstag.

The soldiers saluted and left. Many watched them leave with envy for who wouldn't want to be in their place?

At that time the battle for the Reichstag was in full force.

Crouching down, Egorov and Kantariya ran across the square. The Soviet soldiers watched eagerly their every movement. Suddenly the nazis opened up a murderous barrage and the banner carriers were obliged to duck for cover. Then our troops resumed the attack and Egorov and Kantariya moved out again.

By now they'd already reached the stairway. They stood at the columns supporting the entrance to the building. Kantariya gave Egorov a boost as he tried to attach the banner to the entrance of the Reichstag.

"Hey, it should be higher up!" sighed the onlooking soldiers. As if in response to the wishes of their comrades, Egorov and Kantariya removed the banner and pushed on further. They tore into the Reichstag, disappearing behind its doors.

The battle was already being fought on the second floor. A few minutes passed, then a red flag protruded from one of the windows not far from the central

entrance. It appeared, swung for an instant, then disappeared once again.

The soldiers began to fret: what had happened to their comrades? Had they been killed?

A minute, then two, then ten ticked by. Anxiety was rife among the soldiers. Another thirty minutes passed by without a sign of Egorov, Kantariya or the banner.

Suddenly a cry of joy escaped from the lips of a hundred soldiers. The banner was intact, their friends alive. Bent over, they were racing towards the very top of the building—along the roof. Now they straightened up to their full height, held the banner in their hands and waved to their comrades in greeting. Then they quickly rushed to a glass-enclosed dome which jutted out on the roof of the Reichstag and cautiously began to clamber still higher.

On the square and in the building the battle still raged on, but on the roof of the Reichstag, at its very highest point, the banner of victory already confidently waved in the spring skies over defeated Berlin. Two Soviet soldiers, the Russian worker Mikhail Egorov, and the Georgian youth Meliton Kantariya, and with them thousands of other soldiers of various nationalities, had carried the banner here, through blizzards and hostile weather, to the very den of the nazis, and placed it over the heads of the frightened enemy, as a symbol of the invincibility of Soviet might.

A few days passed before the nazi generals conceded total defeat. Hitlerite Germany had been smashed. The great war of liberation fought by the Soviet people against nazism ended with total victory for us.

It was May, 1945. Spring filled the air. The earth rejoiced. Human beings rejoiced. Salutes thundered over the sky in Moscow. The sky was radiant with the happiness below.

The road leading to the borders of our country, where more than three years before the bloody and cruel war had begun, was a difficult one. But beyond these borders other European countries were staggering under the yoke of nazi oppression. Could the armies of the first workers' and peasants' state in the world deny these peoples the help they were anticipating? Thus began the liberation of Europe...

1. Poland. 2. Hungary.

3. Romania. 4. Bulgaria.

5

6

5. Czechoslovakia.
6. Austria.
7. The Soviet flag
over the Reichs-
tag.

8

9

8. The soldiers who hoisted
the flag over the nazi capital.
9. The time had come for some
hard thinking on the part of
the German soldier—both
concerning his own fate and
that of the future Germany.

10

10. Germany agrees to an unconditional surrender. 11. From the soldier's tureen. A hot meal is given to the residents of Berlin.

11

12. Victory Parade. The nazi banners "arriving" at Red Square in the Soviet capital, before Lenin's Mausoleum.

СЛАВА
ВОИНУ-ПОБЕДИТЕЛЮ!

14

13. Poster by V. Klimashin "Glory to the Victorious Soldier!" 14. Victory salute in Moscow, in honour of the triumphant people who had crushed German nazism in the cruelest of wars, in honour of the 20 million Soviet people who perished in the fiercest war in the annals of mankind. Glory to you, victorious people! Eternal glory to those who fell!

REQUEST TO READERS

Progress Publishers would be glad to have your opinion of this book, its translation and design and any suggestions you may have for future publications.

Please send all your comments to 17, Zubovsky Boulevard, Moscow, USSR.

ИБ № 9286

РЕДАКТОР РУССКОГО ТЕКСТА И. В. ЛОГИНОВ. КОНТРОЛЬНЫЙ РЕДАКТОР Л. Г. АФОНАСЬЕВА. ХУДОЖНИК Л. М. ГОЛЬДБЕРГ. ОФОРМИТЕЛЬ В. И. ЧИСТЯКОВ. ХУДОЖЕСТВЕННЫЙ РЕДАКТОР С. К. ПУШКОВА. ТЕХНИЧЕСКИЙ РЕДАКТОР В. П. ШИЦ. ПОДПИСАНО В ПЕЧАТЬ 10.6.81. ФОРМАТ 70 × 90 1/16. БУМАГА МЕЛОВАННАЯ. ГАРНИТУРА БАСКЕРВИЛЬ. ПЕЧАТЬ ОФСЕТ. УСЛОВН. ПЕЧ. Л. 25,74. УЧ.-ИЗД. Л. 22,68. ТИРАЖ 24630 ЭКЗ. ЗАКАЗ № 005227. ЦЕНА 2 РУБ. 20 КОП. ОРДЕНА ТРУДОВОГО КРАСНОГО ЗНАМЕНИ ИЗДАТЕЛЬСТВО „ПРОГРЕСС" ГОСУДАРСТВЕННОГО КОМИТЕТА СССР ПО ДЕЛАМ ИЗДАТЕЛЬСТВ, ПОЛИГРАФИИ И КНИЖНОЙ ТОРГОВЛИ. МОСКВА 119021, ЗУБОВСКИЙ БУЛЬВАР, 17

ИЗГОТОВЛЕНО В ГДР